PROTEST IN PARIS:
Anatomy of a Revolt

PROTEST

IN PARIS

Anatomy of a Revolt

Bernard E. Brown
City University of New York, Brooklyn

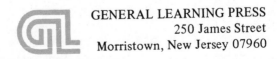

GENERAL LEARNING PRESS
250 James Street
Morristown, New Jersey 07960

Manufactured in the United States of America.

Published simultaneously in Canada.

Library of Congress Catalog Card Number 73–89235

For ELEANOR

PREFACE

This is a book about modern democracies that happens to deal entirely with France. The resurgence of radicalism in the western world is a striking development. But only in France, among the modern democracies, have revolutionary groups triggered a general strike and come close to the seizure of power. When Alexis de Tocqueville wished to study the phenomenon of equality, he chose to do so in America. Equality was more evident in the America of Andrew Jackson than in the France of monarchical restorations, and its effects could be more readily examined. As a topic, modernization and revolt in Gaullist France is comparable in importance to democracy in Jacksonian America.

The point of departure for this study of modernization and revolt is the French uprising of May 1968, one of the most important political events of recent times. "Before" and "after" May 1968 is as current in everyday parlance in France as it is in social science literature. It is often argued that revolutionary upheavals take place only during the breakdown of feudal or traditional societies and in the early stages of modernization. But now there is widespread evidence of the fragility of liberal regimes during later phases of modernization. The May Revolt is an indication of deep tensions within those societies making the transition from an industrial to a scientific civilization, and poses with special urgency the problem of the integration of the intellectual class into the political system.

The treatment here is in the tradition of the critical essay based on historical materials. After an account of the events themselves, there is a review of attempts by several French social scientists to assess the meaning of May. The revolutionary coalition is then broken down into its modernizing and anti-modernizing elements; a sharp contrast is drawn between Trotskyists and Maoists on the one side and anarchists and surrealists (mainly situationists) on the other. Each of these revolutionary groups is placed in historical context; the contradictions within the revolutionary coalition are examined in terms of a theory of political development and the concept of anomie. Since the same groups may be identified elsewhere in the world, this critical perspective is a springboard for comparative analysis. It is my hope that readers will find in this study building blocks for a theory of revolution.

This book is part of an ongoing debate among social scientists centering on the phenomenon of revolutionary ferment in industrial societies. In challenging current interpretations of the New Left my goal is not to score debating points, but rather to get behind rationalizations of power and of claims for power. The analysis offered here is an attempt at demystification.

I was able to observe the last phase of the May Revolt in the summer of 1968, and shortly thereafter wrote a module for General Learning Press entitled *The French Revolt: May 1968*, most of which has been incorporated into this manuscript. A few passages have also been taken from my review of Alain Touraine's *The May Movement* in the *American Political Science Review* (December 1972), and my article "The French Experience of Modernization," *World Politics* (April 1969).

It is a great pleasure to acknowledge the encouragement of colleagues and friends—Benjamin Rivlin, Martin Landau, Roy C. Macridis, Claude Leclercq—and all those who made comments on the earlier module. I am especially grateful to President John W. Kneller of Brooklyn College, who made it possible for me to take a research leave in 1971-72. My thanks also to the Research Foundation of the City University of New York for indispensable support. Finally, my wife, Eleanor, shared in the work as well as the fun.

                                        B. E. B.
                                        Montreal
                                        December, 1973

CONTENTS

Preface		vii
Abbreviations		xi
1.	The Events of May	2
2.	The Meanings of May	3 4
3.	Red Flags, Black Flags	6 6
4.	Toward the Seizure of Power	1 1 8
5.	The Revolt Vanishes	1 5 8
6.	Modernization and Revolt	2 0 4
Bibliography		2 2 6
Index		2 3 5

ABBREVIATIONS

The following abbreviations are used throughout this manuscript.

Student Organizations

FNEF   *Fédération Nationale des Etudiants de France (right-wing)*

SNESup   *Syndicat National de l'Enseignement Supérieur (university teachers union)*

UEC   *Union des Etudiants Communistes (affiliate of PCF)*

UNEF   *Union Nationale des Etudiants de France (leftist dominated)*

Revolutionary Groups

FER   *Fédération des Etudiants Révolutionnaires (Trotskyist)*

I.S.   *Internationale Situationniste*

JCR   *Jeunesses Communistes Révolutionnaires (Trotskyist)*

M.L.'s   *Union des Jeunesses Communistes, Marxistes-Léninistes (Maoist)*

Trade Unions

CFDT   *Confédération Française Démocratique du Travail (Christian Democratic)*

CGT   *Confédération Générale du Travail (Communist led)*

FO   *Confédération Générale du Travail, Force Ouvrière (Socialist oriented)*

Political Parties

Federation   *Fédération de la Gauche Démocratique et Socialiste (electoral alliance of Socialists, Radicals, and political clubs)*

PCF   *Parti Communiste Français*

PSU   *Parti Socialiste Unifié*

UDR   *Union pour la Défense de la République (Gaullist)*

PROTEST IN PARIS:
Anatomy of a Revolt

Nous ne sommes pas en face de besoin de réformes, mais en face d'une des crises les plus profondes que la civilisation ait connue . . . . Cette répétition générale d'un drame suspendu montrait, chez les grévistes comme chez ceux qui les regardaient passer, la conscience de la fin d'un monde . . . . Notre société n'est pas encore adaptée à la civilisation des machines.

André Malraux, *Le Monde*, June 22, 1968.[1]

IN MAY 1968, for the first time in almost a century, barricades were thrown up in the heart of Paris as part of a vast popular movement of political protest. Except during the Liberation, when the French Resistance skirmished briefly with a foreign army on the verge of defeat, no barricades had been seen in Paris since the Commune of 1871. Even in the turmoil of 1934 political violence took the form of riots, and did not proceed to the stage of barricades, dramatic defiance of the state, and a conscious attempt to seize power. Barricades belonged to the age of constitutional instability preceding the creation of the Third Republic, or to the exotic climate of Algiers. Their reappearance in a regime where the opposition can oppose and replace the government through elections was a dramatic indication of a profound crisis within French society, and was so understood immediately by those in power.

Years after the May Revolt took place, controversy still raged over matters of fact and of appreciation. Was the attempt to seize power spontaneous or planned? Why did the police arrest, or give the appearance of arresting the student militants on that fateful Friday afternoon, May 3? Did Pompidou's measures of clemency further stimulate the revolutionaries? Did the Communists sell out the revolution? What transpired when De Gaulle consulted with General Massu at Baden Baden? These are only a few of the thorny questions that continue to intrigue students of the May Revolt; every month brings new revelations by participants, observers, and scholars—and new controversies.

Our immediate concern is not to present a detailed history of the May Revolt, but rather to examine and appraise revolutionary groups and theories within its context. The student and worker movements, far from being united in their opposition to a new ruling class of "techno-bureaucrats," had altogether different political goals and, in addition, were internally fragmented. The May Revolt was not a single explosion of popular anger, but a chain reaction touched off by student and other revolutionary groups and then continued by the workers and middle classes for quite different reasons.

It is essential, then, to distinguish the phases of the crisis as a prelude to further analysis: [1] *the period of gestation, up to May 3*. Student unrest is manifest in many provincial universities, particularly the new campus at Nanterre. [2] *May 3-13*. Students riot in Paris, clash with the police, and occupy most institutions of higher learning. [3] *May 14-29*. Occupation of a Sud-Aviation plant by the workers expands quickly into a paralyzing general strike. General de Gaulle disappears briefly under mysterious circumstances. [4] *May 30-June 30*. General de Gaulle reappears full of fight and vigor. He calls for elections and vows to defend the republic against the menace of "totalitarian communism." Student unrest, student revolt, "contagion" (the term used by General de Gaulle in a television broadcast), and counterattack—these are the turning points in the May Revolt.[2]

Student Unrest (to May 3)

In *Le Monde* of March 15, 1968, Pierre Viansson-Ponté wrote: "That which presently characterizes our public life is boredom. The French are bored .... Youth is bored .... General de Gaulle is bored . . ."—and he went on to call attention to several hundred thousand French who were not bored (unemployed, marginal peasants, pensioners). The formula was striking and captured the spirit of the times. In the spring of 1968 France appeared as an oasis of tranquility in Europe and in the world. Racial and political violence had erupted in the United States; student riots were exploding in Italy, Germany, and Japan; political authorities were being challenged throughout Eastern Europe, especially in Czechoslovakia; and the Irish problem was beginning to preoccupy the British. Gaullist policies seemed to be vindicated by the stark contrast between a world in fever and a France self-assured and calm. Yet, by May and June 1968 France was in the throes of an acute political crisis. How did it happen?

So abrupt was the outbreak of the May Revolt that at first it seemed to have come from nowhere or to have been the product of spontaneous combustion, unplanned and unorganized. Since revolts do not usually occur in this manner, it was then believed that the student organization, the Union Nationale des Etudiants de France (UNEF), and the university teachers union, Syndicat National de l'Enseignement Supérieur (SNESup), had mobilized dissatisfied students, an impression reinforced by the prominent radio and television coverage given to the leaders of these organizations, Jacques Sauvageot and Alain Geismar. Only after the events did it become clear that UNEF and SNESup were without great influence and functioned at the time as restraints rather than stimulants. The revolutionary impulse emanated from other sources.

Protest by students has been an annual event in France virtually every year since the Liberation. Overcrowding, inadequate facilities, insufficient scholarships, impersonal instruction—the catalogue of grievances is long. During the Algerian war protest turned political; conservatives and radicals struggled for control of the student organizations. After the granting of independence to Algeria, student interest in politics waned. But in 1965 a new form of agitation began sweeping through the French universities that was little understood at the time either by university administrators or the general public. The issue was ostensibly petty: the right to entertain members of the opposite sex in dormitory rooms. Militant students at the new residential center at Antony, just south of Paris, blocked construction of a guard house in front of the girls' dormitory. Bewildered administrators at Antony gave in, modifying dormitory regulations so as to permit virtually complete freedom for visitors.

In May 1966 a small group of radicals managed to gain control of the student organization at Strasbourg. Through this official agency they distributed a pamphlet reflecting their anger and passion, *De la misère en milieu étudiant* (On the Poverty of Student Life). It was written for the occasion by a theoretician of the international situationists—a group combining aesthetic surrealism and political radicalism. Although they were expelled shortly thereafter, the radicals had sounded a new note. Most of the themes sprung upon an amazed public during the May Revolt were inspired by the situationists and had made their first appearance during the events at Strasbourg.[3]

Agitation over dormitory visiting privileges flared up again in 1967, this time as part of a national campaign by the Parti Socialiste Unifié (PSU). Students were summoned to mass meetings for debates on sexual liberty and then found themselves engaged in a larger critique of morality and exploitation under capitalism. Dissatisfaction with dormitory restrictions was exploited by the PSU as a means of mobilizing students for the fight against capitalism, the root of all evil. Escalation of demands, beginning with the purely reformist and ending with the purely political, was to be an ever-present feature of the May Revolt.

Nanterre, a newly founded campus just west of Paris, was the launching pad from which the May Revolt took off, to the astonishment perhaps even of the main participants in the events. Discontent at Nanterre, as elsewhere, was first stirred up by the campaign for dormitory privileges. A second wave of discontent followed the reform instituted by Minister of Education Christian Fouchet in 1967, and in particular the promulgation of confusing regulations concerning evaluation of credit for academic work done in preceding years. Under the leadership of a moderate Christian student group, a protest strike was called at Nanterre in November 1967. Student demands at this time related to evaluation of credits, class size, exam standards, and student representation in university councils. After the administration gave in to most demands, the strike was called off. However, it proved difficult to secure faculty cooperation, particularly as regards student participation in decision-making, and the moderate student leaders lost much of their support. The mass of the students had been aroused by the demands for sexual freedom in the dormitories and more rational grading procedures but these issues soon dropped out of sight, to be replaced by the utopian demand for revolution and a totally new society.[4]

A new breed of agitators, typified by Daniel Cohn-Bendit, elbowed the moderates out of the way. Cohn-Bendit first came to prominence when the minister of youth and culture, François Missoffe, visited the Nanterre campus to inspect a new and costly swimming pool. The student militants were prepared for his visit; the minister found his itinerary marked for him by huge phallic symbols and hooting groups of students. Cohn-Bendit emerged from the crowd, asked him for a light, and demanded to know why a recent official report on student life made no mention of sexual problems. The minister retorted: "With your looks, no wonder you have a problem. But you can always take a dip in the swimming pool to cool off." A student voice: "That's a fascist answer!" The minister had scored a debating point but Cohn-Bendit had gained a following.

The radicals now had the Nanterre campus in an uproar. It was rumored that the administration had compiled a blacklist of student militants, who were to be disciplined or expelled for their political activities. On January 26 a group of some eighty students marched up and down the main building, shouting slogans and denouncing the dean, Pierre Grappin, as a Nazi (though, in fact, Grappin had been active in the Resistance). After some university employees had been roughed up, the dean called in the local police. They were greatly outnumbered by the students, who quickly chased the representatives of law and order off the campus. The events at Nanterre were not isolated. By the end of January student protests against dormitory regulations, that ever-popular issue, were taking place all over the country. Hundreds of high school students battled Paris police during a demonstration over the disciplining of a student. More important as a harbinger of things to come, student activists joined with young workers on strike at the Saviem truck factory in Caen and eighteen people were injured in a violent clash with the police. At Nanterre, a group of radical students, calling themselves "les enragés," decided to apply "guerrilla tactics" within the university. In February the militants invaded the girls' dormitory and "liberated the prisoners." Similar incidents took place at a dozen provincial universities.

In February the militants turned their attention from dormitories and exams to a much more serious topic: Vietnam. When the Tet offensive began, students demonstrated outside the American and South Vietnamese embassies. In mid-March bombs exploded at several American banks in Paris; and on March 20 the American Express office on rue Scribe was attacked by roving bands of radicals (mainly Trotskyist). One demonstrator was arrested; he was a student at Nanterre. Word spread that more arrests would follow.

On March 22 some three hundred students at Nanterre held a meeting to protest against police repression. A large group (according to the legend, 142) invaded the administration building and occupied a conference chamber. Modelling themselves on the example of Fidel Castro in the Sierra Maestra, the aspiring revolutionaries founded a "March 22 Movement" (hereafter referred to as M22M) and named a lecture hall after Ché Guevara. After everyone agreed on the need to overthrow capitalism, M22M decided to hold a teach-in the following week on the struggle against imperialism. Around four hundred students participated in this daylong debate on March 28. A now familiar scenario was played out: a liberal university administration oscillated between concession and repression while student activists engaged in a campaign of vituperation and physical violence in an effort to compel the university to discredit itself by calling in the police. During this period of uncertainty there were signs of increasing isolation of the student activists. The major student union, UNEF, issued a strong condemnation of these terrorist tactics. At Nanterre moderate students also spoke out against the cult of violence, as did leaders of Communist youth groups.

But the administration could no longer control the Nanterre campus. On April 25 a Communist deputy and specialist on university affairs was forcibly prevented from speaking at the university by the Maoists. A two-day teach-in on the struggle against imperialism began on May 2. On that day eight members of M22M were given notice to appear before a university disciplinary committee. To heighten tension, rumor had it that a right-wing activist group, Occident, planned to raid the Nanterre campus. M22M, aided at first by the Maoists, prepared to defend their turf, which was soon encircled by a cordon of police. In the midst of this chaos, M22M appropriated an amphitheater for another teach-in. Dean Grappin decided to suspend classes indefinitely.

Meanwhile, on May 2 Prime Minister Pompidou left Paris on a long-planned, nine-day trip to Iran and Afghanistan. Critical tactical decisions were made in his absence by three men who were clearly overwhelmed by events: Alain Peyrefitte and Christian Fouchet, the newly appointed ministers of education and interior; and Louis Joxe, the Acting Prime Minister. On May 3 the Nanterre campus was deserted; the students were converging on the Sorbonne in Paris.

The Student Uprising (May 3-13)

Friday, May 3, was the most important single day of the entire crisis, for on that day the rector of the University of Paris, Jean Roche, called in the police. Several hundred militants had gathered in the courtyard of the Sorbonne at noon to hear speeches by radical leaders (mainly M22M and Trotskyists). After a brief recess for lunch, the rally continued into the afternoon. A series of speakers denounced the closing of the Nanterre campus and the disciplinary procedures initiated against Cohn-Bendit and several others. Some right-wing students of Occident seeking to march upon the Sorbonne were intercepted and rerouted by the police. Fearing attack, the militants in the Sorbonne courtyard prepared to defend their bastion. After discussing the situation with Peyrefitte, the Minister of Education, Rector Roche asked the police to clear the area in order to prevent a clash between the two extremist groups. The police, reluctant to intervene, asked for written instructions, which were forthcoming. "Please reestablish order within the Sorbonne by expelling those who are disorderly," wrote Roche. Thus, the request was merely that the courtyard be cleared, not that arrests be made. At first the operation went smoothly. The would-be revolutionaries agreed to have their papers checked at local police stations. Over five hundred demonstrators filed into police vans and were driven off—although why this was considered necessary remains a mystery, since the effect was bound to be provocative. The onlookers massed around the Sorbonne had no way of knowing the difference between verification of papers and being placed under arrest.[5]

As the vans, chock full of militants, moved out of the Sorbonne area, the crowd intervened; at first they hurled insults, then rocks. The police reacted by charging the crowd, and a battle was on. In the next five hours several hundred people were injured, including over eighty policemen, and six hundred people arrested—almost half of the estimated number of those engaged in the fight. Through an instinct of solidarity the student masses had closed ranks behind the revolutionaries. The public was shocked by the sight of policemen beating up students and innocent bystanders. The police appeared as the aggressors, the students as the victims. Public opinion was on the side of the students (by a margin of eighty to twenty, according to an opinion poll on May 8). UNEF and SNESup called for an unlimited strike, and thousands of students poured into the streets. The chief demand was simply an expression of student solidarity:—"*Libérez nos camarades!*" ("Free our comrades"—namely four students sentenced over the weekend to two months in prison for attacking policemen).

The smell of tear gas hung over the Latin Quarter. The next two weeks witnessed continued street fighting, the construction of barricades, and car burnings. Students occupied school buildings and fought the police, while harried government officials tried contradictory tactics in an attempt to cope with rioters. The student leaders had three demands: dismissal of all charges against demonstrators and release of those who had been arrested; withdrawal of the police from university buildings and surrounding areas; and reopening of university facilities. Within the government the Minister of Education, Alain Peyrefitte, was willing to negotiate with the student leaders, while the Minister of the Interior, Christian Fouchet, took a hard line. General de Gaulle, who believed that dealing with student disorders was the responsibility of his ministers and not of the president of the republic, gave his distant support to Fouchet and the advocates of a tough policy.

On May 6 student protest marchers clashed with the police again, and six hundred people were injured. The incidents continued on the following day, and the government closed the Sorbonne. There then followed the second of the month's three "bloody Fridays." On May 10 twenty thousand students paraded in Paris. The police prevented them from freeing their comrades being held at the Santé prison and from crossing the Seine to storm the central radio station. Gradually the students were pushed back to the Latin Quarter, where they rallied their forces. By midnight about thirty barricades in the Latin Quarter were manned by several thousand determined militants, notably the Trotskyists. In order to avoid bloodshed, the government by this time was willing to meet two demands of the students (withdrawal of the police and reopening of the Sorbonne) and gave assurances that an amnesty would be forthcoming—though it could not be made official until the courts had disposed of all cases pending. In return, the students were to promise that the Sorbonne would be able to function normally.

But serious negotiations were no longer possible. A feverish excitement had taken hold of the student demonstrators behind the barricades, and the hard-core militants were not disposed to compromise. Some student leaders played the game of negotiation—often communicating with government officials via the radio—simply as a way of further arousing the furor of those manning the barricades. Cohn-Bendit declared after a delegation left the rectorate late that night: "We did not engage in negotiations. We said: what is taking place in the street tonight shows that all youth is demonstrating against a certain kind of society."[6] The radicals had succeeded in mobilizing large masses of students (not including, however, a dissident Trotskyist group, the Maoists, and the orthodox Communists, all of whom considered the barricades that night to be a trap), and had no intention of letting an opportunity slip for crystallizing revolutionary consciousness. At 2 A.M. precisely—after most high school students presumably had taken the last métro home—the police proceeded to clear the Latin Quarter. Once again the public was appalled by the well-publicized police practice of beating up demonstrators. The intensity of the fighting in the very heart of a great city caused a profound shock. Almost four hundred people were injured (thirty-two seriously), close to five hundred were taken into custody, and one hundred and eighty-eight cars were destroyed. Was this Paris—or Saigon?

On the following day Georges Pompidou returned from his trip, convinced that sweeping concessions by the government were necessary because public opinion was on the side of the student underdogs. He therefore determined to accept *all* of the student demands so that any future clash between government and students would reveal clearly which side was being unreasonable. After a long session with General de Gaulle, who reluctantly went along, Pompidou announced a policy of conciliation in a television broadcast that night. "These decisions," he said, "are inspired by a profound sympathy for the students and confidence in their common sense." Too late. That very night several thousand students occupied Censier, an annex of the Sorbonne. UNEF issued a declaration denouncing the state, "whose police nature has appeared so clearly." The trade unions and teachers federations called for a 24-hour general strike for Monday, May 13, to be accompanied by mass demonstrations throughout France against police brutality—ten years to the day after the uprising that doomed the Fourth Republic. In spite of squabbling between the Communist Party and the leftists, the strike took place as planned on Monday (though it was far from being general), and several hundred thousand people marched from the Place de la République in the heart of working-class Paris across the city to Denfert-Rochereau. Student revolutionaries urged demonstrators to seize public buildings; but the trade unions kept their troops in line, and most workers simply dispersed.

The students then gravitated toward the Sorbonne and occupied the premises, since the way was no longer blocked by the police. Those who could crowd into the grand amphitheater became the all-powerful sovereign assembly and declared the University of Paris an "autonomous people's university." There then began the unforgettable spectacle of a French-style cultural revolution.

Pompidou's decision to reopen the Sorbonne was crucial, because it enabled the student militants to take over the university. For some observers, his action was a retreat, the cause of the whole tragedy into which France was about to be plunged. It was the breach. But there was no assurance that a policy of repression would have worked either, given the passions aroused by street battles, the determination of revolutionaries to exploit the situation, and the ever-present possibility of intervention by the Communist Party and its well-disciplined troops. Probably nothing would have brought about a return to calm—neither concessions nor repression. Thus, on the tenth anniversary of the overthrow of the Fourth Republic, an insurrectionary force had gained control of a prestigious public building, the Sorbonne, directly challenging the authority of the Gaullist regime.[7]

The Contagion (May 14-30)

General de Gaulle was to leave the country on May 14 for an official four-day visit to Rumania, which had been arranged long in advance. Because of the uncertain domestic situation, De Gaulle had second thoughts about going. The Minister of the Interior, Christian Fouchet, urged him to stay, since he might be needed if the crisis deepened; but Foreign Minister Couve de Murville and Prime Minister Pompidou prevailed upon him to go through with the trip to give the impression of a return to normalcy. Just before taking off, General de Gaulle announced that he would address the country ten days later.[8]

Up to this point the uprising was confined to students only. In Paris, as in Amsterdam, Berkeley, Berlin, Brussels, New York, Rome, and Tokyo (in alphabetical order), the rest of the population, including the workers, remained unmoved by the call to revolution. But on May 14, the day of General de Gaulle's departure for Rumania, the "contagion" spread. Workers in the small aircraft plant of Sud-Aviation, in the suburbs of Nantes, left their machines, occupied the premises, and locked up their director. At the same time workers struck and occupied a small Renault factory near Rouen. Young workers in particular were influenced by the example set by the students. If the tactic of challenging authority was successful in a school, why not in a factory? If autogestion was feasible in a university, why not in a workshop? The strikers fanned out to other Renault plants at Flins and Billancourt to spread the word. The powerful Communist-led union, Confédération Générale du Travail (CGT), joined the movement. It ordered the occupation of Billancourt and flashed the green light for similar actions elsewhere. Thus the protest demonstration of May 13 was followed by a series of wildcat strikes, exploding like firecrackers, on May 14, 15, and 16. Then the movement, canalized and directed by the unions, became a general strike of indefinite duration. Some essential public services, however, in particular the electricity supply, were maintained.

Within one week the unions claimed that there were over ten million workers on strike—estimated by later studies to be closer to six million. Even so, that was more than the number involved in the great sit-down strike of 1936. The workers did not merely picket; they physically occupied factories and converted many into defensive outposts. Red flags flew everywhere. In most cases a small number of workers remained on the premises while the others either stayed home or came to the factory only for meetings, in contrast to the mass occupations of 1936. Nonetheless, the workers had seized control of the means of production! No one knew what to do with the booty, however. Some militants wanted to overthrow the capitalist system; others wanted to force General de Gaulle to resign; the left-wing Christian Democratic union, Confédération Française Démocratique du Travail (CFDT), wanted to negotiate new forms of worker participation in management; and the powerful CGT wanted at first only to secure widespread economic gains for the working class.

The contagion spread throughout the entire society. Now doctors, lawyers, accountants, engineers, researchers, statisticians, journalists, museum curators, actors, film directors, athletes, and shopgirls joined in a general revolt against authority. Hundreds of "action committees" sprang up and through them demands were made for reorganizing the medical profession, the museums, the press, the radio; indeed, for all collective enterprises. The middle and professional classes appeared to be rising up against the bureaucratic structures. through which their lives were governed.

The examples of the cinema and publishing worlds serve to illustrate these middle-class happenings, as well as the atmosphere of unreality in which they took place. Students of photography and cinema, after occupying their school, took the initiative in attacking the film industry. They disrupted the showing of films all over Paris and engaged audiences in debates on the evils of commercialism. On May 26 over a thousand people connected with the cinema attended a "States General of the French Cinema" and quickly agreed that at every stage in the planning, production, and distribution of films they were subjected to degrading commercial considerations. The States General then drew up a "charter" of the future that assumed a socialist transformation of French society. They expected unlimited resources to be placed at their disposal by a socialist state as well as, of course, complete freedom from state control. In a similar spirit, a dozen writers occupied the state-owned headquarters of the Society of Men of Letters, denounced it as decadent, expelled the aging occupants, and founded a Union of Writers. A general assembly of the new union engaged in rambling discussions of Marxism, socialism, revolution, and other hot political topics. Members urged each other to build a new society based on democracy and common ownership of the means of production. But anarchists, revolutionary students, and even the displaced and now irate Men of Letters, began to dispute possession of the building, and the enterprise foundered in confusion.

The film producers and the writers were not trying to devise solutions. They were caught up in a mass movement of protest against the system and yearned for ideals, no matter how contradictory or removed from reality. The fever even spread to a group hardly known for its political expertise, the professional soccer players. About a hundred of these muscular citizens occupied the offices of the French Football Federation, hung a red flag in a window, and put up a sign proclaiming their goal: *"Le football aux footballeurs"* ("Soccer for the soccer players")!

More serious than soccer power from the point of view of the government was the loss of control over its own radio and television system. Many journalists sympathized with the students and pleaded their cause over the public air waves. The Minister of Information cancelled a television show that placed the student rebels in too favorable a light. On May 17 a general assembly of the Office of French Radio and Television (ORTF) employees, including administrators, writers, broadcasters, and technicians, called for a complete restructuring of the ORTF to make it independent of the state. Within five days virtually all of the employees were out on strike; only a handful were authorized to broadcast the news. After the elections in June the government once again took the ORTF in hand and many of the dissidents were fired. The demand for autonomy and self-government was general throughout the society in May and June 1968; but the implications of these demands, and the contradiction between advocacy of socialism for everyone else and laissez-faire for one's own little sector were nowhere clearer than in the sensitive domain of radio and television.

While public attention shifted to the factories, the revolutionary students were busy putting their notion of autogestion into practice. The Sorbonne became a big, booming festival. A jazz band blared forth in the courtyard, while every imaginable political sect produced—as if by magic—stands to display and sell their literature. The walls were covered with graffiti, mostly in the surrealist and dadaist tradition. There were two levels of activity in the occupied universities: the festival, the endless talking in the amphitheaters, the jazz bands, and the "ideological drugstore"; and the gruelling work of controlling and directing the mass of students and elaborating a program, a task that was carried on mostly behind the scenes by the various organized revolutionary groups.

UNEF announced its program on May 16. It was a synthesis of most student demands: "student power" through participation of student representatives endowed with a veto in all collective decisions of the university; autonomy of the universities; extension of the struggle to the press, radio, television, and theater; and collaboration between students and workers. In spite of violent disagreements among the various student groups, one point emerged: the universities were to be independent from the state, that is, they would receive money from the state, and would then use that financial support to subvert the state and overthrow it. Would the universities remain autonomous after the revolution? Would students and

professors enjoy freedom from state control under the new
regime? To pose such questions in the heady atmosphere of the
Sorbonne in May was indiscreet. All indications were that
opponents of the revolution would be considered reactionaries,
to be dealt with in summary fashion.

The revolutionary nature of student demands was under-
lined by the extension of the insurrection from the Sorbonne to
the nearby national theater, the Odéon, signalling a shift from
the goal of an autonomous university to that of a full-fledged
cultural revolution. An action committee at the head of the
mob that flooded into the theater decided that the Odéon
would function as a permanent forum for discussions between
students and workers, a center for "creative revolution." The
director, Jean-Louis Barrault, at first tried to stop the take-over,
then voiced revolutionary slogans himself and went along. At
the Odéon there was only one level of activity—the talkfest;
there was nothing to control behind the scenes.

In the face of this raging storm, the government maneu-
vered for time. There seemed to be no handle; as De Gaulle
remarked later, the situation was *"insaisissable"* (elusive). The
French have had a long experience with revolts; sometimes
the best way to handle an uprising is to let it ripen, give the
ringleaders lots of leeway, let them have their successes—in
the hope that these become excesses—wait for public opinion to
swing against the insurgents, and only then take forceful action.
Provided that the revolutionaries meanwhile do not seize
power! In the days following General de Gaulle's departure for
Rumania, the government's grip on the country weakened. The
strike had spread throughout the nation; the Sorbonne was
occupied; the insurrection spilled over to the Odéon; and the
street disorders continued. General de Gaulle was in a towering
rage when he returned to Paris on May 18, denouncing the
incompetence of his ministers and the fickleness of his
compatriots. *"La chienlit!"*—the French were fouling their own
nest. To begin with, he ordered, clear the Sorbonne and the
Odéon. But his ministers balked; some demonstrators might be
killed and the revolt would gain its martyrs. Better to let the

rebels play themselves out; there were already indications that the public was losing patience with the goings-on at the Sorbonne and with the continuing violence in the street.

Public attention now shifted briefly to Parliament. A motion of censure drawn up by the opposition parties was hotly debated on May 21 and 22, but it fell eleven votes short of the absolute majority. During the debate, Pompidou offered a way out. He declared himself prepared to engage in dialogue with all the trade unions, provided that no political conditions were attached: "The trade unions have no right to substitute themselves for the sovereign people," he said. Leaders of the chief trade unions, including the CGT, immediately responded that they would participate in negotiations to improve the conditions of the working class. It was evident at this point that the Communist leaders did not believe the revolutionary situation was "ripe" and were willing to negotiate with the government rather than seek its overthrow. Pompidou then called for a tripartite conference (government, business, and labor) to be held on Saturday, May 25, at the Ministry of Social Affairs on rue de Grenelle (and known thereafter as the Grenelle Conference). The general strike of 1968 seemed to be heading for the same outcome as the last great strike in 1936—a national agreement negotiated by spokesmen for government, business, and labor to increase wages and improve working conditions, but entirely within the framework of the existing political and economic system.

That is the way it worked out, ultimately, but not before another series of violent clashes and suspenseful episodes. The government announced on May 22 that Cohn-Bendit, who was off on a revolutionary mission to Germany and Holland, was barred from reentering France. Students immediately marched in protest, and once again there were riots in the streets: about 200 persons injured and an equal number taken into custody. Student leaders then announced a mass rally and protest march for the next day, May 24. But the Communists and the CGT were not going to exert themselves for a provocateur like Cohn-Bendit! They announced separate protest marches, so that on that day there were Communist-led demonstrations on both the Left and Right banks in Paris, while about 25,000 people converged upon the Gare de Lyon, a railroad station conveniently close to the Latin Quarter, in response to the call by student radicals.

Friday, May 24—the very day General de Gaulle had picked before his departure for a speech on radio and television. Would he turn the tide again, as he had done during the army *putsch* of April 1961, by simply asserting his authority in an address to the nation? Among those listening were the demonstrators, clustered around transistors, at the Gare de Lyon. But the old Gaullist magic did not work this time. De Gaulle's talk was uninspired and out of touch with reality; his proffered solution to the crisis was yet another referendum that would somehow assure all elements of the population a right to "participate" in decisions affecting them. The offer was accompanied by his customary threat of resignation if the referendum was defeated. De Gaulle was trying to exploit the crisis to achieve a long-cherished goal: a "third way" between grasping capitalism and repressive communism, an association of capital and labor that would transcend class conflict.

The speech fell flat. A graffito at the Grand Palais explained why: "He took three weeks to announce in five minutes that he was going to undertake in one month what he had not succeeded in doing in ten years."[9] De Gaulle himself later admitted: "I missed the target." The speech provoked rather than appeased the demonstrators. That night Paris suffered its third bloody Friday in that May. Gangs of rioters swept through the city and set fire to the Stock Exchange. The bitterest fighting again took place in the Latin Quarter; over five hundred people were injured and over six hundred taken into custody. A police officer was killed that night during riots in Lyon. The government accused "la pègre" (the criminal element) and the anarchists of deliberately fomenting war in the streets. For the first time there seemed to be a change in the attitude of the Parisians, who now showed hostility toward those burning automobiles and chopping down trees for barricades. Nor did they appreciate the spread of street fighting outside of the Latin Quarter.

However, officials responsible for security were disturbed by signs of disaffection within the police forces. As long as the threat to public order came from middle-class students, the police were rough. They resented Pompidou's decision to liberate some of the student rioters, which was considered a disavowal of the police by the very government they were trying to defend. But when millions of workers went on strike, a new note was sounded—policemen were also workers and would be loath to take sides against their class brethren. A communiqué issued by the policemen's union stated that the police were not "privileged," fully understood the motives of those on strike, and hoped that "the government would not systematically oppose police and workers, in which event policemen would be justified in considering certain of their missions as posing grave cases of conscience." It was questionable whether the police force would be a reliable instrument of state policy in the event of a violent confrontation with the striking workers.

The Grenelle negotiations began in this charged atmosphere on Saturday, May 25. Leaders of all the major trade unions were there. The business group was headed by Paul Huvelin, president of the National Council of French Business (CNPF). Prime Minister Pompidou and Minister of Social Affairs Jeanneney represented the government side; hard-line Finance Minister Michel Debré was conspicuously absent. The bargaining was sharp, and on several occasions Georges Séguy of the CGT threatened to walk out. But it was in the interest of all parties to arrive at an agreement quickly: the government was desperately trying to restore its authority; management wanted to get the economy going again; and the CGT was determined not to be outflanked on its left by irresponsible anarchists. Early Monday morning, after round-the-clock sessions, Pompidou announced a settlement: increase of the minimum wage by one-third, general wage increases of seven percent immediately and an additional three percent by October, reduction of the work week, increased family allowances, payment for half the time lost in the strike. It was the most attractive package the trade unions had won in thirty years.

But Pompidou was not yet in the clear, since the union leaders now had to consult the rank and file. The Grenelle accord was to be submitted to the workers in their enterprises. The first such enterprise was the "workers' fortress," the Renault factory at Billancourt. Through a curious set of circumstances, it turned out that the workers were in no mood to hear of compromise. Every day of the strike, a meeting had taken place at 8 A.M. at Billancourt. That Monday the meeting began before the news of the agreement at rue de Grenelle (actually concluded only twenty minutes before) had become known. Twelve thousand workers were assembled, and they were convinced that the unions were going to win all along the line (full pay for all days of work missed during the strike, work week of forty hours without loss of pay, retirement at age sixty, and so forth). The local secretary of the CGT opened the meeting and, believing that negotiations were still underway, called for a continuation of the strike, as he had done each day since the strike had started. His motion was approved boisterously and unanimously. "The strike continues, then, comrades, until satisfaction of our demands." Since Séguy of the CGT had not yet arrived with the good news from rue de Grenelle, the chairman of the meeting gave the floor to Benoît Frachon, who had left the Grenelle meeting the previous evening and was also unaware that the accord had been concluded. André Jeanson of the CFDT spoke briefly, calling for solidarity with the students. Finally, Séguy arrived and presented the main terms of the agreement but it was to no avail. The workers hooted every time management was mentioned, and Séguy quickly realized that the Grenelle agreement would not be ratified by the rank and file. Declaring that the CGT had not called the strike and therefore could not order that it be ended, he in effect registered the failure of his own efforts to remain in control of the situation. Pompidou later remarked that Frachon and Séguy had not "prepared the hall." But workers at meetings all over the country similarly rejected the Grenelle accord. The strike continued and the government now appeared powerless to bring it to an end.[10]

In these circumstances, the opposition parties put themselves forward as an alternative government. PSU and UNEF, with the support of the CFDT, called for a mass rally at the Charléty stadium in Paris on May 27. Although the meeting was boycotted by the Communists, some thirty thousand enthusiastic people attended. It was an impressive demonstration of the strength of the new left. Jacques Sauvageot urged that the movement go forward to socialism. Alain Geismar took up the Cuban theme: "The first duty of a revolutionary is to make the revolution." In a fiery speech André Barjonet, who had resigned from both the CGT and the French Communist Party that week and had joined the PSU, proclaimed: "Today, revolution is possible. But it must be organized quickly, very quickly." Among those in the audience was a former prime minister, Pierre Mendès-France. In the next few days his name was mentioned constantly, especially by the CFDT, as the most likely leader of the left.

At a press conference on May 28 François Mitterrand, leader of the socialist and radical opposition, predicted that the referendum would be defeated, President de Gaulle would withdraw, and Prime Minister Pompidou would disappear. In that event, said Mitterrand, he was prepared to form a provisional government of ten members and would himself be a candidate for the presidency if necessary. Mendès-France also made it known that he "would not refuse to serve" a united left. The PCF found itself threatened on the left by the coalition that sponsored the Charléty meeting, ready to rally behind Mendès-France, and on the right by Mitterrand and the Federation. "It is not serious," said Waldeck Rochet, secretary general of the PCF, "to claim to go forward to socialism without the Communists, and still less so to practice anti-communism as at Charléty stadium." In short, the parties of the left were engaged in the kinds of maneuvers that characterize any change of government. Electoral calculations were being made by the leaders. The Communists wanted to force the Federation to agree to a common program, so that they might reenter the government in a position of strength, while the leaders of the noncommunist left were turning to the center precisely in order to ward off the fervent embrace of the PCF.

The Gaullists were staggering under the blows they had received in the course of one short month. The minister of economy had little economic activity to supervise; the minister of education could not show his face at the Sorbonne; the minister of the interior was no longer sure of his police; the prime minister had made concession after concession and seemed now to have no more cards to play; and the president of the republic was almost an object of pity. Heavy traffic on the roads to Switzerland, where many French have numbered bank accounts, pointed up the crisis of confidence in the regime. Legal authority was collapsing. Would it be followed by anarchy and civil war? If so, anything was possible—a Communist seizure of power, or intervention by the army. Precisely at this point, when the regime seemed to be disintegrating, came the *coup de théâtre*: on May 29 at 11 A.M. General de Gaulle disappeared.

For five hours, and under highly dramatic circumstances, the chief of state dropped out of sight. Since he had last been seen in a helicopter, there was a possibility of an accident, perhaps even that he was dead. In retrospect, De Gaulle's disappearance was a tactical masterstroke. On May 24 his address to the nation had been a flop, and thereafter he seemed to be lost in the shuffle. Attention shifted to Mitterrand, Mendès-France, and the Communists, almost as if the duly elected president had already vacated the premises. All of a sudden, the attention of the entire nation—and of the world—was bracketed upon General de Gaulle. Once again the fate of France was linked irrevocably with his person. Was the whole episode—disappearance, feverish anxiety, reappearance—a carefully produced bit of stage business? At least one reputable journalist contends that it was, and that Prime Minister Pompidou could not have been kept in the dark, in spite of his protestations at the time.[11] The story may never be known in all its details, but for our purposes the play's the thing, not the conscience of the President.

After the failure of the May 24 speech and the rejection of the Grenelle accords, General de Gaulle seemed to be overwhelmed by a feeling of defeatism. Everything was giving way, he later remarked, like the dam at Fréjus (the scene of a recent catastrophe); the torrent was sweeping all before it. Pompidou, in a meeting with De Gaulle on May 28, for the first time voiced the opinion that the Communists might be tempted to seize power. The Communists had just called for a mass protest march that would take them close to the Hôtel de Ville, the traditional site for the proclamation of new republics. There were signs of a hardening attitude within the PCF, possibly because of the fear that Mitterrand and Mendès-France might outmaneuver them, or quite possibly because power seemed to be lying in the street waiting for anyone to come along and pick it up. As a precaution, De Gaulle consulted with the army chief of staff. Several paratroop units were put on the alert and a detachment of tanks was ordered to roam around the outskirts of Paris for psychological effect. Pompidou believed now that the referendum could not be held on schedule and sought unsuccessfully to persuade De Gaulle to call for elections instead. They were to continue the discussion at the cabinet meeting scheduled for the next day, May 29.

On the morning of that day, May 29, General de Gaulle gave his chief military adviser a delicate assignment: to see three generals in charge of the major part of the army's combat units, appraise the state of morale, and find out, quickly, by that evening, whether the army was prepared to carry out any and all orders received from the president of the republic. Shortly thereafter, De Gaulle informed his aides that he was tired and wished to spend a day at home in Colombey. Hence, the regular Wednesday cabinet meeting was cancelled. Pompidou was deeply disturbed and tried in vain to reach the General by telephone. De Gaulle at that time was consulting with his son-in-law, General Alain de Boissieu. At 11 A.M. De Gaulle personally put through a telephone call to Pompidou, a rare occurrence. He repeated the reasons for his trip to Colombey and assured the prime minister that he would return the next day.

Several ministers remained with Pompidou for lunch at his official residence, the Matignon. At 2 P.M. De Gaulle's chief aide appeared, pale and agitated, to report that General de Gaulle had not arrived at Colombey on schedule. In fact, there was no trace of his helicopter! Was he dead? If so, what should be done to stave off the real threat of a takeover by the Communists? A number of parliamentarians arrived at the Matignon on other business, and instead found themselves discussing the disappearance of De Gaulle and the fate of the republic. They drew up a declaration of support for the prime minister. At 4 P.M.—five hours after the presidential helicopter had left Paris—the defense ministry informed Pompidou that General de Gaulle was alive and well and in Baden Baden, conferring with General Massu.

Several years after the event, General Massu, while refusing to reveal exactly what transpired during their meeting, commented: "Even today, I still ask myself why he came to Baden Baden. I've wracked my brains, thought about what he did and said, and I still don't understand why he made that trip." It would have been much simpler, he continued, to have called the generals to the Elysée, where they could go in and out unobserved.[12] But a simple procedure was less important than the symbolic value of De Gaulle's action. The trip to Baden Baden was the equivalent of De Gaulle's gesture in 1944 when, upon entering liberated Paris, he refused an invitation to proclaim the republic from a balcony of the Hôtel de Ville, and instead made his way to the "center of the State"—the ministry of war.

That evening General de Gaulle was back in Colombey and spoke briefly to the prime minister by phone. Meanwhile, loyal Gaullists were preparing to stage a mass rally in his favor the very next day.

The Counterattack (May 30)

The stage was now set for the last act of a Gaullist morality play. The evil were to be punished, the false pretenders to the throne exposed, and the people were to return to their senses. Refreshed by his contact with the only reliable organized force left in the nation, the army, the old warrior was ready to take charge. On Thursday, May 30, General de Gaulle returned to Paris from Colombey by helicopter, arriving at the Elysée just after noon. First a meeting with the prime minister, then the cabinet, then an address to the nation, and finally the mass demonstration—it was a full afternoon! After refusing Pompidou's proffered resignation, De Gaulle briefed him on his speech. Pompidou approved, except for one capital point: there was no mention of new elections. De Gaulle was still not convinced. "You asked me to withdraw my resignation," said Pompidou, "I ask you to dissolve the Assembly." Rather than lose his prime minister in the midst of the battle, De Gaulle agreed.[13] After informing the cabinet, De Gaulle addressed the nation by radio (as in June 1940). "I have made my decision. In the present circumstances I shall not withdraw. I hold a mandate from the people. I shall fulfill it . . . . I today dissolve the National Assembly." He announced that the referendum would be postponed and legislative elections held immediately, unless the French people were prevented by "intimidation, intoxication, and tyranny," from expressing themselves. In that event, he vowed, he would maintain the Republic "by other means than an immediate vote of the country." France, he cried, is menaced by dictatorship, for out of national despair and the maneuvering of the politicians would come the ultimate victory of "totalitarian communism." No! "The Republic will not abdicate, the people will recover. Progress, independence and peace will win along with freedom!"

It was a masterful performance, a political version of the Battle of the Marne. "My center is yielding, my right is retreating. Excellent situation. I attack!" And the enemy was routed. Chaban-Delmas read to the National Assembly the letter decreeing its dissolution; the Gaullist deputies adjusted their tricolor sashes, then walked across the bridge to the Place de la Concorde, ready to lead one of the greatest mass demonstrations in the history of the Republic—prepared in haste by veterans groups and the Gaullist action committees. One million people, according to the Gaullists—in all probability half that number or less—paraded from the Concorde to the Etoile, chanting "De Gaulle is not alone," "Mitterand in the Lido" (suggesting that the latter's talents were more suited to a cabaret than to the presidency) and other slogans more or less disobliging for leaders of the opposition.

After the breakthrough of May 30, mopping up operations went on for about a month. Pompidou reshuffled his cabinet, decreed an increase in the minimum wage, and prepared for the elections, which proved to be a genial tactical move. How could the opposition denounce the government as repressive or unrepresentative when it put its mandate on the line in a general election? Having called for elections ever since the crisis started, the opposition could hardly refuse to accept the challenge. Only student revolutionaries denounced the recourse to the people, and were thus completely isolated. On June 1, UNEF organized a mass march to protest against the "sell-out elections" (*élections-trahison*); some radicals urged that the return to work be prevented by sabotaging the means of production. "Ce n'est qu'un début, continuons le combat" ("This is only the beginning, let us continue the fight"). But this crisis was going to be resolved through the ballot box, not in the street.

Gradually, life returned to normal. Working feverishly, technicians and supervisors managed to restock the gasoline stations. The mass exodus to the beaches and mountains for the long pentecostal weekend was a return to normalcy; the toll was seventy-six killed and six hundred injured in road accidents. Negotiations between employers and unions resumed on a local level, and workers gradually returned to their jobs. Three weeks later only one hundred and fifty thousand workers were still on strike. Serious incidents took place, however, at the Renault works in Flins and the Peugeot factory at Sochaux. At Flins some workers went back, others tried to stop them, and the police intervened. "To Flins" was the battle cry at the Sorbonne; student militants sensed that this could be the occasion for forging a student-worker alliance and restarting the motor of revolution. Thousands of students marched in support of the strike at Flins, though only a handful managed to get to the factory itself. On June 10, in the course of a police charge near Flins, a Maoist high school student either jumped, or was shoved off a bridge, and drowned. When a worker was shot and killed the next day at Sochaux, tempers flared in the Latin Quarter. Protest marches organized by the action committees of high school students and UNEF turned into another harrowing night of barricades and violence. On both sides the tactics of street fighting had been greatly improved. The box score for the riot of June 11: over four hundred injured, eighty-five cars destroyed, twenty-five trees chopped down to build barricades, fifteen hundred demonstrators under arrest. For the first time the public gave active support to the police rather than to the rioters. With the strikes virtually over and elections around the corner, violence seemed to be senseless.

Taking advantage of this shift in public opinion, the government cracked down on the extremists, outlawing eleven organizations—including the March 22 Movement, the JCR, FER and the M.L.'s—and expelling over one hundred and fifty "troublesome" foreigners. Then it was the turn of those revolutionary bastions, the Odéon, Sorbonne, and other occupied university buildings. On June 14 the police evacuated the Odéon; perhaps one hundred people marched out sullenly, among them only one student. Two days later the Sorbonne similarly was cleared. By the end of June, the economy had almost returned to normal and the state was once more in physical possession of its educational system.

The Gaullist momentum carried forward into the election campaign. In a move to placate the right, on June 15 General de Gaulle pardoned General Salan and other officers imprisoned for their terroristic activities in Algeria. The rechristened Gaullist party (Union for the Defense of the Republic—UDR) rang the changes on the theme of law and order. General de Gaulle set the tone in a long radio and television interview on June 7. The explosion, he argued, was the work of a few small groups who were revolting against modern society. These groups had no idea what might replace modern society; they merely "delighted in the negation, destruction, violence, anarchy that is raised by the black flag." But then, "the totalitarian communist enterprise," furious over this autonomous revolutionary uprising, decided to drown it in a general strike, leading to "the ruinous paralysis of the country." He attributed to this "totalitarian enterprise" the desire to bring down the republic, compel the abdication of its president, and seize power.[14]

Following De Gaulle's lead, the UDR candidates denounced the anarchists, accused the Communists of seeking to overthrow the republic, and called on the electorate to vote massively against violence and totalitarianism. The Communists tried desperately to dissociate themselves from the specter of revolution. They contended that the PCF had behaved with scrupulous regard for the parliamentary process, and they vilified the anarchists and Trotskyists as vigorously as did the Gaullists. Party spokesmen denied that they had sought to seize power, and called only for Communist participation in a coalition government. Protested Communist deputy, Mme. Vaillant-Couturier: "We are acting within the framework of legality, with the certainty of defending the interests of the people of France." UNEF tried to discredit the election ("Vote or don't vote, it's all the same"). Some Trotskyists and anarchists urged that the elections be sabotaged by raiding the polling places and destroying ballot boxes; but no one paid heed and the elections went off without incident.

The Gaullist counterattack scattered the opposition parties. On the first ballot, June 23, the UDR elected 152 deputies by an absolute majority, receiving 43.7 percent of the vote (to which may be added another 4.1 percent for pro-Gaullist moderates). The left was disorganized and demoralized. Compared to the previous election, little more than a year before, the Communist vote fell from 22.5 to 20 percent of the total, and that of the Federation (an alliance of Socialists and Radicals) from 19 to 16.5 percent. The PSU vote increased from 2.2 to 3.9 percent, much of this gain due to the larger number of candidates it put in the field. After the second ballot the UDR boasted 300 deputies and the pro-Gaullist moderates another 58, for a whopping Gaullist majority of 358 in an assembly of 485![15]

The prince was back on his throne (for less than a year, as it turned out). But the May Revolt had indeed changed everything. Vast reforms were announced by the government in all spheres of economic and social life, and especially in the universities. A sense of profound unease pervaded French society. All structures, all values, all authority had been challenged by the revolutionaries, who had struck a responsive chord deep within the nation.

NOTES

1. "We do not confront the need for reforms, but rather one of the most profound crises that our civilization has known .... This general rehearsal of a future drama expressed, among the strikers as well as among those who watched them pass, the consciousness of the end of a world .... Our society is not yet adapted to the civilization of machines."

2. The best single account by far of the Events of May is Adrien Dansette, *Mai 1968* (Plon, 1971). Earlier reports still worth reading include: Lucien Rioux and René Blackman, *L'explosion de mai* (R. Laffont, 1968); Philippe Alexandre, *L'Elysée en péril* (Fayard, 1969); J.-R. Tournoux, *Le mois de mai du Général* (Plon, 1969); Patrick Seale and Maureen McConville, *French Revolution, 1968* (Penguin, 1968). A reliable though sparse chronology is in *Année Politique, 1968*, 33-54. Another good recent account, as part of a larger history of the Gaullist regime, is Pierre Viansson-Ponté, *Histoire de la république gaullienne,* vol. II (Fayard, 1971).

3. On the Strasbourg "scandal," see Pierre Feuerstein, *Printemps de révolte à Strasbourg* (Strasbourg: Saisons d'Alsace, 1968).

4. Events at Nanterre are recounted by Dansette, *Mai 1968,* pp. 56-85; Viansson-Ponté, *Histoire de la république gaullienne,* II, pp. 399-420; and at length by Jean Bertolino, *Les trublions* (Stock, 1969).

5. One observer sympathetic to the students comments that M22M

was intent upon escalating incidents until the explosion occurred. Cf. Epistémon, *Ces idées qui ont ébranlé la France* (Fayard, 1968), p. 70. On the student uprising in general, Dansette, *Mai 1968*, pp. 87-158; and Viansson-Ponté, *Histoire de la république gaullienne* vol. II, pp. 437-73.

6. Quoted in Dansette, *Mai 1968*, p. 127.

7. For the view that Pompidou's decision to reopen the Sorbonne was "the breach": Philippe Alexandre, *L'Elysée*, p. 78.

8. The best accounts of the "contagion" are Viansson-Ponté, *Histoire de la république gaullienne*, vol. II, pp. 474-552, and Dansette, *Mai 1968*, pp. 162-278. Also useful are the memoirs of Christian Fouchet, *Au service du général de Gaulle* (Plon, 1971).

9. Cited in Julien Besançon's collection, *Journal mural, mai 1968* (Tchou, 1968), p. 47.

10. The story of the rejection of the Grenelle accord at Renault is well told by Jacques Frémontier, *La Forteresse ouvrière: Renault* (Fayard, 1971), pp. 368-71.

11. Viansson-Ponté, *Histoire de la république gaullienne*, vol. II, pp. 520-52. On the disappearance of De Gaulle, see also Dansette, *Mai 1968*, pp. 301-29.

12. General Massu is quoted by Viansson-Ponté, *Histoire de la république gaullienne*, vol. II, pp. 547-48.

13. Pompidou is quoted by Viansson-Ponté, ibid., p. 541.

14. De Gaulle's interview of June 7 is reprinted in *Année Politique, 1968*, pp. 382-86.

15. Election results are conveniently summarized in *Année Politique, 1968*, pp. 49-53, 395-425.

2

The Meanings of May

"Mai 1968 nous a appris qu'un pays prospère et, finalement heureux, pouvait, du jour au lendemain, se trouver au bord de l'abîme. En dépit du redressement effectué, nous en ressentons encore quelques effets." [1]

Georges Pompidou, December 31, 1972.[1]

T HE STRONG POLITICAL passions that exploded in May 1968 are evident in the literature about that extraordinary event. Whatever else it may have been, the May Revolt was a resounding literary success. Within a few years, over three hundred books and thousands of articles and commentaries were devoted to that episode. And for a revolt that failed! Every conceivable attitude, ranging from lyrical glorification to disdainful vilification, has been advanced in print for the pleasure if not the edification of the public. Most accounts are by partisans who view the student militants as generous idealists seeking to liberate humanity from the constraints of oppressive institutions. Other observers, less numerous and usually less talented, look upon the revolt as a despicable attempt to impose an authoritarian regime upon a free people.[2]

The French continue to interrogate themselves about the lasting consequences of the May Revolt. Was it a flash in the pan, an aberration, or did it usher in a new era of political doubt and instability? Opinions differ, reflecting rival political premises and commitments. Some argue, or hope, that the May Revolt sounded the death knell of the established order, that modern society is coming apart at the seams. As evidence they profess to have seen the questioning of all authority since May 1968 as students challenge teachers, children defy parents, shopkeepers kidnap tax collectors, workers go on strike and imprison their superiors, farmers block roads, priests marry, prisoners riot, and women reject their traditional role. On the eve of the elections that were to register his triumph, in June 1968, Georges Pompidou predicted, "Nothing will ever be the same again." Harsher critics contend that the May Revolt was senseless and reactionary in that it sought to reverse the trend toward the full flowering of the scientific civilization.

In one sense the May Revolt has been buried. Instead of bringing about the overthrow of the Gaullist regime, the specter of violence and anarchy gave the Gaullist parties a new lease on life. A mass of electors swung over to the Gaullists as the most effective barrier to the perceived evil of revolution. After the elections of March 1973, hardly anything specific remained of the May Revolt—apart from a few remnants of the Gaullist university reform that have managed to survive faculty hostility and student indifference.

But it would be a mistake to appraise the May Revolt only in terms of election results and legislation. The ferment expressed by the May Revolt has seeped through all of French society. It is everywhere. In trade unions the notion of worker participation in decision-making has become a major theoretical concern, especially in the ranks of the CFTD. In religion, many Protestant and Catholic clergymen have invoked the principles of the May Revolt in denouncing the injustice and inequalities of French society, calling for a more humane civilization. The educational atmosphere in high schools, as well as universities, has been markedly affected by the resurgence of left wing groups and ideas. Themes of the May Revolt—in particular denunciation of the consumer society and the insanity of modern civilization—have been especially prevalent, even dominant, in the world of cinema and the theater. The "counterculture" of resistance to urban and industrial civilization is so pervasive that it is now practically a part of the culture it hopes to destroy. The industries dealing with dress styles, leisure activities, and popular music have latched onto the counterculture, exploiting some of its most catchy slogans for commercial purposes. The very terms of political debate reflect a growing preoccupation with the issues raised by revolutionary groups. Who would have imagined before 1968 that the poet Arthur Rimbaud's romanticist exhortation— "Changer la vie!"—would be taken over by the once staid Socialist party?

There is another way of appraising the significance of the May Revolt. The revolutionary groups active in May are important not because they seized power (never a real possibility), not because they almost permitted the Communist Party to seize power (a greater but still remote possibility), and not because they set the stage for a conservative victory (as actually occurred), or a future fascist reaction to maintain order (not to be ruled out). Rather, the revolutionary groups are important because of what they tell us about the nature of modern society at the stage of development reached in France in 1968. Anarchism in the nineteenth century also failed, yet it was a highly significant reflection of the social tensions of the time. The anarchist, Pierre Joseph Proudhon lost out to Karl Marx in the contest for domination of the socialist movement, but the ideas expressed by Proudhon—and by the young Marx, for that matter—afford precious insights into the nature of capitalism and industrialization in its early phases. Trotsky was defeated by Stalin, but the phenomenon of party bureaucratization that Trotsky denounced, is still worthy of our attention. Similarly, the May Revolt gives us another way of looking at, and understanding, modernization under the auspices of a liberal regime that the revolutionaries rejected and sought to transcend.[3]

In trying to make sense of the May Revolt, we are fortunate to have at our disposal a few penetrating analyses by eminent French social scientists. Especially interesting are the interpretations put forward by three highly imaginative and skilled observers of the French scene: Raymond Aron, Alain Touraine, and Michel Crozier. Taken together, these three authors raise most of the important questions concerning the causes and meaning of the May Revolt. They share the belief that the revolt must somehow be related to the fact that it took place in a mature industrial society undergoing further transformation at a rapid pace. The May Revolt revealed in a flash that instability and revolution, at least under certain conditions, may accompany or even reverse the headlong rush toward an ever more scientific civilization. Each writer deals with a different aspect of the complex relationship between revolt and modernization—the meanings of May.

Revolt as Psychodrama

Raymond Aron has written more than twenty books, ranging over the fields of philosophy, history, sociology, international relations, and politics. Especially relevant for our purposes are his works on the nature of industrial society and modernization, including *Dix-huit leçons sur la société industrielle (Eighteen Lectures on Industrial Society), La Lutte des classes (Class Struggle), Trois essais sur l'Age industriel (Three Essays on the Industrial Era),* and, in general, *Les Etapes de la pensée sociologique (The Stages of Sociological Thought).* Aron is a seminal thinker, perhaps the leading French social scientist at present, whose encyclopaedic knowledge and acute analytic powers inevitably suggest comparison with Max Weber and Emile Durkheim. He also speaks out regularly on the issues of the day through his widely read column in *Le Figaro.*

As a former professor of sociology at the Sorbonne, Aron was vitally concerned with the May Revolt and the fate of the French university. His first comments appeared during the months of May and June 1968, in his *Figaro* column. Within a few months he published a book, *La révolution introuvable,* which brought his vast erudition to bear upon the events but showed signs of hasty composition. The book consisted of the transcript of Aron's informal replies to questions by an interviewer, Alain Duhamel, about the May Revolt. Aron conceded that his improvisation does not attain the "serenity of science" and that as a sociologist he can better describe the crisis than understand it. At one point he confesses that the events remain for him, in many respects, "mysterious." But a hasty work by Aron is better than ponderous volumes by almost anyone else. *La révolution introuvable*, despite its unfortunate format and incoherence, remains the best single book on the revolt to have appeared to date.

Aron's attitude toward the revolutionaries is one of unconcealed hostility. He recounts how he lived the month of May in "suffering" and "indignation" deeper than anything he had ever felt in his life. No other episode in the history of France, he says, gave him to the same degree such a feeling of the *irrational*; he was "beside himself." Those who greeted the disintegration of French society with such enthusiasm, he allows, "inspired in me an almost physical revulsion." He could not bring himself to believe that French democracy, after surviving the mortal menaces of the Depression, Hitlerism, and Stalinism, might finally collapse because of the dissatisfaction of a handful of students. It seemed unnatural that freedom of thought, parliamentary democracy, economic development, and widely shared prosperity could be repudiated by their principal beneficiaries. He thus characterizes the student revolt as "nihilism of the aesthetes or, better, the eruption of the barbarians, unaware of their barbarity." Where others saw a new form of democratic participation through "contestation" in public meetings, Aron saw the eclipse of rational discussion and "moral degradation" tantamount to a "national catastrophe." The same kind of phrases appear again and again in his narrative: collective delirium, loss of the capacity to reason, wave of conformism, a sad episode in the history of France.[4]

For Aron, then, the problem is how to explain this outburst of collective lunacy. The slogans of the revolution were absurd and the possible consequences of the revolution would have been disastrous because the refusal of economic progress cannot be translated into a political program. Since Aron in effect considers the May Revolt to have been a pathological phenomenon, he at first resorts to psychological explanations. Most striking is his use of the term "psycho-drama," by which he means that the actors in the May Revolt were consciously playing roles, mainly inspired by their glorious political ancestors of 1789. The word psychodrama is used rather than drama because the only organized force actually capable of seizing power, the Communist Party, had no intention of staging an insurrection at that time. There was neither a revolutionary situation nor a revolutionary movement, as evidenced also by the fact that no one was killed during the night of the barricades.

Why was there joyful mass participation in a theatrical performance? Aron contends that the French are usually overawed by a rigid and authoritarian hierarchy, but let the system falter or undergo a crisis and the pent up feelings of resentment suddenly burst forth. The repressed individual gets everything off his chest. For a brief moment there is the illusion of fraternity, and public life becomes a frolic. But after the frolic, the French reconstitute their rigid hierarchies. The profound causes of this phenomenon lie in the emotions. "Instead of taking seriously what the actors *say*, it is necessary to understand what they *feel*." According to Aron the most appropriate approaches to May 1968 are those that most social scientists today consider fallacious or inferior, such as that outlined in Gustave Le Bon's *La Psychologie des foules (Psychology of Crowds)*, or Vilfredo Pareto's concept of "residues." Concludes Aron: "In a period of collective folly, one tries to uncover the causes rather than discuss the pseudo-intellectual content of the delirium."[5]

Aron maintains that, at least partially, we are in the presence of a "biological phenomenon." The pacification of collective life represses man's "aggressive instincts." One expla-nation of May, to use the language of Konrad Lorenz, is that man as an aggressive animal has the need to break out from time to time. Another point is that students achieve emotional and sexual maturity at the age of perhaps fourteen, but continue to be subject to rigorous controls through examinations well into their twenties and beyond. They are condemned to live like children long after they have become adults. Aron even suggests a parallel between students and rats; at a certain point overcrowding among both kinds of animals produces nervous strain and breakdown. To understand the May Revolt, he says, we must "grasp and deal with the emotional states that were at the origin of the acts and the words."[6]

Aron's characterization of the May Revolt as a "psycho-drama" is an understandable expression of his hostility toward the activitists. But it rests on the assumption that a *real* revolution was impossible since the Communist Party, the only force capable of bringing it about, was opposed to the "adventurism" of the student militants.[7] The assumption is at the very least debatable. The Communist Party's tactics were complex and after the middle of May its appreciation of the "ripeness" of the revolutionary situation began to change. At the end of May, Pompidou and other government leaders believed that the Communists were preparing to take power. It was not at all clear at the time that the Communists were counting themselves out of the fight. To consider the May Revolt primarily as a type of theatrical spectacle is vastly to understate its importance. When millions of workers are out on strike, when government ceases to govern, and when the chief of state secretly confers with the commanding general of the armed forces in West Germany to assure himself of support in the event of a showdown, it is not unreasonable to characterize the events that produced such a crisis as genuinely political and not play-acting. The gravity of the events was admitted by General de Gaulle and Prime Minister Pompidou, as well as by opposition leaders; the repercussions were felt in every area of French society. If the May Revolt was simply theater, one may wonder what a real political crisis would be like! Attempts at revolution are real political phenomena even when they fail.

A psychological explanation of the crisis is unsatisfactory. Perhaps the behavior of some individuals might best be understood as deviant or pathological, but certainly not the willingness of so many to follow the alleged psychopaths. The psychological argument might be reversed with equal or greater validity: the deviants were those who refused to follow the militants after the latter had won over the student masses. For some radicals, modern society is "sick," and there must be something wrong with anyone defending it. Counterrevolutionaries, they argue, are frustrated, bitter, personally insecure, and who knows, perhaps insanely jealous of the sexual prowess and pleasures of young militants. Emile Durkheim once remarked that when offered a psychological explanation of social phenomena he was sure of only one thing: the explanation was false.[8] Durkheim's dictum is supported by the controversy over the May Revolt. It is all too tempting, and too easy, to denounce people we do not like as delirious, frustrated, confused, and subject to serious nervous strain; in other words, our opponent is not only wrong, but crazy to boot. The May Revolt involved a struggle for power among, not only individuals, but groups and organized political forces within a society undergoing rapid social change. Unless it can be demonstrated that French society in 1968 had acquired surreal qualities, there is no reason to resort to psychopathological theory.

Aron is too much the compleat social scientist to let his case rest on a literary construction like "psychodrama." Fortunately, overcoming his feeling of physical revulsion, he goes on to analyze the May Revolt as an authentic social and political event, and a deadly serious business. Aron deliberately takes as a model to emulate, the writings of his "master" (to use his own term), Alexis de Tocqueville, on the revolution of 1848. A more appropriate comparison, it seems to the reader, would have been Tocqueville's approach to the revolution of 1789. The question for Tocqueville was why the great revolution took place in France and not in England. In his search for an answer he was led to emphasize the unique qualities of individual political systems as they confront the same general challenges. Similarly, Aron asks why student unrest touched off an acute constitutional crisis only in France among the Western democracies. Here, Aron is at his best and is reminiscent of Tocqueville in his grasp of complex social and political relationships, and in his ability to compare political systems. Bringing Tocqueville up to date, Aron sees the near collapse of the French political system as due to a number of causes: the weakness of intermediary groups between the individual and the state; an accompanying incapacity of individuals to cooperate by themselves, outside of bureaucratic hierarchies; the rigidity of all hierarchical structures; serious economic difficulties (sluggish growth and pockets of unemployment) caused by De Gaulle's desire to build up foreign reserves so as to weaken the dollar; and the accentuation of structural defects within French society by Gaullism, in particular the diminution of the role of Parliament and the elimination of such safety valves as ministerial crises and meaningful parliamentary debates.[9]

The last point mentioned—the defects of the institutions created by General de Gaulle—may well be the most important reason for the spread of the May Revolt to virtually the entire society. Note Aron's renewed appreciation of the virtues of the classic parliamentary system as compared to the rigid, more authoritarian and more highly personal Fifth Republic: "In the long run the French are not intended for a symbolically tough government; they crave men sympathetic to their grievances, even unjustified, and who temper the rigors of administration by concern for private interests—even if these interests do not appear worthy of respect to those devoted to the sole rationality of the collective interest." And he calls for a revival of the "old practice of dialogue and communication deriving from the so much reviled Third and Fourth Republics." We are far removed from the original psychological explanations.[10]

None of the factors mentioned by Aron, however, can explain the original outburst. Taken together, they may account for the inability of the French state to cope with unrest, and the receptivity of the working class to revolutionary appeals. But the unrest itself appears as a kind of mysterious, irreducible first cause. Inasmuch as student revolt and alienation of the intellectuals are widespread phenomena, common to all advanced industrial societies at the present time, they cannot be comprehended in terms of the idiosyncratic features of French society.

In the course of his argument, Aron raises the question whether the May Revolt signifies "the end of a civilization," to use the phrase made popular by André Malraux, who was then minister of culture, and repeated subsequently by General de Gaulle and Prime Minister Pompidou. Initially, he scoffs at the notion, considering it a way of excusing the political gaffes of the Gaullist regime. Obviously, one cannot be expected to deal effectively with a problem of "universal history." Bringing the May Revolt down to the human dimensions of a power struggle, Aron observes, is displeasing to Gaullists and to revolutionaries. Nevertheless, Aron himself expresses concern that the May Revolt heralded the end of an era.

> I do not claim to prophesy: a civilization without religion, with a Church that questions itself and sometimes denies itself, deprived of the values of country and tradition, is perhaps entering into the ultimate phase that precedes death. A society founded on the voluntary cooperation of millions and millions of individuals in rationalized organizations risks being paralyzed by the violence of minorities and the disaffection of the many. Perhaps the events of May will appear tomorrow as revelatory of the fundamental precariousness of a liberal order in a scientific civilization. I do not state that those who admire the revolution of May are wrong. Perhaps the future will bear them out and the historians will see in what appears to me a play [*une comédie*] the surging forth of subterranean and destructive forces.[11]

Aron is thus torn between his preferences as a citizen and his instincts as a sociologist. "One of the lessons I drew from the events," he observes, "is that modern societies are more fragile than we used to think."[12] This fragility may vary from country to country, but all modern pluralist societies—and probably nonpluralist ones as well—contain elements of weakness. In short, modern societies and especially those based on liberal values are highly vulnerable to pressure from organized minorities.

Here is the most exciting part of Aron's analysis. The problem as he sees it is how to explain the alternation between periods of apparent tranquility when individuals are completely caught up in their private concerns and periods of agitation. In his exasperation with the activists, Aron never quite abandons psychological theories. "I am tempted by two explanations, one quasi-biological or psychological, the other sociological." But even his sociological explanation is really a variation of the psychological one. "The sociological explanation places emphasis on the alternations; the individual is apparently reduced to the condition of a private person, without belonging to a community of religious faith or of political belief; then suddenly, these isolated beings, enamored of comfort and prosperity, are seized by passion—it is an attack of fever with clearly defined objectives that lead to political or social upheavals or an attack of fever without clearly defined objectives and such is the present case. In the absence of a model that satisfies our aspirations, the attacks of fever have an essentially negative, nihilistic, or destructive character."[13]

But elsewhere Aron is inspired not by psychologists, not even by Tocqueville, but—and this is unacknowledged—by Emile Durkheim. He points out that modern society, because of its increasing complexity, requires more and more cooperation and the acceptance of voluntary discipline; it becomes easier for minorities to bring about paralysis through obstruction. "What characterizes the days of May—and I do not underestimate its significance—is the apparent rejection of modern society itself in order to bring about a general crisis of authority and obedience . . . . " Who are the people rejecting modern society? Aron singles out in particular the young bourgeois, brought up by indifferent or indulgent parents, "liberated from all sexual, patriotic or traditional taboos," who obtain without effort all the benefits of material civilization that they then denounce as unfit for others. In short, Aron is describing the phenomenon analyzed by Durkheim as *anomie*. But Aron barely begins the analysis of consensus and anomie in modern society; he is so carried away by his distaste for the activists that he never really develops his sociological explanation of the relationship between revolt and modernization. His treatment is only a beginning, marred by internal contradictions and theoretical deadends. But it is a beginning.[14]

Perhaps Aron's greatest contribution to the study of the May Revolt is his refusal to accept any political slogans at face value. He argues that every society requires a system of constraints and a hierarchy; that any people wishing to progress must submit to the discipline required by modernization; that the will to create a revolutionary situation cannot be a substitute for rational analysis of politics. More important than any of his explanatory theories is Aron's refusal to abandon critical faculties in the presence of political rhetoric.

Revolt as Wave of the Future

The contrast between Raymond Aron and his fellow sociologist, Alain Touraine is complete in almost every respect. Touraine, a professor at Nanterre in 1968, was a participant in many of the critical negotiations involving students, faculty, and government. If Aron cannot conceal his contempt for the student militants, Touraine in his book, *Le Mouvement de Mai ou le communisme utopique*, applauds their "holy anger against phoniness, lies, and silence." Aron quotes Cohn-Bendit with a shudder, while Touraine presents a sympathetic portrait of his former student turned revolutionary. Aron denounces the violence of the "barbarians"; Touraine characterizes the groups of demonstrators behind the barricades as a "people's society." Aron exclaims that the revolt is "psychodrama," perhaps even a farce; Touraine hails the same event as a "thunderbolt announcing the social struggles of the future" in France and all other advanced industrial societies.[15]

For Touraine the May Revolt is the specific French expression of the instability and conflict inherent in postindustrial societies. Capitalism, he argues, is evolving into a new phase. Economic power today "belongs not to private holders of profit, but to large organizations, private or public, nourished more by self-financing or public credit than by private capitalists holding the right to make economic decisions." Control of the economy is now vested in a "technocratic bureaucratic class." The new ruling class has a new ideology, exalting economic growth and modernization instead of mere profit-making. Part and parcel of the new ideology is the hope that the old clash between capitalist and working classes can be eliminated or transformed through rapid modernization and that political problems in the future will be dealt with pragmatically, through negotiations among groups on the basis of their interests. The new ruling class encourages the notion that nineteenth-century ideologies are no longer relevant to the problems of industrial societies. In this view conflict and "ideology" are characteristic of early modernization while conflict or tension management is the dominant trend in late modernization.[16]

But, says Touraine, there is neither a decline of ideology nor an end to the class struggle, which is mere wishful thinking on the part of the techno-bureaucracy and its hired ideologues. Rather, a new form of political conflict erupts during late modernization, transcending and replacing the former class struggle between workers and capitalists. "The stake in the struggle is no longer merely profit-making, but control of the power to make decisions, to influence, and to manipulate." For Touraine the importance of the May Revolt lies in the fact that it signifies a rupture within the society, a rebellion not by marginal elements (ethnic minorities or the oppressed and demoralized poor, as predicted by Marcuse) but by those at the very heart of the productive process—the students being groomed for positions of command in the technocratic society. The new revolutionaries refuse to accept the dehumanizing consequences of technology, although Touraine maintains that they do not reject modern society as such. "This technical civilization is not in itself an instrument of domination," he observes. "But," he continues, in a burst of sociological jargon, "it simultaneously propagates, transmits, depersonalizes, and masks the power of ruling forces that reduces individuals and groups to their place in an integrated hierarchy of production and consumption."[17]

The students who oppose the "authoritarian-rationalism" of technocracy and the utopia of the ruling class form their own "anti-society" and "counter-utopia." To change society and to change life by enabling individuals to control their own destiny are their goals; hence Touraine's characterization of the May Movement as "utopian communism." Autogestion—self-government or participation of individuals in the making of decisions that affect them—is considered by Aron to be an empty slogan, totally incompatible with the discipline required by modernization; for Touraine autogestion is the great hope of the future libertarian society and the central message of the May Revolt, the procedure whereby the power of technocracy will be broken once and for all.

Most observers of the May Revolt distinguish between a student phase and the strike by millions of workers, and conclude that the students played the role of a "detonator." Touraine flatly rejects this thesis. Both students and workers were rebelling against the same evil—control of society by a technobureaucracy. Despite the participation of a variety of revolutionary organizations, he sees the May Movement as unified. "The profound unity of the movement was due to the fact that it was no longer fighting a ruling group defending private interests but generalized power over social and cultural life." The rebellion was not against modernization as such, but only against its bourgeois-technocratic or authoritarian-rationalist form. "The May Movement did not reject industrial society and culture, but revealed their internal contradictions and new social conflicts. It did not stand outside society but at its very center. Its leaders were neither victims of economic development, misfits, nor romantics nostalgic for past revolutions."[18]

One major drawback of Touraine's argument is the ambiguity of the key concepts. He assures us at first that modern society is controlled by "generalized power," which elsewhere becomes a "techno-bureaucracy," and at still another point, "large organizations." There is quite a difference among these propositions and, to boot, no evidence is presented to support any of the conflicting assertions—or exhortations. He also states that class conflict in the new society will be between "technocrats" or sometimes "techno-bureaucrats" and "professionals." But are not bureaucrats also professionals, and cannot professionals become bureaucrats? This is not to mention professional revolutionaries who have been known to create bureaucracies. Touraine's general theory of modernization and revolt is on such a high level of abstraction, and involves such ambiguity, that it is virtually unusable.[19]

It must also be pointed out that Touraine's description of the structure of the May Movement simply does not square with reality. This may be of little concern to militants, who wish to change reality in order to attain political goals, but it may be annoying to social scientists and even to ordinary citizens just trying to put the pieces together. In Touraine's account the unsuspecting reader catches a glimpse of such exotic creatures as situationists, Trotskyists, Maoists, and anarchists. But, aside from affirmations about their "profound unity," it is never explained who they are, how they viewed modernization, and how the individual achieves self-government in the authoritarian systems admired by at least some among them. That all the activists were in favor of modernization is at variance with the facts. Even Touraine occasionally lets slip that some participants in the May Revolt took pleasure in opposing all social machinery. In actuality, the May Movement was riven by conflict over every major issue of political and social life, including the larger goals of economic development.

Touraine does not demonstrate that the mass of the students were conscious of their role as rebels against generalized control of society by the techno-bureaucracy. This may have been the perception of the *enragés* at Nanterre and of the situationists; but Trotskyists and Maoists scoffed at the notion that intellectuals could replace workers as gravediggers of capitalism. The great majority of students, including those who fought for the liberation of their imprisoned comrades, seemed to be unconcerned about the evils of the techno-bureaucracy. A poll of student opinion in September 1968 asked each respondent to place himself in one of the following categories: [1] those who wish not only to change the university but radically to transform society; [2] those who seek actively to reform the university, and its programs and methods of instruction; [3] those who wish above all to pass their exams. The results, after a period of intense politicization: in category one—12 percent; in category two—54 percent; in category three—31 percent; no answer —3 percent. The first group of 12 percent probably is either revolutionary or receptive to revolutionary appeals; such a group can accomplish a great deal under favorable circumstances and might even be able to create a revolutionary situation. But the student mass does not seem to be a consciously revolutionary force as described (or desired) by Touraine. Such a mass might be manipulable, but that is another kind of enterprise.

Nor is Touraine's enthusiasm for the new revolutionaries widely shared by the public at large. In March 1970, a poll asked: "On the whole are you rather favorable or rather hostile to the student demonstrations now taking place in France?" The results: among adults, 9 percent favorable as opposed to 80 percent hostile (11 percent no opinion)! Even among young people, only 22 percent were favorable as opposed to 69 percent hostile (9 percent no opinion). This is hardly the profile of a people eagerly awaiting a signal from Cohn-Bendit to throw off their bonds.[20]

As if to reply to criticism ahead of time, Touraine states that any departure from his type of analysis (for example, to view the May Revolt as a crisis of French society or an ensemble of crises of modernization and change) would be "inspired by conservatism." To consider the May Movement in any sense as resistance to changes imposed by the logic of industrialization, he continues, would serve the interests of the "rising ruling class" (presumably, the technocrats or "generalized power"). Such an interpretation would impoverish and falsify social reality and "succumb once again to ideology."[21] Let us assume for the sake of argument that conservatism is inherently evil. Is it being conservative to point out that some of the active participants in the May Revolt repudiated modern life, questioned science, rationality, and technology, and glorified instead the unity of primitive societies, the mysterious, the

accidental, the emotional, and the surreal? Surely it is not
wicked to call attention to an intriguing phenomenon that must
somehow be explained. Suppose we observe that many self-
styled libertarians in the May Movement were actually quite
authoritarian, in spite of their slogan, *"Il est interdit d'interdire"* ("It is forbidden to forbid"). One student leader, for
example, singled out Raymond Aron as a bourgeois apologist
who would not be permitted to teach in the future. If we take
note of such expressions of intolerance do we become malicious
conservatives? Touraine's logic may lead to the absurd conclusion that opposition to modernization is progress, suppression
of freedom of thought is liberation, and political ideology is
political analysis. On the last page of his book Touraine calls for
theoretical work that will "develop a social movement and
foster its conflict with the powers that rule society"; and in the
next paragraph he says that his goal is to grasp the meaning of
what happened in May. He not only fails to resolve the
contradiction between these two goals; apparently he is
unaware even that there may be a contradiction between them.

Revolt as a Style of Protest

Michel Crozier, who was also a member of the ill-fated
Department of Sociology at Nanterre in 1968, does what his
colleague Touraine warns *against*: he views the May Revolt as a
crisis of change and modernization. The great advantage of
Crozier's approach is that he avoids making metaphysical
generalizations that are beyond proof or disproof. He calls our
attention to concrete phenomena such as political institutions
and administrative structures, and to a process of social change
whose characteristics can be analyzed with reference to a
variety of indicators and historical situations. Leaving the realm
of exhortation and speculation over motives we return to the
real world.

In his attitude toward the events, Crozier is more hostile
than sympathetic, that is, closer to Aron than to Touraine. The

enragés at Nanterre delighted in disrupting Crozier's classes, and his resentment may well have carried over into his analysis. Yet, some students urged Crozier to support the revolt, pointing out that he, too, was a sharp critic of French society and believed that change in France comes about through crisis. Crozier replied that his "repugnance to follow their lead was certainly the expression of an instinctive reaction." In a "Letter to Students," dated May 20, 1968, he saluted those "courageous enough to say no" to French institutions, but he rejected the notion that the rigidities of French political and administrative structures could be remedied through collective delirium or such slogans as "autogestion."[22]

Crozier entitled his book on the May Revolt, *La société bloqueé* (or *"the stalemate society"*), thereby acknowledging his debt to Stanley Hoffmann, who first used this phrase in 1963 to describe French political life. Writing in 1970, Crozier rather disarmingly begins: "That French society is a 'stalemate society' is now admitted by everyone, even if not openly stated." There may be much talk about change in a stalemate society, he explains, but there is a refusal, in spite of revolutionary appearances, "to envisage the slightest real change." The best example, the very archetype of the stalemated French system for Crozier, is the French administration, which has not changed in its essentials since it was described in a devastating manner by Alexis de Tocqueville in his study of the *ancien régime*. Basic characteristics of French adminstration are extreme centralization (power is formally concentrated at the top of the pyramid, but in fact cannot be effectively exercised since those at the top are completely cut off from subordinates) and stratification (compartmentalization on the basis of positions within the hierarchy, favoring structural rigidity and routine). Because centralization and stratification are barriers to communication, it takes a long time to perceive the consequences of decisions and to correct errors. Change erupts in the form of crises that weaken the whole system but leave its rigid structures untouched.

The French university, says Crozier, is a replica of the total administrative system and of the stalemate society—centralized and highly stratified. "The consequence of such a system," he observes, "is that it constitutes a bloc impervious to change. The university thus isolated is blind. It can neither adapt itself to new demands from the environment, nor even perceive them." Through an examination system that theoretically offers all an equal chance to compete but in fact favors the children of the already educated, the university maintains the stalemate society.[23]

For Crozier, the May Revolt fits perfectly into his analytic scheme: a massive, rigid structure provokes a total challenge in an atmosphere of crisis, but leaves the system itself intact in the end. The *enragés* went off on an emotional binge, but failed to face up to the real problem of reforming the university to serve the needs of modern society. They rejected everything, which means that, in the end, nothing happened. "The French did not rebel in order to put an end to capitalist exploitation or to build a classless society, they plunged into the crisis in order to bring into question a system of human relations, a style of action, and a model of management to which they were subjected. The crisis of May appears, then, first as a questioning of a French style of action and an instinctive revolt against what we have called the stalemate society." The French, according to Crozier, dream of a new means of communication among themselves, but always within their system. "When they returned, drunk and exhausted from their adventure, nothing had changed, nothing in fact could have changed."

Yet there is hope, says Crozier, that the May Revolt will mark a departure from the model of the stalemate society, not because of any direct results obtained, but rather in signalling a change in French behavior. As evidence, he cites loss of faith in the system by the top-level decision-makers and bureaucrats, and the beginning of the liberalization of French society. If the elites seek to reinforce their special privileges through continued centralization and stratification, then the French will have yielded once more to their "old demons" of bureaucratic corporatism and irresponsible radicalism. But if the elites gamble on an open society and accept change, then "the crisis of May will quickly appear as the last great fling (*'le dernier grand cinéma'*) that this old incurably romantic nation must absolutely offer itself before entering the world of responsibility."[24]

What Crozier has in mind is reform that will enable the French to resolve the real problems of the modern world rather than cherish the illusions derived from a preindustrial era. His prescription is to replace the present rigid, overly centralized structures with an open, simple, and responsive system, based on permanent dialogue and negotiation between state and citizenry. Everything would be interrelated—decentralization and innovation in university life, transformation of the administrative system, a new role for the state, development of the social sciences—all pointing toward a liberation of individual energies within a rapidly modernizing society. To Crozier's critics his proposals sound suspiciously like the dread prospect of Americanization.

Crozier's argument rests upon one key assumption: that France is indeed a "stalemate society." If this assumption is unwarranted, then the entire argument collapses. First, it must be pointed out that Crozier uses the term in a somewhat different manner than does Stanley Hoffmann. For Hoffman the stalemate society does not mean that France is paralyzed but that it is a unique mixture of feudal-agrarian and industrial societies—"a halfway house between the old rural society and industrialization." Neither sector could completely eliminate the other, and the political system of the Third Republic reflected the fact that the fundamental equilibrium of the society would not be changed by the state. However, writing in 1962, Hoffmann concluded that "the stalemate society is dead"—though many of the old tensions remain. It was killed by the transformation of French society during and after World War II—by the emergence of fully industrial attitudes, the more active role of the state in planning economic development, a reorientation of the French business class, and structural changes in the working class. In a later commentary, Hoffmann points out that the May Revolt was largely due to the transformation of French society. But he also argues, as does Crozier, that the revolt was a flare-up of French individualism. Nonparticipating citizens when dissatisfied, Hoffmann contends, behave as rebels rather than reformers; their whole way of life prepares them for "wild utopianism, intransigeance, and self-righteousness."[25]

Hoffmann's use of the term "stalemate society" is puzzling in terms of his own argument. How could an industrial sector have emerged in the first place if there really had been a stalemate, and how could the stalemate society suddenly be pronounced dead in 1962? Surely there had been a process of change, beginning even before World War II, in the course of which French society was transformed. Surely the state had played a role in this transformation. The use of ideal types (like agrarian and industrial societies, and "halfway house") as literary devices makes French society appear to be far more static than was the case under the Third and Fourth Republics, and more dynamic than it actually was under the Fifth Republic. Far from being a stalemate society, France took on the characteristics of all modern societies at roughly the same pace as the other countries of Western Europe.

Crozier goes even further than Hoffmann in his use of the term "stalemate society." He states flatly that in France there is never any "real change," the system is paralyzed. In particular, the university constitutes a bloc that is "impervious to change." But if, as Hoffmann asserts, "the stalemate society is dead" (as of 1962), how can Crozier continue to refer to France as a stalemate society in 1970? For Hoffmann the May Revolt was caused by widespread transformations of French society, while Crozier concludes that it was really a protest against the stalemate society. Something is wrong with the thesis. Part of the difficulty is purely stylistic, since Crozier admits that some change has taken place—but it is not "real" change. The implication is that the only features of political life in France that count are centralization and stratification, and even if the entire economy and society are transformed, the change is not "real" as long as the administrative system remains intact. The confusion appears to be total between change and the mechanism through which it is realized.

To add to the confusion, Crozier himself does not always proceed on the assumption that French society is stalemated in the sense of being paralyzed. Thus, he observes in another context that France is now entering a world of rapid change, that the Planning Commission under Jean Monnet introduced a new administrative style into French politics, and that in the past twenty-five years "we have gone from an economy of stagnation to an economy of growth." He concedes that "considerable modernization has been accomplished," but in confusion, irresponsibility, and at the price of much tension. If, in fact, France has gone from an economy of stagnation to one of growth—which is necessarily accompanied by corresponding changes in every sector of the society and culture—then a major transformation has taken place. Crozier states that the French, ill-adapted to an industrial society, already confront the problems of the postindustrial society. But how did the French manage to reach this phase of development in the first place? Crozier continually laments the manner in which modernization has taken place; but this is another issue entirely. That the French experience of modernization has been distinctive is evident; but a unique political style should not be confounded with the process of modernization itself.[26]

Take, for example, the problems of the French university. At the outset Crozier gives the impression that it is impossible to change or even to budge. Yet, in fact, a great deal budged and changed within the French university in the period following World War II. The number of students more than quadrupled between 1950 and 1968, growing from 135,000 in 1950 to almost 400,000 in 1965, and over 500,000 in 1968. This immense increase in the student population was accompanied by such innovations in methods of instruction as seminars and group research. There was also a dramatic reversal of the numerical ratio between those of professorial rank (*professeurs* and *maîtres de conférences*—corresponding to professors and associate professors in the United States) and those below professorial rank (*maîtres-assistants* and *assistants*— roughly equivalent to nontenured assistant professors, lecturers, and teaching assistants in the United States). In 1956 the balance was 56 percent to 44 percent in favor of the professorial ranks; by 1963 the balance was 67 percent to 33 percent in favor of the nonprofessorial ranks. The great expansion of the nonprofessorial ranks led to a weakening of the authority of those who traditionally ran the university, namely the full professors, and strengthened the radical elements within the university. Thus, the student population, composition of the faculty, and educational structures underwent a considerable evolution in the period following World War II. One of the changes, in fact, was the creation of an experimental university at Nanterre. The crisis of May came about in the context of movement, not stalemate.[27]

Nor is it convincing to draw such a sharp contrast between authoritarian structures and French individualism as an explanation for the violence of the outburst of protest in May. It must be kept in mind that the French are among that dwindling band of peoples in the world to sustain a liberal democracy, which should limit the emphasis placed on authoritarianism as a distinctive trait of their political system. The evidence offered in support of the proposition that the French are more individualistic than their neighbors is fragmentary and highly impressionistic. Members of the French Communist Party, to take one example among many, have not exactly been noted for their fierce individualism. Also, to present the May Revolt as the expression of a peculiarly French style of authority and protest fails to explain the eruption of similar crises elsewhere. French Trotskyists, Maoists, and situationists are no more wildly utopian, intransigeant, or self-righteous than their opposite numbers in Germany, Italy, Japan, or the United States.

Curiously, Crozier raises searching questions about the nature of modernization and revolt in the United States, but drops this promising line of inquiry when he turns to France. He points out that the American system is highly vulnerable now not because it is more oppressive or less efficient than, say, the Soviet system, but rather because change is occurring more rapidly in the United States. The more modern a society, he continues, the more tensions are generated and the more difficult it is for individuals to shoulder the burden of freedom. Even the greater participation of Americans in their decision-making process becomes a source of weakness, since as citizens they know that they must blame themselves, not distant authorities when things go wrong.[28] The same kind of analysis could readily be applied to France. Rapid social change and liberal democracy are characteristics of both the American and French political systems. We suggest, then, that the May Revolt was produced not by paralysis, stalemate, or rigid administrative structures, but precisely by the kind of swift modernization that has been so unsettling everywhere else.

Some Necessary Distinctions

We could add many more studies of the May Revolt to the three just considered in detail. Particular mention might be made of the work of Henri Lefebvre, Edgar Morin, Claude Lefort, and Jean-Marc Coudray, and Epistémon, which present somewhat different interpretations of the events.[29] There is a tendency in the literature on the May Revolt to oversimplify a complex event by lumping together quite divergent phenomena. Observers are fascinated by the student militants, or the tactics used to provoke the crisis, or the sudden collapse of political authority, or the spread of dissent to the workers, the unhappiness manifested by the middle classes and professionals, or the final defeat of the revolt. It is all too tempting to explain the entire episode in terms of one of its aspects. Thus, because one observer may be repelled by the endless palaver at the liberated Sorbonne, or outraged when militants disrupt classes and beat up opponents, he may quite naturally resort to a psychological explanation of behavior that seems to him deviant or pathological. Yet this theory would not account for the receptivity of the student masses to the initiatives of the militants. Another observer may see his youthful dreams of a more just society on the way to realization; he may be caught up in the May Movement as an active and enthusiastic participant and may quite understandably characterize the Movement (and himself along with it) as the wave of the future. But this would not explain why the revolt failed. Those in positions of authority, or in sympathy with authority, and who feared that the most precious values of Western civilization were in danger of destruction, might feel that the fault was not in themselves because they were inept but rather in the irresistible trends of world history. Yet only in France among the modern democracies did a student revolt touch off widespread social disorder and a general strike and almost bring about the over-throw of the regime. The crisis of Western civilization did not produce similar results elsewhere.

We cannot begin to make sense of the May Revolt unless we draw necessary distinctions: among the groups engaged in the revolutionary action; the phases through which the revolt passed; the areas of French society affected by the revolt; the levels of power and authority at which revolutionaries and antirevolutionaries acted and reacted; and the various political consequences of social change. Each level of analysis must be dealt with separately before any attempt can be made to relate them all.[30] We shall, therefore, enumerate at the outset a few propositions concerning the May Revolt.

1. Explanations of the May Revolt must satisfy one minimum requirement—they must relate to the specific events as they occurred, and not to some imagined or heroic clash between the forces of good and evil (on whichever side of the barricades these forces may be presumed to exist). In the specific historical situation of May-June 1968 the revolt was not a single explosion, but rather should be perceived as unfolding in several clearly marked stages. This point, crucial for any explanatory theory, has already been argued in the preceding chapter.

2. It is misleading to talk about *the* May Movement, *the* students, or *the* revolutionary elements as if they constituted a monolithic group. One striking feature of the revolutionary movement in May was that it was diverse to the point where the major groups were more opposed to each other than to the liberal state they all vowed to destroy. The despised liberal state allowed them to continue to exist while their revolutionary rivals, if victorious, would not have been so indulgent or foolish. Any theory concerning the May Revolt that fails to take into account the deep divisions within the revolutionary movement simply does not refer to the real situation.

3. It is a misconception to think of the May Revolt as a nondirected act of spontaneous combustion, even though there was an element of spontaneity in the tactics used. The militants within the revolutionary coalition had elaborated a theory concerning the seizure of power before the event, and refined the theory subsequently. They deliberately attempted to create a revolutionary situation, and to seize power. Not everyone who participated in the events had a design in doing so; indeed, most did not. Although the masses of factory workers, clerical workers, professionals, and students had many grievances, they did not themselves take the initiative. Once these masses were set in motion, however, the revolutionaries lost control of the crisis they had provoked. Again it is important to distinguish among groups, social sectors, and phases of action in order to come to grips with the May Revolt.

4. The revolt was not mere play-acting, but a serious event that has marked the postwar history of France. It failed, however, and the reasons for failure are just as important as the causes of the crisis in the first place. Chief among the reasons for the failure of the revolutionaries is the role played by the Communist Party within the French political system, which is one

of the most important questions of interpretation raised by the May Revolt.

5. The May Revolt is best understood in the context of rapid social change rather than stalemate or paralysis. Relating modernization and revolt is an exceedingly difficult task since it involves correlations between highly complicated sets of factors. One approach is to focus interest on the "entry into politics" of social groups as they are generated or enlarged by the process of modernization. Students may be viewed as part of the intellectual class that becomes increasingly important in the scientific civilization and is simultaneously placed under intense pressure by new demands. Integration of social groups into the political system leads directly to the question of consensus or its lack, which is far more important for an understanding of the May Revolt than an administrative or political style of transacting public business.

These propositions will be developed at greater length in the chapters that follow.

NOTES

1. "May 1968 has taught us that a prosperous, and ultimately happy country, could, overnight, find itself at the edge of the abyss. In spite of the recovery since then, we still suffer from some of the conquences."

2. Pierre Viansson-Ponté comments: "More has been written about the days of May-June 1968 than on the entire French Revolution; more than on 1848 or the Commune, perhaps as much as on the four years of the First World War and almost as much as on the five years of the Second World War." *Histoire de la république gaullienne* (Fayard, 1971), vol. II, p. 393.

3. For a classic analysis of an ideology and social movement primarily as a means of understanding the nature of social change: Emile Durkheim, *Le socialisme* (Presses Universitaires de France, 1969).

4. For his feelings of revulsion toward the revolutionaries: Raymond Aron, *La révolution introuvable* (Fayard, 1968), pp. 13-15, 26-27, 69, 133.

5. On the "psychodrama": ibid., pp. 33-37, 65, 131.

6. Biological explanations: ibid., pp. 47, 53, 54.

7. On Communist Party tactics: ibid., pp. 33-36.

8. Durkheim's dictum on psychological explanations in *Les règles de la méthode sociologique* (Presses Universitaires de France, 1968), p. 103.

9. Aron's debt to Tocqueville, *La révolution introuvable*, pp. 23, 30. On the reasons for the near collapse of the regime, pp. 39, 44 (weakness of intermediary corps), pp. 91-92 (economic difficulties), p. 95 (building up foreign reserves), p. 97 (institutions of Fifth Republic), p. 129 (rigidities of administrative structures).

10. Citations on the Fifth Republic, as compared to Third and Fourth, ibid., pp. 129-30, 131.

11. Ibid., p. 134.

12. Ibid., p. 44.

13. Ibid., p. 47.

14. On increasing complexity of modern society, ibid., p. 89; on rejection of modern society, p. 109; on young bourgeois liberated from taboos, p. 148.

15. Alain Touraine, *The May Movement, Revolt and Reform* (New York: Random House, 1971), pp. 79-80. All page references are to American edition.

16. On economic power belonging to large organizations, ibid., p. 220; on the new ideology of the ruling class, pp. 23, 30, 265-66.

17. On the stake in the struggle, ibid., p. 24; students at the heart of society, p. 26; on technical civilization as an instrument of domination, p. 59.

18. On autogestion, ibid., pp. 60-61; on the profound unity of the movement, p. 58; on May Movement not rejecting industrial society, p. 22.

19. On "generalized power," ibid., p. 58; techno-bureaucracy, p. 40; large organizations, p. 220; on conflict between technocrats and professionals, p. 40. In a "postface" written in 1972, Touraine refers to the new forms of domination as "quasi-exclusive control of the means and effects of social and economic change by large organizations of production and management," adding another bit of confusion to his key terms.

20. The poll of student opinion in 1968, published in *Réalités*, November 1968, cited by Philippe Bénéton and Jean Touchard, "Les

interprétations de la crise de mai-juin 1968," *Revue Française de Science Politique*, 1970, xx:3, p. 525. The IFOP poll of March 1970 is in *Sondages*, 1970, nos. 1 and 2, p. 124.

21. Citations on criticism of his position as conservative, Touraine, *The May Movement*, p. 77.

22. Michel Crozier's *La société bloquée* (Seuil, 1970), pp. 237-41. On his reluctance to join the student militants, ibid., p. 225.

23. The disarming statement, ibid., p. 7; on the characteristics of French bureaucracy, pp. 94-96; on the French university as a bloc impervious to change, p. 148.

24. On why the French rebelled in May, ibid., pp. 170, 172; "the last great fling," p. 179.

25. For the original use of the term stalemate society, see Stanley Hoffmann, "Paradoxes of the French Political Community," in Hoffmann, ed., *In Search of France* (Harvard University Press, 1963). For his interpretation of the May Revolt: Hoffmann, "The French Psychodrama," *The New Republic*, August 31, 1968, pp. 15-21.

26. For his comments on rapid change in France, Crozier, *La société bloquée* pp. 108, 118, 136, 175.

27. On the changes in the structures of the university and ratio between the professorial and non-professorial ranks, Bénéton and Touchard, "Les interprétations de la crise . . ." pp. 507-10.

28. Comments on modernization in the United States, Crozier, *La société bloquée* pp. 190-93; on the burden of freedom, ibid., p. 209.

29. Henri Lefebvre, *L'irruption de Nanterre au sommet* (Anthropos, 1968), Edgar Morin, Claude Lefort, and Jean-Marc Coudray, *Mai 1968: la brèche* (Fayard, 1968), and Epistémon, *Ces idées qui ont ébranlé la France* (Fayard, 1968).

30. The need to draw distinctions is well argued in Bénéton and Touchard, "Les interprétations de la crise . . . .", pp. 539-43.

3

Red Flags, Black Flags

La société dominante qui se flatte de sa modernisation permanente doit maintenant trouver à qui parler, c'est à dire, à la négation modernisée qu'elle produit elle-même.

De la misère en milieu étudiant (1967)[1]

A CENTURY AGO, the red and the black referred to the struggle between two Frances, one anticlerical, socialist, universalist; the other Catholic, conservative, nationalist. The Republic and the Church, symbolized by the village schoolteacher and the parish priest, fought for domination of the minds of the young. Two Frances represented two different views of the world—innovation versus tradition, science versus mystery, secular versus sacred, and for some, workers versus owners. Today the historical rivalry between Republic and Church has been downgraded, surviving as a relatively minor political conflict over the legal status of Church schools. But by 1968, red and black had come to designate a different kind of conflict. Those who paraded behind red flags during the May Revolt represented one or another brand of communism in power (now or in the past), while those who proudly displayed black flags were anarchists in fact or in tendency. Red flags and black flags flew together in defiance of the bourgeois state, but they were borne by separate contingents of revolutionaries and were symbols of sharp disagreements and deep hatred.

Who were these revolutionaries massed behind red and black flags? A first impression was that the disorders "just happened"; the revolutionaries appeared to be everybody in general and nobody in particular. Then the public became vaguely aware that within the mass of students on the barricades were highly organized revolutionary groups with leaders, troops, in some cases, arms, and plans for the seizure of power. Strange acronyms began to crop up in press reports: JCR, FER, and M.L.'s, along with references to a mysterious International of Situationists. It was only after the May Revolt that serious analyses on the nature of the revolutionary coalition began to appear.

The "detonator" of the May Revolt was fashioned by student militants. But—and this point is crucial for an understanding of the course of events—these militants were fragmented politically; were working at cross purposes; and were striving to attain wholly contradictory goals. For a brief moment they were united in their desire to bring down the bourgeois university, but even on this relatively minor aspect of their far-reaching programs they disagreed on tactics. The various student revolutionary organizations and movements reflected two wholly opposed outlooks. One set of organizations wished to create a corps of professional revolutionaries (in the tradition of Lenin, Trotsky, and Mao) who would overturn the regime, establish total control of the society, and then drive on to more complete industrialization. These included two Trotskyist organizations (Jeunesses Communistes Révolutionnaires or JCR, and Fédération des Etudiants Révolutionnaires or FER) and the Maoists (Union des Jeunesses Communistes, Marxistes-Léninistes or M.L.'s).

On the other hand, a loose, diffuse "movement" of anarchists and assorted surrealists distrusted all organizations, denounced Lenin and Trotsky, expressed reservations even about Mao, Ho Chi Minh, and Castro, and in effect sought to destroy the whole infrastructure of the modern economy. This heterogeneous collection included long-established anarchist societies, the situationists, and many students in the March 22 Movement. Their goal was not industrialization but a state of complete, untrammeled individual creativity. Neither set of groups could possibly have existed in a society created by the other; but the future struggle for power was subordinated to the immediate task of liberating students from the oppression of their bourgeois environment.

The revolutionary student groups are not to be confused with the three major student unions. These were the Union Nationale des Etudiants de France (UNEF)—wracked and weakened by internal strife and in 1968 controlled by leftists; the Fédération Nationale des Etudiants de France (FNEF)— patronized by the government, and pro-Gaullist; and the Union des Etudiants Communistes (UEC)—created by the French Communist Party in 1956. UNEF originally had been a nonpolitical federation of local student service organizations concerned with such mundane matters as housing, cafeterias, social security, and bookstores. The organization was plunged into a political crisis during the Algerian war, when students in favor of maintaining the integrity of the national territory and those opposed to a colonial war fought for control with no holds barred. In 1956 leftist opponents of the Algerian war ousted the moderate leaders. Some students even participated in the underground opposition, aiding the rebel cause. Moderate students found it impossible to remain within the new UNEF. They created the rival FNEF, which soon was the beneficiary of the state subsidies that previously had gone to UNEF. Although FNEF never had much support from students, its very existence served to fragment and weaken the student movement.

UNEF lost not only its financial support, but also most of its members, who drifted off into apolitical indifference. In 1967 left-wing socialist (PSU) students managed to gain control of the UNEF general assembly after a violent confrontation with the Communists. Their success was hollow, since the dues-paying membership by that time had declined officially to 70,000, in actuality probably close to 15,000 (out of 600,000 students). Indeed, an official inquiry was scheduled to be launched into UNEF's financial situation. It proved impossible to secure sufficient agreement at the general assembly in 1968 to elect a president, so that a vice-president had to assume these functions. He was Jacques Sauvageot, an art history student and member of the PSU. After the riots of May 3, Sauvageot was in the thick of the fight, engaging in negotiations with officials of the university and government, issuing communiqués, marching in the front ranks during mass demonstrations. In the confusion of the time UNEF appeared to the public as the organizing genius of the French student movement. But the appearance was deceptive; UNEF had little to do with the riots at Nanterre and in fact had taken a public position against the "cult of violence."[2]

The Communist Party's student organization, the UEC, played even less of a role than UNEF in the events of May. Its chief importance was as the mother movement that gave birth to three dissident revolutionary student groups (two Trotskyist and one Maoist). From its founding in 1956, the UEC was rent by crisis, since many students opposed Communist Party policy on Algeria, especially after the party joined in the vote of full powers to the Guy Mollet government. The first sizable defection took place in 1961, when Trotskyist students withdrew and formed the Comité de Liaison des Etudiants Révolutionnaires (CLER). In the growing dispute between the Soviet Union and China, many student members of UEC openly sympathized with the Chinese and lampooned the pro-Soviet line of the PCF leadership. The militants were especially outraged by the decision of the PCF to support François Mitterrand during the presidential elections of 1965, and the accompanying emphasis on the possibility of a "peaceful transition" to socialism. They also demanded that the party fight for victory in Vietnam (as urged by the Chinese), not merely "peace in Vietnam" (the slogan of the PCF). The party leaders asserted their authority by purging the troublemakers, but in so doing they eliminated the most dynamic elements in their own student organization. In April 1966 another Trotskyist group withdrew from UEC and founded the JCR. A few months later a pro-Chinese group formed the M.L.'s. While the parent UEC languished, the three groups created by party-dropouts—CLER, JCR, and M.L.'s—rapidly recruited new members, set in place viable structures, and flourished. It was a demonstration, in miniature, of the lack of dynamism of orthodox Communist parties in advanced industrial societies throughout the world, and the rising popularity of Trotskyists and Maoists.[3]

Red Flags: Trotskyists and Maoists

Rival and then companion of Lenin, genial tactician of insurrection, creator of the Red Army, victor in the Russian civil war, archenemy of Joseph Stalin, finally a "prophet outcast"—Leon Trotsky is inextricably linked with the coming of communism to the modern world. Trotskyism for its followers today is neither historical romance nor anachronism, but rather a means of coping with an agonizing intellectual problem that haunts a whole section of the revolutionary movement: if communism is such a worthy goal, how can one account for that unpleasant reality which is the Soviet Union? Trotskyism is a way out, since it explains why the revolution remains pure and good despite the horrors of Stalinism.

The central theme in Trotsky's attack on Stalinism is the exploitative nature of bureaucracy. In this view, the Soviet Union is incapable of fully realizing socialism because of the formation of a bureaucratic layer at the apex of the social pyramid. The Soviet Union continues to be a workers' society with a socialist base, since the means of production have been collectivized. But the Stalinist bureaucracy is a new ruling caste, playing the same role as the old capitalists, with one important difference: for Trotsky the bureaucracy is a dominant and privileged group but not a class since it has no base in the productive process. Hence he considered the Soviet Union a "degenerate" workers' society, deformed by an irresponsible bureaucracy. Such a situation could not endure and had to evolve either toward true socialism or a return to capitalism.

After Trotsky's assassination in 1940, his disciples continued his relentless criticism of the Soviet Union. Nevertheless, many French intellectuals saluted Stalinism as the salvation of humanity during and after the war. At the time, J. P. Sartre, for example, wrote paeans of praise to the Communist Party. Only the Trotskyists kept hammering away at Stalinism and the Soviet regime, outflanking it on the left. Yet deficiencies abounded in the Trotskyist analysis. It was never explained how a workers' society with a "socialist base" could possibly have produced such a monstrous bureaucracy. Surely, many critics suggested, there must be something even more basically wrong with the Soviet regime than the accidental emergence of a bureaucratic clique. Trotsky refused to trace the evil beyond the great divide of 1923. He recoiled from the suggestion that the seeds of Stalinism were perhaps to be found in the very nature of Leninism itself, in the notion that a party of professional revolutionaries speaking on behalf of the proletariat should displace the workers and arrogate to itself the power to make decisions. Yet Trotsky himself, along with Rosa Luxemburg and many others, had warned of the danger of creating an irresponsible bureaucracy when Lenin first put forward his views.

In spite of inconsistencies and contradictions within the Trotskyist view of the world, the conditions were "ripe" (to use a favorite Marxist term) for a revival of Trotskyism in the 1960s. Khrushchev's denunciation of the "crimes of Stalin" seemed to offer conclusive evidence of the justice of Trotsky's indictment. Criticism of the Soviet Union turned to revulsion among many young intellectuals after the repression of the working class in Berlin in 1953 and especially in Hungary in 1956. Greater freedom of travel enabled western revolutionaries to come into contact with the reality of Soviet society, which many found still backward and depressing half a century after the revolution. Yet these same intellectuals remained fervent communists.

Trotsky's love-hate relationship with his own creation, the Soviet Union, reflected the ambivalence of many intellectuals throughout the world. He believed that progressive forces would eventually undermine Stalinist despotism and permit a resumption of the march toward universal freedom. Through Trotskyism, convinced socialists could cheer the Bolshevik Revolution and damn the Stalinist regime; they could affirm their belief in the beneficence of revolution and express their deep revulsion for forced labor camps, repression of dissent, and other awkward features of the "episodic relapse" (Trotsky's term for Stalinist bureaucracy). An incidental advantage of Trotskyism was that it explained the menace of bureaucracy as a general phenomenon everywhere, including capitalist societies, a subject of considerable concern to students and intellectuals as the use of the computer and practices of automation became more widespread.

In May 1968 *two* Trotskyist youth groups—the FER and JCR—played an important role in the revolt. Each group reflected the orientation of a larger movement. Why should there have been two separate and mutually distrustful groups, each claiming Trotsky as an inspiration? To understand this curious situation, we must make a brief excursion into the prolific factionalism of the Fourth International, and the split in France between the Lambertists and the Frankists.

Trotsky himself founded the Fourth International in 1938 as a rival and challenge to the Stalinist Third International. Although largely a paper organization, it provided a pole of attraction for the numerous Trotskyist sects that proliferated after the death of its founder. Dissension and sectarianism plagued the Fourth International from the outset. Virtually all of Trotsky's followers agreed with the old master's contention that capitalism was on the verge of collapse, ripe for overthrow by determined revolutionaries. But every other key point in Trotsky's program provoked controversy. Was Soviet bureaucracy merely a social group, capable of being toppled by a swift revolutionary blow, or had it become instead a social class, deeply rooted in the very structure of Soviet society? Was Stalinism merely an episode, or did despotism derive from faults in the Soviet system, perhaps even from Leninism itself? Before his assassination, some of Trotsky's American followers raised the question whether Trotsky did not share with Stalin the responsibility for bureaucratic tyranny, exemplified by his role in crushing the rebellion of the Kronstadt sailors in 1921. Thus, they turned the Trotskyist analysis upon Trotsky himself. When Trotsky refused to condemn the occupation of Eastern Poland by the Red Army in 1939, and called for "defense of the Soviet Union" on the grounds that it remained a "workers' state," many followers were shaken and confused. The result was a fragmentation of the Trotskyist movement.

In 1952 Pierre Lambert and his followers were excluded from the French section of the Fourth International, whereupon they founded a rival party, the Organisation Communiste Internationaliste (OCI). Lambert criticized the official thesis at the time that capitalism was demonstrating a capacity to reform and strengthen itself. He also rejected the idea that the Stalinist bureaucracy might undergo a process of liberalization. In the 1960s Lambertists remained skeptical of the role of the Third World in promoting revolution, holding that only in highly industrialized societies could authentic revolution take place. They considered Castro and Guevara "petty bourgeois," and denounced the Cuban and Vietcong regimes as Stalinist in orientation. Lambertists take literally Trotsky's transitional program of 1938 in which he urged defense of the immediate interests of the proletariat in order to gain their confidence. They therefore participate in trade union activities to the fullest possible extent, regardless of the orientation of the union leadership; Lambert, himself, is an active member of the Force Ouvrière. Their favorite tactic is to make use of the unions in mobilizing workers for mass demonstrations before public buildings.

In 1961 Lambertist sympathizers created the Comité de Liaison des Etudiants Révolutionnaires (CLER) as a student group within a larger youth movement, and in April 1968 it was rebaptized the Fédération des Etudiants Révolutionnaires (FER). Like its parent group, FER stressed the importance of fighting for the immediate interests of workers within existing trade unions (or in the case of FER, the interests of students within UNEF), as a means of converting everyday demands into a radical orientation. FER emulated the Lambertist technique of staging mass demonstrations in front of public buildings. For FER, the students in early 1968 were not revolutionary but rather were concerned about professional problems, such as exams, admission procedures, and physical facilities. Students were urged to rally behind UNEF (which, if all worked out, would be controlled by FER), and thus be ready to participate along with the workers in a revolutionary upsurge.

The difference between FER and other student groups became increasingly manifest after the May Revolt broke out. FER ridiculed the idea that students could get anywhere by isolated action, either through a "critical university" or on the barricades. Intellectuals could not presume to give advice to workers. On May 10 a large group of FER militants marched to the barricades, only to warn the students that they were risking isolation, and called instead for a combined student-worker mass demonstration. FER also refused to take part in the occupation of the Sorbonne, again because it feared being cut off from the workers. The turning point, for FER, was the start of the general strike on May 13. For the first time it seemed possible to realize their dream of union between students and workers. FER militants were in the forefront of strike activities, especially in Nantes, where they had a sizable following. But FER remained aloof from the other revolutionary groups, refusing to coordinate tactics.

The parent Trotskyist organization in France, the Parti Communiste Internationaliste (PCI)—from which the Lambertists split off in 1952—has remained under the control of Pierre Frank and Ernest Mandel, the head of the Belgian secretariat ever since Trotsky's death. The Frankists have turned their attention increasingly from the industrial nations to the Third World. The Cuban and Vietnamese revolutions were seen as the forerunners of world revolution, and students were hailed as participants in the process. In its approach to students the PCI applied the old Trotskyist tactic of "entrism": a distinction was made between an advanced sector of the party, openly Trotskyist, and a clandestine sector consisting of militants secretly planted within nonparty organizations. It is not clear whether the UEC was deliberately infiltrated by the Trotskyists or, conversely, whether the policies of the UEC led to disillusionment among its militants who then turned naturally to Trotskyism. Whatever the case, a "left faction," led by Alain Krivine, a history student of middle-class origins, was expelled from the UEC in March 1966. This group created the Jeunesses Communistes Révolutionnaires (JCR), which was closely linked with the PCI or Frankist tendency.

The members of the left faction within the UEC were in disagreement with Communist Party leadership on a number of matters, including the party's decision to support Mitterrand for the presidency (vilified as "reformism"), Khrushchev's policy of peaceful coexistence (considered a sell-out of the revolution), and Soviet intervention in Eastern Europe (denounced as imperialism). Krivine later confided that he first had doubts about the party during a trip to the Soviet Union, when he saw that the country was "far from being a paradise on earth"; he was also scandalized when party officials pressured him not to make his critical views public.[4]

But the most important reason for the defection of radical students from the UEC was dissatisfaction with official Communist Party policy toward the Third World. The capitalist world was relatively quiescent and stable; it was in the developing countries that the radicals saw revolutionary possibilities. The guerrillas of Latin America and of Vietnam—not the bourgeoisified working class of the industrial nations—were carrying the revolutionary impulse. As one young Trotskyist later commented, it was especially with reference to Cuba and Vietnam that his group realized the inevitable result of Communist Party policy would be betrayal of the world revolution. It was urgent to stop imperialism and support the forces of revolution everywhere. One of Alain Krivine's brothers, for example, toured North Vietnam with a group investigating American "war crimes" and made his contribution to the cause by testifying before the Bertrand Russell tribunal in Stockholm. Ché Guevara's slogan—create two, three, more Vietnams—was electrifying. It meant that militants everywhere could participate in the battle against imperialism. On the other hand, Maoism seemed to be a deadend, since the notion of the conquest of the cities by the countryside reduced the western proletariat to inaction.[5]

Trotskyism, as interpreted by Frank and Mandel, thus provided the global view for which many radical students were looking. The starting point is the Leninist organization of professional revolutionaries that would bring political knowledge to the proletariat. Hence, students and bourgeois intellectuals are destined to play the role of revolutionary vanguard, after freeing themselves from class prejudices. It was comforting for radical students of middle-class origins to know that they were not condemned to follow behind the proletariat in the march toward socialism. Building upon the insights of Trotsky and Rosa Luxemburg, the JCR worked out an explanation of the nature of Soviet communism that was satisfactory to radical students: Stalin went wrong when he suppressed the Workers' Opposition and created a despotic bureaucracy, but the Soviet Union is still basically a workers' state. The JCR was able also to take advantage of the enthusiasm generated among students by the Cuban and Vietnamese revolutions, calling for unity in the struggle against imperialism at home and abroad.

One way professional revolutionaries prepare the proletariat psychologically for the ultimate violent showdown with the bourgeoisie is to provoke clashes in factories and in the street. To equip itself to play such a role, the JCR created a disciplined fighting force for street combat. Militants were carefully selected and had to prove themselves before being elevated from "observer status" to full membership. As part of its "entrist" tactic, JCR helped to found and then participated actively in the March 22 Movement, but deliberately refrained from using its muscle to take over. It had a fully developed theory concerning the seizure of power—creating a revolutionary organization, sparking a popular insurrection, setting up strike committees, forming a "dual power," conquering power in a direct confrontation with the state, and finally installing a new type of Soviet democracy, free from the blemishes of

Stalinism. Of all the revolutionary organizations in the field in May 1968, JCR was the only one that conceivably could have wielded power.

Several smaller Trotskyist groups contributed to the ferment of ideas in the May Revolt. The Tendance Marxiste-Révolutionnaire, led by Michel Pablo, formerly a secretary of the Fourth International, contended that the initiative in world revolution has now shifted to the countries of the Third World. For Pablists the peasant masses of the Third World play the same role today that the proletariat of the industrial nations played in the nineteenth century; guerrilla war is thus the most appropriate form of class struggle. In advanced countries Pablists urged revolutionaries to emphasize the qualitative needs of the proletariat, as opposed to material conditions or the standard of living. Chief among these needs is autogestion, the right to participate in decisions that affect one's life. Another Trotskyist group, Union Communiste (sometimes also known by the name of their journal, *Voix Ouvrière,* or *"Workers Voice"*), that was founded in 1940, presented a sharp contrast. *Voix Ouvrière* denied that the Third World was in any way privileged to lead the global revolution, which could only be accomplished by the working classes of the advanced nations. The task is then to organize and educate the workers within factories and enterprises and to bring about revolution through a general strike. At first dubious about the revolutionary credentials of the students, *Voix Ouvrière* swung around, after May 13, to a sympathetic position, calling for close collaboration between students and workers. The minor Trotskyist sects helped popularize the conflicting notions of the unity of world revolution, displacement of revolutionary initiative toward the Third World, autogestion, and revolution through a general strike—all of which were thrown into the simmering ideological pot in May.[6]

In addition to the Trotskyists there was another detachment of young revolutionaries brandishing red flags: the Maoists. Like the Trotskyists, the Maoists were inspired by Marxism and Leninism—but there the resemblance ended. For the disciples of Mao Tse-tung, Stalin continued the glorious heritage of the Revolution and Trotsky was a renegade. The Maoists condemned the "revisionism" of Khrushchev precisely because it called into question the great merits of Joseph Stalin, and started the Soviet Union down the road to a degrading form of social democracy.

The Maoist student group, like the Trotskyist groups, had their origin in the radical wing of the UEC. Many had been students at the prestigious Ecole Normale Supérieure, where they were influenced especially by the pro-Chinese philosopher, Louis Althusser, who undertook a new reading of the classics of Marxism. When Althusser was censured by the Communist Party, the radical students withdrew from the UEC in protest and in December 1966 created the Union des Jeunesses Communistes, Marxistes-Léninistes (M.L.'s). A few months later the young Maoists repudiated their master, Althusser, on the grounds that he was a philosophical idealist. They turned instead directly to the writings and thought of Mao Tse-tung. Their political goal, as suggested by the very title of their journal, was *Servir le Peuple.* The M.L.'s were profoundly skeptical of any attempt to exploit student grievances for revolutionary purposes, since they were convinced that only the workers could make a revolution. In order to experience class exploitation, it was incumbent upon militants to live among the people and share their existence. Many M.L.'s gave up their studies and took jobs in order to be able to proselytize more effectively. They fought alongside young workers during the vicious wildcat strikes at Caen and Le Mans in early 1968. By then many Maoist students were in the factories as workers, participating actively in local trade unions, especially the CGT, and discussing in study groups the lessons to be drawn from their factory experience. Thus, the Maoists spread the gospel of a proletarian revolution within the very citadel of the "reform-ist" CGT. They were also active in the formation of committees to support the Vietnamese revolutionaries (Comités Vietnam de Base).

In early 1968 the M.L.'s turned once again to the student sector, following the appearance of an article in the Chinese press urging work among the student masses. But their aim at this point was to persuade the students to join the proletariat, not to encourage them to spearhead a revolution. The Maoists were surprised by the outbreak of the student revolt and played only a small role in the events. On the other hand, they incontestably helped spread the "contagion" to the working class after May 13.

The Maoist students, in contrast to their Trotskyist comrades, were not closely linked to a political party. In the first place no orthodox Maoist party existed in France until December 1967 when the Parti Communiste Marxiste-Léniniste de France (PCMF) was created. Before that date there were "study groups" of self-styled Marxist-Leninists, most of whom originally had been members of the PCF but took the side of China and Albania against the Soviet Union in the great debate within the international communist movement. These study groups first sprang up in 1963 and exchanged views through a pro-Chinese journal, *Révolution.* Curiously, the M.L.'s opposed the creation of a full-fledged Maoist political party, in spite of the endorsement of the Chinese themselves, on the grounds that it was premature. In the early part of 1968 the PCMF devoted most of its efforts simply to getting organized and publishing its newspaper, *L'Humanité Nouvelle.* It had few members, was weakened by dissension, and enjoyed little influence within the revolutionary coalition in May.

Maoist political action—through the M.L.'s—was especially attractive to students and intellectuals who wished to revive, or further, a tradition of revolutionary violence for which the French Communist Party was no longer a vehicle. The M.L.'s *refused to obey*—parents, professors, foremen, bosses, the army, the state, everybody. Of all the revolutionary groups, Maoists were the most likely to appeal to young people intent upon flouting authority without reverting to primitive or preindustrial models of social organization. They were especially active in denouncing conditions of labor in the factories, and in resisting the cadence imposed upon workers on assembly lines. The M.L.'s were thus able to exploit two venerable traditions among French workers: revolutionary violence, and antipathy toward factory work. But unlike anarchists and surrealists, the

Maoists were not opposed to modernization. Had not Mao himself preached the necessity of work, transformation of nature by man, and rapid industrialization?

The increased popularity of the Maoists after the May Revolt attests to the appeal of this amalgam of the negative (first step) and the positive (second step). To be destroyed was the inhumane system of capitalist industrialization. To be created was a more humane industrial civilization, in which problems of authority would no longer exist. Mass spontaneity and a highly moral Communist Party would combine in some unforeseen way to make possible a more livable society. Details were unimportant. As Alain Geismar later explained to his judges: "No thinker, even were he a genius and a revolutionary, could discover today the way in which a socialist democracy can function. The new democracy and the liberty of the people will be born and develop in the revolutionary practice of the masses." Especially gratifying to students was the clear implication that intellectuals would not have to negotiate with reformist trade union leaders, faceless bureaucrats, or scheming politicians. They would be able to reshape French society virtually by themselves, spontaneously approved of course by the popular masses and unencumbered by the dead weight of the traditional intermediaries.[7]

Black Flags

The groups so far described—Trotskyists and Maoists—shared a belief in the need for a corps of professional revolutionaries. They accepted Marxism *and* Leninism as a starting point, FER and JCR adding Trotsky to the ideological base and the M.L.'s opting instead for Mao. A great divide separated these groups from the other factions within the revolutionary coalition—anarchists and surrealists, who generally repudiated Leninism (and, perforce, Trotskyism and Maoism) in the name of either orthodox Marxism or other exponents of socialism in the nineteenth century, or sometimes even in the name of art! Anarchists and surrealists worked mainly within the March 22 Movement (M22M) and the International Situationists.

M22M was a sort of holding company created by representatives of most of the revolutionary groups already described, particularly the JCR (though not the FER) as well as anarchists, and including even some Maoists. No common organization or ideology could be sustained by these disparate groups. Making a virtue of necessity, the founders of M22M proudly proclaimed their refusal to draw up a program or create structures, though in fact a rudimentary organization proved to be unavoidable. There was only one way to keep these completely opposed groups working together: by identifying immediate political objectives on which everyone could agree and by subordinating differences in a common effort. Action replaced both organization and ideology. One militant explained the way in which it worked: "If a bunch of guys get together and talk about Marx," he said, "they disagree and start to argue. 'You are a shit, you are a counter-revolutionary, you don't understand anything about Marx, etc.' But if you give them a specific task, like the occupation of a building, then they either do it or not; that is, they are either revolutionary or not . . . . Who gives a damn what you think about Marx?"[8]

M22M was able to exist only because leaders of the various groups found it a convenient mechanism for coordination of tactics and radicalization of student masses who might otherwise have been unreceptive to a political appeal. Technically, it had no leader, but in the eyes of the public and of most students, the chief spokesman of M22M was Daniel Cohn-Bendit, and this impression was not entirely false. Cohn-Bendit had been born in France of German-Jewish parents. Bilingual, he had opted for German nationality and studied in Germany. He was strongly influenced by Rudi Dutschke and the Federation of German Socialist Students, or SDS. (K. D. Wolff, president of the SDS, was among the 142 students who created the M22M at Nanterre.) The fighting tactics of the SDS— especially the use of insults, ridicule, and violence—were thus channelled into France by the anarchists as well as the JCR. Cohn-Bendit was very close to his older brother, Gabriel, a professor at Nantes, an anarchist, and a French citizen. The younger Cohn-Bendit had rare ability to dominate meetings—by his oratorical skill, sense of drama, and flair for converting immediate issues into revolutionary doctrine. He was the Trotsky of the student soviet, although there was no Lenin to back him up, no revolutionary proletariat to carry him forward, and no Kerensky in the Elysée to make things easy.

The public was amazed at the time by the political sophistication of this twenty-three year old sociology student, and by his presentation of an ideology that seemed to be coherent, comprehensive, and novel. Cohn-Bendit denounced all existing political systems. No hierarchy, nor any other form of constraint should be imposed upon free men and women, he said. He damned with equal vigor the bourgeois state and the Communist Party, or any other party professing to speak on behalf of the workers. "What we propose is very difficult to understand. People imagine that, somewhere, someone decides for them, leads them toward a goal, and they believe that a central structure of authority must exist. We want to prove to them that they are wrong. Order such as we know it can disappear. The taking over of the schools has proved it . . . . The movement creates itself as it moves forward."[9]

The first task of the true revolutionary is to demonstrate that all authority is ridiculous, and for this purpose any tactic is valid. Cohn-Bendit and his friends set about joyously to create trouble, stir up students, insult opponents, all to prove that emperors at every level of the system were without clothes. But this did not mean opposition to industry and civilization. "I am not against civilization. That doesn't mean anything. I am against the nature of our society and against its forms of expression. And our civilization is nothing but the form of expression of the nature of the system in which we live." What follows the overthrow of the bourgeois state? For Cohn-Bendit the workers must take over the means of production, not only occupying premises but above all assuming managerial functions as well, through "action committees." The final goal is the unimpeded liberty of the individual. As the brothers Cohn-Bendit phrased it in their book, "The revolutionary process of the months of May-June has only reinforced the certainty that one day we shall ourselves organize our own lives. We will not be doing it for our children—sacrifice is counter-revolutionary and comes from a Stalinist-Judeo-Christian humanism—but ultimately in order to have untrammeled enjoyment."[10]

The sudden reappearance of black flags and anarchist ideology stunned political observers in May 1968. Anarchism, which flourished in France in the nineteenth century, had almost ceased to exist after World War I. Yet, every element in the ideology propagated with such assurance and flamboyance by Cohn-Bendit derived from the anarchist tradition. Perhaps the most astonishing thing about Cohn-Bendit was this very attempt to revive a doctrine dormant for forty years. The Fédération Anarchiste and Fédération Communiste Libertaire had long discouraged young militants by their stodginess as well as their authoritarianism (a curious feature of life among anarchists). But these old-line organizations had at least kept alive the central notions of anarchism through such publications as *Le Libertaire* and *Le Monde libertaire.* More lively was the periodical *Noir et Rouge,* which became the official organ of a neoanarchist group taking the same name in 1956. The central concern of *Noir et Rouge* was to ensure the triumph of libertarian over bureaucratic socialism. Its militants denounced the menace of bureaucracy (pointed out by Bakunin and later by Trotsky) and urged instead that libertarian socialism be created through workers councils. Cohn-Bendit was a member of the *Noir et Rouge* group, which was only one faction among many within the anarchist movement, and the only one to play an important role (through M22M) in the May Revolt. At the annual conference of the Fédération Anarchiste in September 1968, Cohn-Bendit and associates attended only to denounce that organization as outmoded, arousing the indignation of those who had been tending the flame for decades. Nonetheless, Cohn-Bendit was giving expression to a vital tradition of anarchist theory.[11]

When he was the center of attention during the May days,

Cohn-Bendit told an interviewer: "I am still an anarchist . . . in the line of the socialism of councils." He specifically acknowledged Bakunin as the greatest single influence, declaring himself a Marxist in the same sense as Bakunin. Equally important was the defeat or betrayal of the Bolshevik Revolution. As an anarchist Cohn-Bendit accepted Trotsky's critique of Stalinist bureaucracy—although he condemned Trotsky for his role in crushing the Kronstadt revolt. He was also anti-Leninist, since democratic centralism is a device for maintaining hierarchical control. "Contrary to the affirmations of Trotskyist historiography," commented the brothers Cohn-Bendit in their book, "it is not in 1927 nor 1923 nor even 1920, but as of 1918 and under the direction of Trotsky and Lenin that the Russian Revolution degenerated." What's left, then? Said Cohn-Bendit: "I am . . . for a democratic federalism, for federated autonomous groups which act together, but which always retain their autonomy"![12]

The sources of neo-anarchist thought are thus manifold. Proudhon and Bakunin, the founders, contributed a profound hatred of the state and of any power wielded over man by man. They glorified libertarianism, the organization of society from the base upward, and not from the top down. Bakunin in particular warned against the dangers of authoritarian communism and the "red bureaucracy." In 1870 he prophesized: "Take the most radical of revolutionaries and place him on the throne of all the Russias or confer upon him a dictatorial power . . . and within a year he will have become worse than the Tsar himself." From Bakunin, too, derives the neo-anarchist glorification of individual liberty, which is not to be confounded with nihilism. Individuals are mutually dependent, he conceded, the products of the actions of society. But society should exert its discipline through voluntary and freely consented association. What happens when some individuals refuse to accept this discipline? The hard infighting and bitter struggles among anarchists, to say nothing of their attitude toward political opponents, are ominous signs.

Proudhon is a major source of anarchist theory concerning

the role of the masses in bringing about the revolution. Struck by the revolutionary upsurge in 1848, Proudhon concluded that revolutions are *not* brought about by "initiators." All revolutions are accomplished by the "spontaneity of the people," whose instinct is always more accurate than that of their leaders. A real revolution, product of universal life, is not the work of anyone. The theme was later taken up and developed by Bakunin. Revolutions come "like a thief in the night," he said, produced by the "force of things," germinating for a long time in the depths of the popular consciousness. " . . . Then they explode, touched off in appearance often by trivial causes." They can be predicted and sensed, but the explosion can never be hastened. In the experience of the Paris Commune, Bakunin found confirmation of anarchist theory concerning the seizure of power, "the actions of individuals being practically nil, the spontaneous action of the masses must be all." Neo-anarchists, inspired by Proudhon and Bakunin, engaged in a searching reexamination of Marxism, downgrading the implications of "economism" and the inevitability of the triumph of the proletariat. They returned to the early manuscripts of Marx, emphasizing the alienation of man in his daily existence and the importance of voluntarism, as opposed to determinism, in bringing about change.

But Proudhon and Bakunin were also vaguely aware of the limits of spontaneity and the need for political knowledge and action coming from the "outside." At times they anticipated Lenin in calling for the creation of a corps of revolutionaries who would educate and lead the masses. Anarchists were to be "invisible pilots," directing the activity of the masses but without any of the usual appurtenances of power. They should propagate ideas corresponding to popular instincts. Who is to say which leaders are correctly interpreting the instincts of the masses? What happens in the event of disagreement between leaders and masses? These questions could not be avoided during the Russian Revolution, and as a result the anarchist movement was shattered.[13]

In demanding "all power to the Soviets," the Bolsheviks

appropriated an anarchist idea. But when it became apparent that anarchism called into question the basic structure of the revolutionary regime, the Bolsheviks arrested and imprisoned anarchists en masse. Neo-anarchists today are especially moved by the epic of Nestor Makhno, an anarchist of peasant origins who proclaimed a rural anarchist society in the Ukraine shortly after the revolution. Makhno spread the gospel of people's control of rural communes, soviets, and even the army—although in practice key decisions were made by a small military clique. A libertarian movement could hardly be tolerated by the Bolsheviks, and the Makhnovites were wiped out by the Red Army in 1920. The same political aspirations reappeared during the revolt of workers and sailors at the Kronstadt fortress in February 1921. Carried forward by the spirit of striking workers in Petrograd and Moscow at the time, the Kronstadt rebels called for an end to the Bolshevik monopoly on power and the authoritarianism that had been imposed on the nation. They posed a grave threat to the regime by demanding "all power to the Soviets," "the Soviets without the Bolsheviks," restoration of liberties and free elections. Trotsky was given the unpleasant chore of subduing the Kronstadt rebels; his Red Army attacked, gave no quarter, suffered and inflicted huge casualties, and finally occupied the fortress. Makhno and the Kronstadt rebels, glorious resisters of Bolshevism, became heroes of anarchism; their ghosts haunted the leaders of the Soviet regime, as well as the Trotskyists.

For the anarchists, the failure of the Bolshevik Revolution to establish libertarian socialism required a reexamination of the role of the workers in a socialist society. Proudhon had considered the most important aspect of 1848 to be the flowering of workers associations, in which he saw the future basis of a "non-state" organization of power. Here was the germ of the neo-anarchist theory of autogestion. The despotism of the Communist Party can be prevented by one force only—the people themselves. For neo-anarchists the communism of the party must be replaced by the communism of councils or soviets. They have taken as their model the Paris Commune of

1871, the soviets of 1905 and 1917, and the workers' councils
that sprang up in Germany in 1918, Italy in 1920, and Hungary
in 1956. The French neo-anarchists admire Rosa Luxemburg
(rather than her contemporary and rival, Lenin), and also Anton
Pannekoek, who is considered the most important theorist of
workers' councils in the period following the Bolshevik Revolution. Most ideas that later appeared in neo-anarchism can be
found in Pannekoek—including the spontaneous nature of
revolution, the way to structure workers' councils (with
delegates revocable at every instant), the origin of councils in
strike committees, and the reliance upon the workers themselves for their own emancipation.[14]

Anarchist students in 1968 had been especially influenced
by such contemporary theorists as Henri Lefebvre whose *La
Proclamation de la Commune* (1965), glorified the creative
spontaneity of the commune, and *La Vie quotidienne dans le
monde moderne* (1968), which emphasized the dehumanizing
impact of modern society; and above all by Jean-Paul Sartre's
La Critique de la raison dialectique (1960), with its glorification
of the revolutionary group, born in violence, as the agent of
history. Herbert Marcuse was not among these seminal influences, though his ideas may have been transmitted indirectly
from Rudi Dutschke and the German SDS. Alain Geismar later
commented: "Many people refer to Marcuse. I must say that, to
my knowledge, none of the militants of my union, of UNEF or
of any other organization, or perhaps one in a thousand, ever
read a single line of this author . . . . " Cohn-Bendit agreed: "No
one among us has read Marcuse."[15]

The neo-anarchist ideology offered a view of the world of
1968 that many French students found congenial because of its
even-handed rejection of capitalism and communism in its
Soviet form; contempt for the Communist Party and distrust of
all other dissident communist organizations; reliance upon
spontaneity and workers councils as a way of solving the
problem of authority—combined with a willingness to retreat
altogether from the modern world if the authority problem
proved too difficult. Bakunin especially appealed to some

students because of his trumpet call for action and destruction of the existing order, and his repudiation of all those—including workers—who allowed themselves to be bourgeoisified. Bakunin's identification of the *lumpen* (dregs) and the criminal element as the source of the coming revolution made sense to some intellectuals who feared that the workers had become hopelessly enmeshed in materialistic and reformist trade union activity.

The neo-anarchists, and especially Cohn-Bendit, gave the student movement an unusual flavor. In their wake came the people of fantasy—the nonpolitical artists, writers, and other intellectuals who wanted nothing more than the opportunity to act out the role of artist-kings. The neo-anarchists were opposed to *all* of their revolutionary allies. They denounced everyone—Stalinists, Trotskyists, Maoists—and even went so far as to suggest that such beloved figures as Ho Chi Minh and Fidel Castro had betrayed their revolutions by creating bureaucratic structures. The neo-anarchists, in turn, were considered by all the other groups to be hopeless idealists and reckless adventurers. Had the revolution actually succeeded, there doubtless would have been a struggle between the neo-anarchists and the Trotskyists similar to that between the Kronstadt workers and sailors and Trotsky's Red Army, and with the same outcome. But the showdown never came.

Surrealpolitik

Bemused visitors to the liberated Sorbonne and other university buildings were struck in particular by the graffiti emblazoned on the walls. It was as if the Chinese cultural revolution had suddenly erupted in the middle of Paris. On the wall-newspapers that French universities now boasted, all existing values were turned upside down. Many spectators found this reversal of perspective refreshing. There was condemnation of modern society: "The forest precedes man, the desert follows him"; repudiation of the consumer economy and society of spectacle: "Merchandise—we'll burn it"; "Let us banish applause, spectacle is everywhere"; "Are you *consumers* or real *participants*?" Vigorous protest against the degradation of life under capitalism: "Look at your work, nothingness and torture are what it is"; "People who work are bored when they don't work. People who don't work are never bored." For those who might not have gotten the message, a very direct: "Never work!" Most surprising was the even-handed condemnation of capitalism and communism: "Humanity (down with *L'Humanité*, counter-revolutionary rag) will never live free until the last capitalist will have been hanged with the guts of the last bureaucrat." The tactic to be used against existing society? "Insolence is the new revolutionary arm." The goal is to change the condition of life and permit total freedom: "Those who speak of revolution and class struggle without referring to daily reality speak with death in their mouths"; "Enjoy without being shackled. Live without killing time." And the students added passion to their politics: "The more I make love, the more I feel like making the Revolution; the more I make the Revolution, the more I feel like making love."[16]

In the confusion and tumult of the May Revolt the slogans and shouts of the students were considered expressions of mass spontaneity and individual ingenuity. Only afterward was it evident that these slogans were fragments of a coherent and seductive ideology and had virtually all previously appeared in situationist tracts and publications. Situationism since then has been popularized in the theater, cinema, and literature, as well as in the universities. Many intellectuals who went down to political defeat in June 1968 have taken their sweet revenge upon repressive political and social institutions in their writings and films, exalting sheer lust for life, emotionalism, and gratification of desires. Some recent films are simply vehicles for situationist theory, subjecting to remorseless criticism the consumer economy and society of spectacle, and unintentionally demonstrating that films inspired by situationism can be even more boring than the usual Hollywood fantasy.

Of all the revolutionary groups active in the May Revolt,

however, the least noticeable at the time was the Internationale Situationniste (I.S.). In retrospect, however, the "spirit of '68" was perhaps best captured, one might even say incarnated by the situationists. The Situationist International, created in July 1957 in Italy, was the result of a merger of one faction of the Lettrists with two obscure groups: the Mouvement pour un Bauhaus Imaginiste (MBI) and the Psychogeographical Committee of London. The Lettrists, directed shortly after World War II by Isidore Isou (Jean-Isidore Goldstein), were outraged by the way in which art was being contaminated by the world of commerce and business. They sought to shock people into thinking about the degradation of modern life. In 1952 some young Lettrists, led by Guy Debord, disrupted a press conference at the Hotel Ritz held by Charlie Chaplin (who had been one of the darlings of the surrealists after World War I). When disowned by an irate Isou, the dissidents split off and founded the Internationale Lettriste. The new organization rapidly turned political, on the assumption that only through revolution could the artistic way of life become a reality. In 1957 Debord published a report calling for the creation of "situations" and of an international situationist movement.[17]

Heeding this call were a small number of architects, artists, and urbanists (members of the previously mentioned MBI and Psychogeographical Committee) whose goal was a new life style brought about by cultural and architectural revolution. Common to all three major components of the I.S.—Lettrists, MBI, and psychogeographers—was hostility to capitalism, belief in revolution as the transformation of the conditions of daily existence, and emphasis on the spontaneity and creativity of art.

The French section of the I.S. immediately began to publish an extraordinary journal, the *Internationale Situationniste,* whose first issue appeared in June 1958. Subsequent issues came out irregularly thereafter, on the average of once every six to eighteen months. The journal offered philosophical discussions and acid commentary on current events, interspersed with political comic strips and erotic photographs.

Headquarters of the organization were established in a seedy hotel in the heart of the Latin Quarter. Guy Debord, who served as director of the journal until July 1968, has the reputation of being the revolutionary spirit and conscience of the I.S.—sitting in judgment on the qualifications of aspiring members and presiding over constant purges, as guardian of the pure revolutionary faith.

In the first few years of their existence, the situationists worked quietly, out of public view, elaborating their revolutionary theory. Outside of a limited circle of artists and poets, they were unknown. In the first issue of their journal they sounded the themes deriving from the three components of the organization: surrealism as an approach to politics and as a shock tactic, the need for a new urbanism, and for a revolution that would convert daily existence into an art form. The I.S. also sought to explain the name by which they wished to be known, defining a "situation" as "a moment of life, concretely and deliberately constructed by the collective organization of a unitary environment and a play of events." Out of this obscure definition came a central message of situationism: do not submit to the degradation and insanity of the modern world, rather deliberately create *situations* in which the individual at last can free himself of repressive influences and live as a creative artist.[18]

A larger public became aware of the I.S. through the Provo movement in Holland, one of whose leaders had been a full-fledged situationist before being expelled in 1960 in one of Debord's frequent purges. A number of situationist ideas were taken up by the Provos, including the notion of provocation through irony and play. The I.S. eventually repudiated the Provos who too willingly succumbed to the evils of hierarchy and commercialism. But the situationists were pleased to see in the appearance of the Provos confirmation of their analysis of the crisis of European youth.[19]

The situationists emerged from obscurity in 1966 during the student revolt in Strasbourg, which was a dress rehearsal for the May Revolt two years later. Around a hundred students at

Strasbourg in 1966 had been converted to situationism without actually being members of that exclusive group. Taking advantage of the general student apathy and disinclination to vote in elections, this handful of radicals managed to gain control of the local student organization. They contacted I.S. headquarters after their victory and were advised to publish a manifesto with the funds so opportunely made available by a bourgeois institution. One of the leaders of the I.S., Mustapha Khayati, wrote the manifesto, though he did not sign it. Entitled *De la misère en milieu étudiant, considérée sous ses aspects économique, politique, psychologique, sexuel et notamment intellectuel et de quelques moyens pour y remédier* (On the Poverty of Student Life, a consideration of its economic, political, sexual, psychological and notably intellectual aspects and of a few ways to cure it), it was an immediate hit. Over 20,000 copies were distributed at Strasbourg alone, and it has since been reprinted many times and translated into several languages. The manifesto was a brilliant piece of action literature, summarizing situationist theory in forceful and easily comprehensible language. Proclaiming that all organization is repressive, the radicals at Strasbourg demanded the liquidation of the student organization under their control, and also of UNEF, in order to pave the way for the final victory of the international power of workers' councils.[20]

The Strasbourg revolt was soon quashed, since more was at stake than the right to distribute a pamphlet. A student cafeteria, a university co-op, and a summer vacation camp—with a total budget of almost a half million dollars—had been placed in the trust of a faction dedicating itself to destruction of all existing authority and to international revolution. The matter went to the courts, the radicals were charged with fraudulent election practices and embezzlement of funds, and the solid Strasbourgeois soon recovered control of their association. Nonetheless, the Internationale Situationniste had suddenly surfaced in the world of student activism, and its journal along with the manifesto on *The Poverty of Student Life* became a fount of political wisdom. In addition, two books appeared in

1967 which attracted a great deal of attention among student radicals. One was by the acknowledged leader of the situationists, Guy Debord, who subjected modern capitalist society to a withering analysis in his *La société du spectacle: La théorie situationniste.* More comprehensive, since it combined criticism of reality with groping toward utopia, was the *Traité de savoir-vivre à l'usage des jeunes générations,* by a member of Debord's editorial committee and an active situationist, Raoul Vaneigem. Most of the slogans chalked on the walls of French universities in May 1968 came straight out of the books by Debord and Vaneigem, and the manifesto by Khayati.

Among the students influenced strongly by situationist literature were the *Enragés* of Nanterre, who took their name from the proto-anarchists led by Jacques Roux during the French Revolution. The Nanterre group consisted of a half dozen determined agitators (of whom the best known was René Riesel), and perhaps twenty to thirty followers during the period from January through May. They deliberately created "situations" by shouting down professors or hurling oranges and tomatoes at them, and at one point by invading and looting administrative offices. Immediately after participating in the occupation of the Faculty Council chamber at Nanterre on March 22, they fell into a violent dispute with the Trotskyists, Maoists, and anarchists present. The *Enragés* left in a huff and proceeded to paint their slogans on the inviting blank walls of the Nanterre campus. For the *Enragés* the M22M slogan, *"l'imagination au pouvoir"* ("Imagination in power") assumed the continuation of a power relationship between leaders and followers; the slogan thus betrayed a readiness, even an eagerness to make compromises in order to gain power and perhaps to create new forms of exploitation. The *Enragés* countered with a situationist refrain, *"Prenez vos désirs pour la réalité"* ("Take your desires for reality"), so that art would triumph over politics.

Shifting their activities to Paris, the *Enragés* joined enthusiastically in the street battles of early May. They established close contact with the I.S.; the relationship was formalized on May 14 by a "Comité Enragés-Internationale Situationniste," which immediately began to issue ringing communiqués to the public. René Riesel of the *Enragés* was one of the fifteen members of the first occupation committee at the liberated Sorbonne. After the collapse of direct democracy at the Sorbonne, *Enragés,* situationists, and some sixty other like-minded revolutionaries formed a Council for the Maintenance of Occupations, with headquarters at a teachers institute. The Council turned away from the students and toward the workers. "Our sole program is the total destruction of the university, along with the destruction of all institutions, of all forms of oppression, the only point of departure possible for the realization of art and philosophy."[21] The situationists had come a long way from Charlie Chaplin's press conference at the Hotel Ritz.

Situationist ideas after the May Revolt gained in popularity, but Debord was displeased by what he called his "revolting celebrity" and declared that he and his friends were going to become "even more inaccessible, even more clandestine. The more our theses become famous, the more will we ourselves become obscure." The four-man committee that replaced Debord as editor of the I.S. journal in July 1968 was not able to put out another issue, and Debord has since stated that it would be desirable to cease publishing a journal whose success had become too "routine." Those who used to anxiously await each issue for tips on reality, he commented wryly, will now have to begin thinking for themselves, in the best situationist tradition.[22]

After attending a disappointing situationist conference in Venice, in September 1969, Debord decided that the I.S. should be weakened not strengthened. A year later he deliberately provoked a split within the organization by announcing his intention to attack personally all those who were insufficiently active or effective (as he defined the terms). By 1972 virtually every situationist who had been prominent in the preceding decade had either resigned or been expelled. Mustapha Khayati left in 1969 to take part actively in one of the radical Palestine liberation groups; Raoul Vaneigem resigned in a huff in November 1970, after accusing himself of failure; René Viénet left in 1971 "for personal reasons"; and René Riesel was expelled after Debord denounced him as a "buffoon" and an "ordinary crook." Despite the purges, Debord claims, with good reason, that situationist theories are more influential than ever: "The theory, the style, the example of the I.S. are adopted today by thousands of revolutionaries in the principal advanced nations, but, more profoundly, it is the totality of modern society that appears to be convinced of the truth of situationist perspectives, either to achieve them or to combat them."[23]

Situationism is the exact reverse of social science, which may account for its enormous popularity among students of literature and art. Consider the major assumption made by most social scientists: that the procedures of the natural sciences (elaboration and verification of conflicting hypotheses) are a model for the study of society, enabling us better to understand the world and prepare the way for intelligent reforms. Since Durkheim's time it has also been an article of faith among French social scientists that increasing division of labor (that is, modernization) makes it possible for individuals to enjoy a measure of autonomy and freedom. Man in a simple or primitive society is merely an extension of the group, hemmed in by taboos, without a mind or will of his own. Science and technology perform a positive function in bringing about the transition from traditional to modern societies.

On every one of these points the situationists, drawing primarily upon their surrealist heritage, were in violent disagreement. For the situationists, man in primitive society is part of a single universe, marked by unity of beliefs, productive activity and harmonious social relations. He lives in close contact with the cosmic forces that govern humanity, the earth and the stars. Time has a deep and personal meaning, measuring the ascension of man's radiant soul to heaven. With division of labor comes division within society. The unity of the world is shattered, men are pitted against one another, labor becomes a burden instead of a pleasure, the integrated universe is replaced by man alienated from his activity and from nature. As the world becomes more modern—that is, more specialized and scientific—so does it become more mad, more horrendous, and unlivable. The merchandise provided in such abundance by industrial society is poisoned, just as the air is polluted. Reason creates unreason. The supreme achievement of modern technology—the consumer economy—reduces man to the level of a commodity. He is bought and sold and eventually becomes a mere spectator, totally drained of feeling and love. As for the social scientist—his function is to condition people to accept their lot. He makes the world an object of study instead of a place of pleasure. Only revolution is true, all else is ideology and false. In opposition to the "realpolitik" of social scientists is what may be called the "surrealpolitik" of situationists. Following the lead of Raoul Vaneigem, we will consider surrealpolitik in three aspects, as [1] a radical critique of modern society; [2] a prescription for transforming modern society through revolution; and [3] a new perspective made possible by revolution.[24]

The situationists have adopted the Marxist notion that the exchange of money for commodities and back into money is the dominant value of a modern capitalist society. Marx's strident commentary on the fetishism of commodities and the reduction of human beings to their exchange value is repeated and embellished by the situationists. Thus, Debord recounts that under capitalism good is identified with production and ownership of merchandise, and evil with its absence, wholly apart from the question of human enjoyment. But an economy based on merchandise is empty, devoid of human warmth and loyalty. The consumers in a consumer economy in fact consume a void. Ultimately, man shows his superiority over merchandise by destroying it, as in the pillage and looting during the riots in Watts and other American cities.[25]

The "society of spectacle"—a phrase popularized by the title of Guy Debord's book—is the social equivalent of a consumer economy. Just as commodities are the rationale of the economy, so do spectacle and imagery become the motifs of the society. Man becomes alienated from both commodities and spectacle. Says Debord at the outset of his study: "The entire life of societies where modern conditions of production prevail may be considered an immense accumulation of *spectacle.* Everything that is directly lived is turned into a performance." Spectacle represents the "nonliving," a false consciousness, mere external appearance divorced from reality, the incarnation of passivity, the unreal heart of the real society, the opposite of life. When an individual enjoys himself and gives free play to his emotions, he lives and has no need of spectacle. In the society of spectacle everything is artificial and inhuman—intellectual life as well as daily existence. "To be" is replaced by "to have," which finally becomes "to appear."[26]

A root cause of spectacle is the increasing specialization of labor and social function that takes place as a society modernizes. Men become separated from one another in the productive process and consequently in their perceptions as well as their roles. In primitive society the individual feels himself part of the group and at one with the universe. Modernization disrupts the unitary synthesis and sets the individual adrift. Comments Debord: "The origin of spectacle is the loss of the unity of the world and the gigantic expansion of modern spectacle expresses the totality of that loss . . . ."[27]

In the modern world one of the extreme forms of spectacle is bureaucracy. The bureaucrat enters into contact with the economy, that is, his merchandise, only through the intermediary of the whole bureaucratic community. To ensure respect for decisions, the masses must be left with little or no margin of choice. In a highly specialized society, the bureaucrats decide and the masses passively obey.

For the situationists, the most important division within a society is between those who cannot modify their "social space-time," or situations, and those who organize conditions of life for themselves and for others. The only revolution that matters is one that suppresses hierarchy, radically changing the manner in which decisions concerning "social space-time" are made. But how can the revolution possibly succeed unless the masses are organized? Vaneigem distinguishes between "leaders" and "chiefs," between the poetry of "agitators and leaders" and the authority of directors. It is possible to have organization without hierarchy, leaders who do not become chiefs—by making the revolutionary organization a merry fellowship of artists who poke fun at themselves, participate joyously in a common endeavor, and seek pleasure rather than obedience.

Following from the repudiation of bureaucracy is a natural disdain for the kind of planning considered a salvation by the technocratic left. Planning of any sort furthers specialization of function, depriving the individual of the last bit of his autonomy and freedom. And of all the kinds of planning to which mankind is subjected, perhaps the most atrocious is urban planning—a technique used by capitalism, argues Debord, to refashion the environment in its own image and to serve its own purposes. Thus, the workers are atomized and scattered throughout the suburbs so that they are unable to organize. The city is destroyed and replaced by a wholly artificial "pseudo-countryside" lacking the natural warmth of human relationships in either countryside or city.[28]

Rather than plan through bureaucracy, modern man should create his own environment; the city should be a place for social encounters, encouraging especially the accidental and the haphazard. Central to the situationist view of urbanism is the *"dérive"*—literally, being adrift, or wandering aimlessly through a section of the city. Typically, a small group of like-minded individuals would roam around a neighborhood for a few hours or several days. The purpose of such a *dérive* is to wrench the individual out of his customary role, to open his eyes to new relationships, and ultimately to enable him to reshape his "situation" in his own image.[29]

It follows from the situationist view of hierarchy that the communist model of revolution is no improvement. The horror of capitalism is simply replaced by the horror of hierarchic communism; if anything, the worker has even less control over his destiny. Communism everywhere—in Cuba, North Vietnam, and China, as well as in the Soviet Union—creates another form of spectacle, with the *image* of the working class as interpreted by an all-powerful and exploitative bureaucracy replacing real, live workers. The Bolsheviks have become the party of the "proprietors of the proletariat." Stalinist bureaucracy is a prolongation of the society of merchandise and spectacle. In effect, the situationists accept Trotsky's criticism of the Soviet Union, but then turn the argument against Trotsky himself, seeing him as a supreme bureaucrat outmaneuvered by Stalin in the struggle for power. Nor do the situationists share the Trotskyist veneration of Lenin. On the contrary, according to the situationists, Lenin is probably the real villain of the piece, since he created a force of professional revolutionaries outside of the proletariat, thus forming a class of decision-makers separated from the masses. The situationist critique of modern communism is total: anti-Lenin, anti-Stalin, anti-Trotsky, anti-Mao, anti-Ho, and anti-Castro. The debt to anarchism is obvious, except that the situationists repudiate the anarchists as well.[30]

To destroy modern society, then, is the object. As a first step, a man must say, "No!" He must refuse to accept the modern world, for only then will it be possible to transcend it. Nihilism is the beginning of the revolution; but by itself is self-defeating, since it does not go beyond refusal of existing reality. The next step, suggests Vaneigem, is Dada, which was a laboratory for the rehabilitation of daily life. Dada led to a rediscovery of joy and a reversal of perspective. Dadaists lacked a critical sense of history, however, and so fell easily into the trap of Stalinism. The point is to assimilate the technique of nihilism and Dada, but only as part of a truly revolutionary action.[31]

An essential element of the surrealist technique of refashioning the existing world is *"détournement"* (or distortion), which is given a special meaning by the situationists. It designates the reemployment in a new context of preexisting artistic elements. *Détournement* should take place in a playful spirit; to make fun of the world is to help along its disintegration. It is both negation and prelude, repudiating existing culture, yet salvaging some of it in order to point the way toward a new culture. Situationist experiments with *détournement* include a film documentary by Debord entitled, "On the passage of some persons through a rather short unity of time," which had the unusual merit of claiming to show the longest sequence of completely black frames in the history of cinema. Probably the most catchy use of *détournement* so far has been comic strips that convey revolutionary messages. Closeups of a man and a woman about to embrace are punctuated by the following captions: "Look at the Paris Commune . . . " (lips approach); "That was the dictatorship . . . " (noses almost touch); " . . . of the proletariat" (passionate kiss).[32]

It is hardly enough for a handful of intellectuals to preach the necessity of revolution; there must also be a revolutionary instrument. At first the situationists appealed only to artists and other "producers of culture"—a rather narrow base for a revolutionary movement. At a conference of situationists in September 1960, in London, Debord proposed that each delegate present a written response to the question: "Are there any forces in society from which the I.S. can draw support? Which forces? Under what conditions?" Although some delegates contended at first that only avant-garde artists are truly revolutionary, the situationists eventually discovered the working class on the basis of this questionnaire.[33]

It was not until the following year that the I.S. called for the creation of "Councils of Workers," and not until 1963 that the term "proletariat" gained currency in situationist literature. It was given a new meaning, however, in conformity with the situationist view of the modern world. "One can consider as proletarians those people who have no possibility of modifying the social space-time that society allocates to them for consumption . . . . The directors are those who organize that social space-time." That is, the new proletarian is not simply the factory worker creating value appropriated by the capitalist, he is any person driven to a condition of alienation because he has nothing to say about the decisions affecting his life. The class struggle cannot be eliminated by economic planning or any other bureaucratic process, but only by generalized autogestion through workers councils. By 1967, with the publication of books by Vaneigem and Debord, the proletariat became the privileged instrument of revolution, "the negation at work in the society." In theory almost everyone is proletarian since almost everyone has lost control over the conditions under which he lives. But situationists, regardless of the implications of their definition, began to identify the proletariat exclusively with the traditional working class.[34]

What kind of society will replace that of exploitation and spectacle? The very opposite of today's, making possible a life of creativity, love, poetry, pleasure, and communication. Each individual will be an artist, in that he will shape his "social space-time" as he wishes and develop all of his faculties to the fullest extent. Like the neo-anarchists, the situationists find the model of organization for the future libertarian society in the revolutionary experience of the proletariat—the Paris Commune, the soviets of 1905 and 1917, and the councils created by workers in Italy in 1920, East Berlin in 1953, and Hungary in 1956. A negative lesson derives from study of reformist trade unions and Bolshevism: to avoid at all costs the creation of a bureaucracy or any group pretending to speak or act on behalf of the workers themselves. Once separated from the decision-making process the workers become passive spectators. Total democracy requires the end of specialization and hierarchy.[35]

But the situationists repudiate the anarchist conception that there be *no* organization whatsoever; some form of organization is a necessity. What does total democracy mean in practice? During the May Revolt the situationists offered some guidelines. Through their Committee for the Maintenance of Occupations, they warned against collaboration with Maoists, Trotskyists, or anarchists. The workers are rather to take possession of the economy directly, through workers' councils, without intermediaries like politicians, unions, or anyone else. "What is distinctive about the power of councils? The dissolution of all external power; direct and total democracy; unification in practice of decision and of implementation; the delegate revocable at any moment by his constituents; abolition of hierarchy and of independent specialization; permanent creative participation of the masses; international extension and coordination .... Autogestion is nothing less." Subsequently, Vaneigem pointed out that eventually the councils would require an extensive organization, including committees on equipment and production, information, coordination, and self-defense. The ideal size for local councils, he suggested, is around eight to ten thousand people![36]

In striving to achieve total freedom for all, the situationists do not recoil from the use of violence against those who oppose progress. No compromise is possible, asserts Vaneigem, with the enemies of liberty, no pity will be shown to the oppressor. The class enemy will be executed without trial. Terrorist anarchism of the nineteenth century, while shortsighted and superficial, at least had the merit of disrupting the self-regulating mechanism of an oppressive society, of ripping the veil that concealed its criminal nature. The proletariat, argues Vaneigem, has no other recourse but to liquidate those who block its way to total liberation. "It must destroy them totally, as one destroys a particularly prolific vermin."[37]

The role of the situationists is to help the proletariat become conscious of the new conditions under which it is exploited. The I.S. defines itself as the conscience of the revolution, not a hierarchy of professional revolutionaries. It hopes to lead a long march toward revolution, beginning with the creation of a parallel society, going on to a coalition of microsocieties carrying on guerrilla war against the power structure. The revolutionaries make clear that the alternative to workers' councils is insurrectional chaos, pillage, terrorism, and repression. Vaneigem's "urban guerrilla" will "liquidate" policemen, stage riots, disrupt the economy, challenge all authority.[38] Thus beckons the new society of love, creativity, and untrammeled liberty.

The situationists boasted among their small membership

some brilliant tacticians and gifted polemicists, but this can hardly account for their widespread influence in the May Revolt and in French cultural life since then. Situationist ideas were the most unusual feature of the May Revolt. But it is remarkable that situationists are themselves not original thinkers. Every aspect of situationist theory (and, by extension, of the ideology of the May Revolt that so impressed the public) can be found in the older surrealist movement: repudiation of science and technology; questioning of abstract logic and reason along with a parallel interest in magic, the occult, and the orient; longing for the unity of primitive societies; provocation as a tactic; and the demand for unlimited liberty coupled with a penchant for authoritarian practices. Situationism is surrealism resurgent. Wherever modernization takes place, it is accompanied by counterpressures of various sorts. Surrealism may be viewed as part of the dialectical opposition to transformation of society by science and technology. The May Revolt in France cannot be understood without taking into account the surrealist refusal to accept the condition of man in the modern world.

Surrealism as a movement refers to the activity of the artists and writers who grouped themselves around André Breton between the two world wars. Along with Breton were three other "musketeers": Louis Aragon, Paul Eluard, and Benjamin Péret, who later went their separate ways but share the distinction of founding and shaping surrealism in its first years. Included in the movement were a great many intellectuals of the period, such as the poets Philippe Soupault, Tristan Tzara, and Robert Desnos, and the painters Francis Picabia, Max Ernst, René Magritte, Joan Miró, and Salvador Dali. Contemporary literature and art have been profoundly marked by their work. The political implications have also been far-reaching.[39]

Breton spoke of the "surrealism" of the Greeks, of Dante and Shakespeare, of Swift, Sade, Hugo, and many others, by which he meant there is an eternal surrealism that is part of the human spirit. In all ages there are some who turn the world topsy turvy, rejecting that which prevails and glorifying that which is considered absurd. As Breton remarked, the idea of surrealism, among other things, is " . . . perpetual promenade in the middle of a forbidden area."[40] In the twentieth century surrealists turned away from logic, rationality, and science, and emphasized the human faculties of imagination and the senses. They drew sustenance from the traditions of romanticism, the Gothic novel, and the literature of the fantastic. By far the most important single influence is that of Lautréamont (Isidore Ducasse), the object of a veritable cult among surrealists. This tormented genius, who wrote his *Chants de Maldoror* and *Poésies* as an adolescent and died at the age of 24, blazed the way through his constant reversal of the values of good and evil and a self-deprecating humorous style.

Surrealists echo the renunciation of the poet Rimbaud: "Real life is elsewhere. We are not in the world." But they do not simply admire the past; they seek to invent a future inspired by the past, in which man can live to the hilt, encountering adventure, and exploring the vast reaches and depths of humanity. Rimbaud's phrase is sounded again and again: *"Changer la vie."* One expression of the quest for a new life was Dada, which denigrated everything then in existence in order to affirm the supremacy of disorder over order.

Dada was the total repudiation of the modern world. It is hardly surprising that it should have flourished during and immediately after World War I, when European society seemed to be committing suicide. Everything was rational—technologies, economies, social structures, diplomatic policies, military establishments—except for the total result, world war, which was utterly insane. Modern civilization was bankrupt, not merely because of the war in 1914, but in its fundamentals. The devotees of Dada dedicated themselves to devastation and destruction—by disrupting theatrical performances, staging noisy demonstrations at art exhibits, holding mock trials of literary enemies—any act that would provoke, shock, shake up the intellect. But sheer negativism eventually alienated even the alienated. By 1924 the creators of Dada abandoned their "hobby horse" and evolved into surrealists. Yet they always retained a trace of nihilism and negativism from their Dada days. Surrealism was an extension, not a negation of Dada.[41]

In the early 1920s the surrealists experimented with such artistic techniques as automatic writing in order to transcend reality by unleashing the unconscious. Free association of words and ideas as in dreams (induced by drugs, if need be) embodied the supreme value of spontaneity. Poetry was conceived not as an exclusive literary activity, but rather as a way of life for all men. "Poetry," as Lautréamont said, "must be composed by all." The ambition of the surrealists was to transform daily life into an exciting adventure. As Breton put it in 1946: "Transform the world, change life, recreate human understanding from scratch."[42]

In order to expand the mind, surrealists developed the juxtaposition of disparate objects as a shock tactic. Lautréamont's aesthetic became an inspiration: "Beautiful as the accidental encounter, on a dissecting table, of a sewing machine and an umbrella." Defiance of logic, suggestion of sexual symbolism, exaltation of emotion and dream—out of this combination the situationists later fashioned the tactic of *détournement*. The surrealist goal was absolute and unlimited freedom for the individual to explore anything and do anything, including the kind of liberation from sexual restrictions advocated by Sade and the psychologist Wilhelm Reich. In a world supposedly governed by laws and regulations, surrealists vaunted the values of chance and accident, leading to a whole new view of the city as the most congenial setting for fortuitous encounters (the basis of the situationist theory of urbanism and the *dérive*). Life was approached playfully, as a game, in an effort to recover a sense of joy through participation (reappearing among situationists as the playful spirit, provocation, and the happening).

Repudiation of the modern world requires an inexorable war against rationality. Logic and science are intolerable restrictions upon the human spirit. Proclaimed Breton, " . . . logical processes today no longer are applied to anything but the resolution of problems of secondary interest . . . . Imagination is perhaps on the point of coming back into its own."[43] More important than science in the modern world is the treasure trove of magic, the occult, alchemy, and astrology. The world is an enigma wrapped in a mystery. Primitive man could participate directly in the mystery of the universe through his rituals and his art, creating poetry as Lautréamont had urged. Western rationality has separated man from the universe, leading to the alienation of man from his society and himself.

Another way to redemption is through the great religions of the Orient, which consecrate the unity of the individual with the world, in such pleasing contrast to the compartmentalization engendered by modern science. Asia is the "citadel of all hope," the mysterious source of opposition to the West which will ultimately realize the dream of all creative artists by crushing modern civilization. "Western world, you are condemned to death," proclaimed Aragon during his surrealist period. "We are the defeatists of Europe. Let the East, your terror, finally answer our call . . . . We are those who will always stretch out a hand to the enemy." Revival of interest in oriental religions has always been a counterpoint to modernization in the West.[44]

Dada and surrealism were carried along by the same current that produced anarchism, both the extreme libertarian variety and the kind of terrorism that flourished at the turn of the century. André Breton once confided, "Where surrealism first recognized itself . . . was in the black mirror of anarchism . . . . A great fire smouldered there." In 1951 the surrealists were accorded a literary column in *Le Libertaire,* the official journal of the Anarchist Federation. Breton explained on this occasion that, for him, anarchism represented "true socialism, the expression of desire on the part of exploited masses to create a classless society."[45]

The surrealist goal has always been vague: transform the world, change life, dream of a future and shape it according to one's dream—all excellent slogans for tearing down an existing society but hardly blueprints for a new order. Yet these sharp critics, these uncompromising opponents of discipline, these fearless champions of liberty almost all had flopped into the communist camp by 1927. The surrealists were carried toward communism above all by their contempt for the morality of the bourgeois world from which almost all of them had come. Capitalism glorified profit, led to the supremacy of material things over human and artistic values, reduced men to cogs in the machinery of the economy. In the conformist atmosphere of the 1920s, who but the Communists were against capitalism and bourgeois morality? To be a revolutionary in literature and art meant also to be a revolutionary in politics, and everyone knew that the Soviet Union, under the sterling leadership of Stalin, incarnated the revolution. The enemy of my enemy is my friend. Marxism for surrealists became the solution to the problem of attaining liberty through discipline; creative artists were perceived as fellow sufferers and natural allies of alienated workers. Thus, the surrealists in one easy hop went from sheer nihilism to enthusiastic acceptance of the discipline of the Communist Party; some even stuck it out through the entire Stalinist period.

The ambiguity of the surrealist attitude toward revolution and communism is evident in the careers of three of the founders of the movement. Breton broke with the Communist Party within a few years of joining. He was too much of an individualist to be comfortable as a dutiful member of a party cell. His admiration for the duo Lenin-Stalin was replaced by enthusiam for the duo Lenin-Trotsky, finally yielding to the anarchism that he had found so attractive as a youth. On the other hand, Eluard (who had moments of doubt but overcame them after the Liberation) and Aragon swung over to active membership in the Communist Party and militant Stalinism.[46]

The case of Louis Aragon is particularly interesting. Aragon and Breton became fast friends during World War I, when both served in the medical corps of the French army. They worked closely together thereafter, putting out surrealist journals and even collaborating on a joint literary endeavor. Aragon later remarked that his accord with Breton was a "natural phenomenon." Aragon was one of the first of the surrealist group to achieve literary fame. He scandalized the bourgeoisie with his anti-militarist, anti-patriotic, and anti-religious writings. In 1920 he proclaimed in a celebrated Dada manifesto during a protest demonstration:

> "Plus de [no more] peintres, plus de littérateurs, plus de musiciens, plus de sculpteurs, plus de religions, plus de républicains, plus de royalistes; plus d'impérialistes, plus d'anarchistes, plus de socialistes, plus de bolchéviques, plus de politiques, plus de prolétaires, plus de démocrates, plus d'armées, plus de police, plus de patries, enfin assez de toutes ces imbécilités, plus rien, plus rien, rien, RIEN, RIEN, RIEN."

Aragon at first dismissed communism as another "vague ministerial crisis" that did not get to the heart of the matter. In a talk in Madrid he lumped capitalists and workers together and went on to express an ideal surrealist sentiment: "I shall never work, my hands are pure . . . . I curse science, that twin sister of work." Along with the other surrealists, Aragon joined the Communist Party in 1927—but played no active role, and did not give up his surrealist views. Rather, he saw party member-ship as a natural act of defiance of the bourgeoisie by a surrealist. Then, one day, Aragon and his companion, Elsa Triolet, decided to take a trip to Moscow as tourists. It turned out, fortuitously, that a Congress of Revolutionary Writers was to be held in Kharkov, in October 1930, during their stay in Russia. An invitation to attend was hastily arranged. Aragon went to Kharkov as a surrealist in the service of the revolution. With hardly a murmur, he accepted a declaration of the Congress condemning Freud and Trotsky, along with the "errors" of Breton's Second Manifesto. He also agreed to submit his writings thereafter to party control. Aragon returned from Kharkov a convinced convert to communism, accepting the Third International as the anointed agent of world revolution. He definitively quit the surrealist camp and became one of the most effective of French propagandists for the Communist Party and the Stalinist regime. In an initial burst of

enthusiasm he even called for the assassination of French
political leaders and social democrats.[47]

In the heyday of Dada, Tristan Tzara had rivalled Aragon
in the ferocity of his attacks on all shackles upon the
individual's freedom of expression. And, like Aragon, Tzara
went from nihilism to obedient membership in the Communist
Party. Once the surrealists had cut their moorings from
liberalism in the name of liberty, nothing prevented them from
drifting hither and yon, in and out of Stalinism, Trotskyism,
anarchism, and apathy. The plea for unlimited liberty was easily
converted into a justification of unlimited discipline.

Situationists may castigate those who swung over to
orthodox Communism, but they have still to formulate a clear
relationship between surrealism and political revolution. The
situationist debt to surrealism is specifically emphasized by
Raoul Vaneigem, who writes: "Since the time that there have
been men, and that they read Lautréamont, everything has been
said and few have come forward to take advantage of it."
Debord, on the other hand, considers situationists in the
tradition of surrealism, but well beyond it. Surrealism is only a
beginning; "the point is to go further." Debord later phrased it
as follows: "Dada wanted to *suppress art without creating it;*
and surrealism wanted to *create art without suppressing it.* The
critical position elaborated since by the *situationists* has shown
that the suppression and the realization of art are inseparable
aspects of the same *transcending of art.*" The aim is to make
daily life itself a work of art.[48]

Whether or not the situationists have succeeded in transcending art, they have performed admirably the task of
transmitting a valuable heritage to the present generation of
revolutionary intellectuals. Mainly through their agency there
welled up in the May Revolt an immense force of protest
against the modern world and all its works, blending passion,
mystery, and the primeval. Trotskyists, Maoists, and anarchists
dominated the scene during the May Revolt. But in the long run
the most significant feature of the revolt may well have been
the sudden resurgence of surrealism as an armed vision.

NOTES

1. "The dominant society that flatters itself on its permanent modernization now finds with whom it must deal, that is, with the modernized negation that it produces itself." From the situationist pamphlet, *On the Poverty of Student Life* (Strasbourg, 1967), attributed to Mustapha Khayati.

2. On UNEF, see Adrien Dansette, *Mai 1968* (Plon, 1971), pp. 43-45, 93-98, 414-417.

3. On the troubles of the UEC: Alain Schnapp and Pierre Vidal-Naquet, *Journal de la commune étudiante* (Seuil, 1969), pp. 377-385; and Patrick Seale and Maureen McConville, *French Revolution, 1968* (Penguin, 1968), pp. 37-56.

4. In an interview reported by Jean Bertolino, *Les trublions* (Stock, 1968), pp. 106-107.

5. Cf. Bertolino's interview with the Trotskyist militant (Jean Schalit), ibid., p. 100; on Alain Krivine's brother, ibid., pp. 104-106.

6. On Trotskyism in general, the three volume life of Trotsky by Isaac Deutscher is indispensable, especially volume 3, *The Prophet Outcast* (Oxford University Press, 1963). Among the best treatments of Trotskyism in France are: Richard Gombin, *Le projet révolutionnaire* (Mouton, 1969), pp. 43-107; Richard Gombin, *Les origines du gauchisme* (Seuil,

1971), pp. 31-48; Seale and McConville, *French Revolution,* pp. 37-56; Schnapp and Vidal-Naquet, *Journal,* pp. 315-346; M.-A. Burnier and B. Kouchner, *La France sauvage* (Publications Premières, 1970), pp. 196-215; Dansette, *Mai 1968,* pp. 45-53; and J.-C. Mouret, "La famille Trotskiste," *La Nef* (June-Sept. 1972), pp. 57-75.

7. Geismar quote from *Minutes du procès d'Alain Geismar* (Editions Hallier, 1971), p. 63. For a useful collection of texts and documents on Maoism in France: Patrick Kessel, *Le mouvement "maoiste" en France,* vol. 1 (Union Générale d'Editions, 1972). Also: Schnapp and Vidal-Naquet, *Journal,* pp. 346-64; Gombin, *Le projet,* pp. 109-128; Burnier and Kouchner, *La France sauvage,* pp. 154-94; Dansette, *Mai 1968,* pp. 45-52; Jean Moreau, "Les 'Maos' de la Gauche Prolétarienne," *La Nef* (June-Sept. 1972), pp. 77-103. On the appeal of the Maoists in France, see Michèle Manceaux, *Les Maos en France* (Gallimard, 1972), especially the foreword by J.-P. Sartre.

8. Cited by Philippe Labro et al., *Ce n'est qu'un début* (Publications Premières, 1968), p. 57.

9. Cited, ibid., p. 36.

10. Cohn-Bendit on civilization, interview reprinted in J.-L. Brau, *Cours, camarade, le vieux monde est derriére toi!* (Albin Michel, 1968), pp. 189-90. On the final goal of the movement: Daniel et Gabriel Cohn-Bendit, *Le gauchisme, remède à la maladie sénile du communisme* (Seuil, 1968), p. 130. On the March 22 Movement in general, see: Mouvement du 22 Mars, *Ce n'est qu'un début, continuons le combat* (Maspero, 1968); Jean Bertolino, *Les trublions, passim.;* Dansette, *Mai 1968,* pp. 71-76; Schnapp and Vidal-Naquet, *Journal,* pp. 415-24.

11. On anarchist organizations in France: Gombin, *Les origines,* pp. 99-151; Burnier and Kouchner, *La France sauvage,* pp. 216-20; André Laude, "Les anarchistes," *La Nef* (June-Sept. 1972), pp. 117-28.

12. Cohn-Bendit quotes are from: interview reprinted in J.-L. Brau, *Cours, camarade,* pp. 189-90; D. and G. Cohn-Bendit, *Le gauchisme,* p. 260.

13. On Proudhon, Bakunin, and general background of anarchist thought, see: George Woodcock, *Anarchism* (Penguin, 1963); and Daniel Guérin, *L'anarchisme* (Gallimard, 1965).

14. On anarchism and the Bolsheviks: Woodcock, *Anarchism*, pp. 376-400; Guérin, *L'anarchisme*, pp. 96-126. For an excellent treatment of Pannekoek and the origins of autogestion: Gombin, *Les origines*, pp. 114-51.

15. Geismar and Cohn-Bendit quotes on Marcuse in Jacques Sauvageot, Alain Geismar, and Daniel Cohn-Bendit, *La révolte étudiante* (Seuil, 1968), pp. 47, 70.

16. Graffiti conveniently collected by Julien Besançon, *Journal mural, mai 68, passim.*

17. For a general view of the origins and the doctrines of the situationists: Gombin, *Le projet*, pp. 27-42; Gombin, *Les origines*, pp. 73-98. The first twelve numbers of the I.S. journal, now almost impossible to find, were reprinted as a book by a Dutch publisher, Van Gennep, in 1970. Indispensable are the books by Guy Debord, *La société du spectacle* (Buchet-Chastel, 1971); Raoul Vaneigem, *Traité de savoir-vivre à l'usage des jeunes générations* (Gallimard, 1967); and René Viénet, *Enragés et situationnistes dans le mouvement des occupations* (Gallimard, 1968). One of the first observers to note the significance of the situationists in the May Revolt was Alfred Willener, in his *L'image-action de la société* (Seuil, 1970), which includes chapters on Dada and surrealism by a poet, Pierre Gallissaires. Willener becomes so involved with the subject matter that his sociology takes on the character of a surrealist happening.

18. The definition of a situation is in *Internationale Situationniste* (henceforth referred to as I.S.), no. 1 (June 1958), 13.

19. On the Provos: I.S., no. 11 (Oct. 1967), pp. 65-66.

20. On the Strasbourg revolt: I.S., no. 11 (Oct. 1967), pp. 23-31, and Pierre Feuerstein, *Printemps de révolte à Strasbourg* (Strasbourg, Saisons d'Alsace, 1968), *passim.*

21. On situationists and enragés in the May Revolt: René Viénet, *Enragés et situationnistes;* and I.S., no. 12 (Sept. 1969), pp. 3-34.

22. See Guy Debord and Gianfranco Sanguinetti, *La véritable scission dans l'internationale* (Champ Libre, 1972), p. 79.

23. Debord quote on the influence of the I.S. in ibid., p. 11. For a rundown on the purges within the ranks of the situationists, see J.-J. Raspaud and J.-P. Voyer, *L'internationale situationniste* (Champ Libre, 1971).

24. For the situationist view of primitive man and modern society: Debord, *La société du spectacle*, pp. 19-23; Vaneigem, *Traité de savoir-vivre*, pp. 76-93. On social science and false ideology: Debord, ibid., pp. 146-76; Vaneigem, ibid., pp. 239-40.

25. The situationist attack on the consumer economy: Debord, *La société*, pp. 25-37; and Vaneigem, *Traité*, pp. 13-187 for a general critique of modern society.

26. Cf. Debord, *La société*, p. 9.

27. Ibid., p. 22.

28. On the distinction between leaders and chiefs, Vaneigem, *Traité*, pp. 269-73. On urban planning: Debord, *La société*, pp. 135-45; and Vaneigem, *Traité*, p. 234. Also, *I.S.*, no. 6 (August 1961), pp. 33-37.

29. On the *dérive*: *I.S.*, no. 1 (June 1958), 19; *I.S.*, no. 2 (Dec. 1958), pp. 13-17, 19-23.

30. On communism as a form of spectacle: Debord, *La société*, pp. 54-101.

31. On Dada: Vaneigem, *Traitè*, pp. 167-87; Debord, *La société*, p. 156.

32. On *détournement*: Vaneigem, *Traité*, pp. 191-95, 272-78; Debord, *La société*, p. 167; and *I.S.*, no. 3 (Dec. 1959), pp. 10-11; *I.S.*, no. 11 (Oct. 1967), pp. 32-36.

33. The 1960 London conference is summarized in *I.S.*, no. 5 (Dec. 1960), pp. 20-21.

34. Definition of proletariat: *I.S.*, no. 8 (Jan. 1963), p. 13.

35. The future society: Debord, *La société*, pp. 97-100, 146-76; Vaneigem, *Traité*, pp. 190-287.

36. On the meaning of autogestion and total democracy: *I.S.*, no. 12 (Sept. 1969), pp. 74-79. Also, Debord, *La société*, pp. 97-101.

37. On the use of violence, Vaneigem, *Traité*, pp. 25-26, 31, 282.

38. On the urban guerrilla: ibid., pp. 284-87; *I.S.* no. 12 (Sept. 1969), 77. Role of the I.S. in the revolution: Vaneigem, *Traité*, pp. 275-76, 286-87; also, *I.S.*, no. 11 (Oct. 1967), pp. 37, 54-55.

39. Useful critical works on surrealism include: Yvonne Duplessis,

Le surréalisme (Presses Universitaires, 1971); Robert Bréchon, *Le surréalisme* (Armand Colin, 1971); Maurice Nadeau, *Histoire du surréalisme* (Seuil, 1964); Gérard Durazoi and Bernard Lecherbonnier, *Le surréalisme* (Larousse, 1972); J. H. Matthews, *An Introduction to Surrealism* (Pennsylvania State University Press, 1965); and Michel Sanouillet, *Dada à Paris* (Pauvert, 1965). For a fascinating personal memoir emphasizing political activities of the surrealists, see André Thirion, *Révolutionnaires sans révolution* (R. Laffont, 1972).

40. André Breton, *Manifestes du surréalisme* (Gallimard, 1971), p. 92.

41. Michel Sanouillet argues persuasively that dada and surrealism (which he calls dada without laughter) were both manifestations of a vast movement of subversion that turned the world of letters upside down after World War I. Cf. his *Dada à Paris*, pp. 420, 432. In general, see Bréchon, *Le surréalisme*, pp. 26-27; Durozoi and Lecherbonnier, *Le surréalisme*, pp. 28-32; and Nadeau, *Histoire*, pp. 9-11, 21-32. The term "Dada," according to Nadeau (p. 21), was chosen by opening a dictionary at random. One meaning is "hobby horse."

42. Jean-Louis Bédouin, *Vingt ans de surréalisme* (Denoel, 1961), pp. 91-92.

43. André Breton, *Manifestes*, p. 18.

44. On the importance of magic and the occult, in general see Bréchon, *Le surréalisme*, chap. 2; and Durozoi and Lecherbonnier, *Le surréalisme*, pp. 11-16. Aragon quote on Western world, in Nadeau, *Histoire*, p. 76.

45. Breton on the link between surrealism and anarchism, in Bréchon, *Le surréalisme*, p. 119; also Bédouin, *Vingt ans*, pp. 203-05.

46. On surrealists and the Communist Party, see: Bréchon, *Le surréalisme*, chap. 4; Durozoi and Lecherbonnier, *Le surréalisme*, pp. 215-26; Nadeau, *Histoire*, chaps. 2 and 3; and André Thirion, *Révolutionnaires, passim.*

47. Aragon quote, "plus de . . . " from Nadeau, *Histoire*, pp. 26-27; Aragon quote in the Madrid speech, ibid., p. 76; see also, ibid., pp. 140-47. André Thirion, who knew Aragon well during the surrealist period, offers a perceptive analysis of Aragon's sudden conversion, *Révolutionnaires*, chaps. 27, 28. For an official party view: Roger Garaudy, *L'itinéraire d'Aragon* (Gallimard, 1961).

48. Vaneigem quote on Lautréamont in his *Traité*, p. 8. The very first article in the first issue of the *I.S.* (June 1958) is entitled, "The Bitter Victory of Surrealism." Citation from Debord is in his *Société*, p. 156.

4

Toward the Seizure of Power

Le Pouvoir avait les universités; les étudiants les ont prises. Le Pouvoir avait les usines; les travailleurs les ont prises. Le Pouvoir avait l'ORTF; les journalistes lui ont pris. Le Pouvoir a le Pouvoir. Prenez-le-lui.

(Graffito, entrance hall, Institut d'Etudes Politiques)[1]

THE MAY REVOLT was not a sudden, aimless outburst of popular energies; it was a conscious attempt to seize power, however farfetched such an act may have appeared before May. Each revolutionary group placed the problem of power at the center of its preoccupations. Even those revolutionaries who advocated a spontaneous popular uprising were working tirelessly to bring it about, so that in effect "spontaneity" was contrived.

Although everyone wanted revolution there was no agreement on how to go about it. Organization versus spontaneity, Bolsheviks versus Mensheviks, Lenin versus Rosa Luxemburg, Trotsky versus the Workers Opposition: the minuscule revolutionary groups in France acted out the historic debate of the whole European social-democratic movement, to which was added the modern controversy over guerrilla war versus peaceful coexistence. For some, it was chimerical to wait for workers to become revolutionary on their own, or to seize power impulsively. Workers required knowledge "from the outside," that is, from the professional revolutionaries who could best appreciate the requirements of an historical situation. Otherwise the workers became mere trade unionists and uprisings degenerated into uncontrollable adventures. For others, the professional revolutionaries would become bureaucrats and always find reasons to postpone the revolutionary gamble. If, by accident, revolution actually occurred, the hierarchy arrogating to itself the power to direct the working class quickly would evolve into an irresponsible, new ruling class. Spontaneity would lead to reformism and adventurism, organization would result in postponement of action or dictatorship.

To work out a "correct" policy for the seizure of power is never easy under the best of circumstances. In a country like France the century-old debate on revolutionary tactics seemed to be taking place in a void. France, after all, was a highly industrialized society, its proletariat largely integrated into the social system and its peasantry hardly a revolutionary force. The revolutionaries did not number more than a few thousand altogether (the most generous estimate would be fifteen thousand), and were opposed by the organized forces of the society, including the major trade unions and the Communist Party—not to mention the police and army. Most revolutionaries before May hoped at most to create a "prerevolutionary" climate of opinion; but some, undaunted, believed that revolution was a real possibility.

By the end of May, as a result of a chain reaction in which all groups participated, in some cases unwittingly, the "impossible" revolution was at hand. Even though working at cross-purposes, the revolutionary groups generated a rapid-fire crescendo of activity. Arch-rivals turned out to be objective allies in spite of themselves and their wholly incompatible goals. The revolutionary situation had been created by amalgamating the tactics of all the groups. The key steps, approximately in the order in which the revolt unfolded were: "contestation," or permanent, relentless criticism of the existing order; exposure of the violent nature of bourgeois society through provocation; extension of the revolt to the working class; conversion of campuses and factories into revolutionary bastions; and creation of a "dual power."

Contestation, largely the contribution of the anarchists

and situationists, means repudiation of all existing values, institutions, and authority, from the immediate (for example, professors, university officials, policemen) to the global (De Gaulle, capitalism, reformist communism, bureaucracy, modern society). One popular form of contestation is to disrupt lectures and hold professors up to ridicule. At Nanterre, for example, a highly successful technique was simply to occupy a lecture hall and refuse to permit classes to be held there. On one such occasion the M22M appropriated a lecture hall assigned to the distinguished historian René Rémond (subsequently to be president of a restructured Nanterre) for a "debate" on Vietnam and other political topics. When Rémond opened the door, he was insulted and pushed out. The anarchists thus expressed their contempt for authority figures and dramatized the irrelevance of university instruction in a revolutionary world. Anarchists and situationists, devoting themselves to criticism and destruction of contemporary society, especially admired and emulated the techniques of contestation perfected in Germany by the SDS and in Japan by the Zengakuren.[2]

After the existing society has been attacked and weakened, the next step is to expose the inherently repressive character of liberal and bourgeois-democratic institutions, even of that most liberal of all institutions, the university. As explained in one of the first pronouncements of M22M, the revolutionaries are conscious of being a small minority. So their problem is to arouse the political consciousness of the inert or apathetic masses. Their action, explained the revolutionaries, " . . . was a matter of making the latent authoritarianism come out (cf. the carloads of police ready to intervene) by showing the true face of the proposed 'dialogue.' As soon as certain problems are posed, the dialogue yields its place to the billy club." The sight of policemen beating students illuminates in a flash the repressive nature of the entire society. Then, through a spontaneous instinctual movement of solidarity, the masses enter the fray. For example, on the critical day of May 3, most of the revolutionary leaders were in the custody of the police and were being escorted peacefully from the courtyard of the

Sorbonne. The silent mass that watched the proceedings suddenly intervened, and the spark of revolt was struck.[3]

In the eyes of the anarchists the events of May 3 were a vindication of the theory of spontaneity, since the students unexpectedly and on their own rose up in a show of solidarity. By continually applying pressure, the revolutionaries had forced the state into a repressive act; the rest could be left to chance. But not all revolutionaries shared the anarchists' enthusiasm for spontaneity. For Trotskyists of FER the barricades of May 3 were convincing proof of the need for a highly disciplined organization to prevent "adventurers" from leading unsuspecting students to a slaughter. Trotskyists of JCR were more flexible, concluding from the same events that political attitudes are conditioned by the structures through which they are expressed. A working class will be "spontaneously trade unionist" if led by reformists, said two JCR theoreticians, and "spontaneously revolutionary" if led by revolutionaries.[4]

Whatever their position regarding tactics, anarchists, Maoists, and Trotskyists were agreed that the working class remained the indispensable agency of revolution. FER and Maoists were so convinced that at first they denied the utility of agitation among students at all, devoting themselves instead to organizing the workers. JCR and anarchists freely conceded that students could not accomplish the revolution by themselves, but hoped that a student revolt would set a good example for the workers to follow. Spokesmen for M22M talked of their action as exemplary—a means of creating a new situation, in turn leading to escalation of revolutionary activity. The very first act of the students after the occupation of the Sorbonne on May 13 was to open the university to workers. Then came the news of the occupation of Sud-Aviation; it was an electric shock, for it seemed to signal the transformation of a student riot into a socialist revolution. Jacques Sauvageot summed up the appraisal of the student leaders:

> The student movement played the role of detonator, posing early the problem of power . . . , which permitted a certain number of

students to assume a political posture. In a second phase, the movement was extended to the mass of the workers and the problem of the university became secondary or rather became part of the common struggle. Now the student movement is strictly dependent upon the workers' movement. If the latter stops, then ours is condemned because it will find itself isolated in the face of brutal repression, because the students cannot carry on a political struggle alone.[5]

Once the general strike began, all revolutionaries agreed that the traditional practice of picketing was not enough; a "dual power" had to be created. Here the influence of Trotsky was most evident, although some revolutionaries preferred not to mention his name for doctrinal reasons. The tactics to follow were: first, create a strike committee; then, under the direction of the strike committee, occupy the factories and convert them into armed camps; finally, transform the strike committee into a general workers council (or soviet) responsible for the management of the factories and other enterprises. Autodefense thus evolves naturally into autogestion and the liberation of popular energies through truly democratic councils. The bourgeois state would then have to face up to using violence to regain control of its means of production and nerve centers. The orthodox Marxist view would be borne out—it is the bourgeoisie and not the working class that resorts to violence in a revolutionary situation. And if the army and police were ordered to fire upon students and workers, would they do so? Wracked by dissension, the mercenaries would probably swing over to the side of the people. There would thus come into existence a "dual power": the "real" power of the workers and the "apparent" power of a frightened and increasingly isolated bourgeoisie. The victory of the proletariat and the overthrow of capitalism would be inevitable.[6]

Despite violent disagreement among themselves on every important issue concerning tactics and goals, student leaders by the end of May believed that they had successfully adapted the theory of people's war to an advanced country. Industrial societies, they argued, cannot be overthrown by frontal assault. Guerrilla war based on the peasantry is obviously unfeasible. But an *urban* guerrilla force, made up of students and young workers, can provoke an industrial people's war (occupation of factories, self-defense, and workers control) that will topple the bourgeois regime.

The problem of the seizure of power also has an international dimension. Over half the world's population is under communist or self-styled revolutionary rule. Convinced revolutionaries can hardly be expected to renounce aid from brethren fortunate enough to be in power elsewhere. Since revolutionaries do not make it a practice to publicize the sources of their funds, nor their contacts with foreign powers, it is virtually impossible to know for certain whether or to what extent French militants were aided or directed "from the outside" (to use Lenin's phrase in a different context). They have been linked by observers to an impressive array of foreign intelligence agencies, including: the American C.I.A. (to get back at De Gaulle for pulling out of NATO); the Soviet KGB (uneasy over De Gaulle's popularity in the East European satellites); and the Israeli foreign office (to punish De Gaulle for his pro-Arab diplomacy). One of the most elaborate of such theses assigns a key role to the East German intelligence service, working through Cohn-Bendit in France and Rudi Dutschke in West Germany to stir up trouble in the West, heighten international tension, and strengthen the hand of hard-liners in the communist world. The same source contends that the North Vietnamese provided large subsidies to the JCR in return for vigorous support of their policies.

In a book published shortly after the May Revolt, Raymond Marcellin, the Minister of the Interior, claims that the French revolutionary movement was coordinated, directed, and financed by the "Tricontinental Organization of People's Solidarity" in Havana. The Tricontinental was created in January 1966 at a Havana congress attended by six hundred delegates, including a number of French militants later in the forefront of the revolt. According to Marcellin, the Tricontinental boasts an efficient secretariat, a financial committee, and other services operating out of Havana for the express purpose of coordinating revolutionary activity in advanced countries and the Third World. Under the prodding of the Tricontinental, European revolutionary leaders had met a number of times: in Liège in October 1966, Brussells in March 1967, and Berlin in February 1968. A large number of French students, mainly Trotskyists, returned from the giant rally in Berlin full of admiration for the fighting tactics of the SDS and resolved to create "two, three Berlins."[7]

According to other observers China was the guiding genius and source of aid for at least some French revolutionaries. PCF spokesmen have asserted that the French Maoists receive substantial financial subsidies from China. *Le Monde* correspondent Michel Legris concurs. Prime Minister Pompidou hinted darkly during the crisis that the Chinese were behind all the trouble. In a statement to the National Assembly on May 11 he referred to the presence of "determined individuals disposing of important financial resources, of equipment suited to street fighting, depending evidently on an international organization . . . that seeks not only to create subversion in Western countries, but to disturb Paris at the very moment when our capitol has become the rendezvous of peace in the Far East." Only the Chinese fitted this description. That there was a centrally coordinated international conspiracy of some sort behind the leftists was widely believed by the French public—according to an IFOP poll in June 1970, by almost half of those with opinions.[8]

How much credence can be placed in these allegations? Among the most reliable historians of the May Revolt, Adrien Dansette is skeptical and Pierre Viansson-Ponté derisive. International links exist among the revolutionary groups, Dansette concedes, but he sees no evidence of a foreign plot to set off a revolt in France. Viansson-Ponté scoffs at the notion of a "secret conductor" of the revolutionary orchestra. Even Christian Fouchet, minister of the interior in May 1968, alluding to Pompidou's comment on foreign involvement, confesses: "As

for myself, I never believed that there was a real conspiracy."
No one has yet come forward with convincing proof that the
Cubans, or Chinese, or anyone else plotted to overthrow the
Gaullist regime or "teleguided" the student revolutionaries. The
May Revolt was a surprise to most participants, to say nothing
of intelligence agents in either Havana or Peking. Nor would it
have been an easy task to manipulate or orient such a diverse
and quarrelsome mass as the French student revolutionaries
either at a distance or on the scene.[9]

Nonetheless, it is likely that Chinese and especially Cuban
intelligence agents had contacts with individual French revolutionaries, that activities were coordinated and that money
changed hands—none of which would be viewed as reprehensi-
ble or abnormal in a revolutionary movement. There are many
healthy precedents. Lenin lavished money upon the Communist
parties abroad after coming to power. That there is an
obligation both to give and receive financial aid among brother
parties was made clear by Trotsky in 1921: "International
solidarity would only be despicable hypocrisy, a simple mask
concealing rank chauvinism . . . if the sections that could help
refused to do so or if, on the contrary, those who need financial
aid refused to accept it out of fear of bourgeois public
opinion." At first Komintern reps actually carried large sums
around in cash, but the arrest of one of them in 1921 led to
more efficient methods of transferring funds. Annie Kriegel, an
exceptionally well-informed observer, estimates that four-fifths
of the operating expenses of the French Communist Party in
the prewar period were covered by the Soviet Union. In
addition to financial aid, the Third International offered foreign
communists a way out of the otherwise insoluble dilemma of
organization versus spontaneity—by locating the revolutionary
spark in the Soviet Union and thus eliminating the incon-
venience of interminable debate on how to seize power.[10]

It would not be surprising if French revolutionaries today
had links with revolutionaries in other countries, including Cuba
and China, profiting from the same happy combination of
subsidies and revolutionary inspiration enjoyed by Communist

parties everywhere during the Stalinist period. Indeed, shortly after the May Revolt, Alain Geismar and a group from M22M left for Havana to recount their experiences to Cuban leaders and discuss the lessons to be drawn. But fraternal aid cannot account for the existence of a revolutionary situation. The Soviet Union presumably financed the Communist parties of both France and Great Britain in the 1920s—with widely different results. The question is how the French revolutionary groups managed to set off a revolt in May 1968 when the rival political forces, including the Communist Party and the bourgeois state, had immense financial resources at their disposal and the benefit of close alliances with foreign powers. If Cubans and Chinese were indeed involved in the May Revolt, a little money went a long way.

The classic debate over spontaneity and organization, as well as the polemic over the role of foreign intelligence agencies fade out of sight when we turn to the way in which the revolutionary groups actually went about the business of seizing power in May 1968. Far more important were the precedents established in the last French experience in overthrowing one republic and creating another, specifically in overthrowing the Fourth Republic and creating a new one under General de Gaulle's leadership just ten years before, almost to the day. The most striking parallel to the May Revolt is not Russia in 1905, nor China in 1948, nor Hungary in 1956, nor even Cuba in 1959—but rather Algeria in 1958.

The student revolutionaries were consciously inspired by the example of the Front de Libération Nationale (FLN). The six "historic chiefs" of the FLN, opposed by the organized Moslem parties, determined to change the course of history themselves. At first accused of mad and irresponsible "adventurism," they successfully unleashed the revolution that led to the independence of Algeria. An even more important source of inspiration (unacknowledged, of course) was the confused collection of dissident groups of French that managed to overthrow the Fourth Republic. In the May Revolt the student militants used the language of the heroic FLN, but followed the practices of the French settlers, whom they despised.

The coup that led to De Gaulle's return to power was not accomplished by a direct attack upon the state; it was rather the result of a chain reaction, initiated by small, well-organized groups in both Algeria and France. The "detonator" in May 1958 was composed mainly of right-wing university students in Algeria led by Pierre Lagaillarde, along with veterans' associations and a number of occult societies. The goal of the activists was to create a situation in which a greater power would be compelled to intervene. It was accomplished by occupying the largest administrative building in Algiers (the Gouvernement Général, or GG) on the initiative of the university students and the secret societies, and with the precious help of the high school students (another interesting similarity to the events ten years later). Once the GG was occupied, the government was compelled either to accept the situation and lose face, or resort to force. Under these circumstances, the army—which had not started the revolt—stepped in to restore order and take power. This was precisely what the right-wing activists wanted.

In May 1958 the revolutionaries were reactionary, inspired by fascists and conservatives; they sought the overthrow of parliamentary democracy and its replacement by an authoritarian regime. Ten years later the revolutionaries were leftist radicals, inspired by Communists; they sought the overthrow of parliamentary democracy and its replacement by a people's democracy. The ideological goals were total contrasts, but the tactics used for the seizure of power were strikingly similar. A network of small, secret, and well-organized revolutionary societies planned to occupy public buildings (in 1958 the GG, in 1968 the schools and universities). This occupation would create an intolerable situation for the government. "Another force" (in 1958 the army, in 1968 the workers) would intervene to make the revolution. The leaders of the May Revolt borrowed more extensively from the tactics of *Algérie française* than they knew, or perhaps cared to admit.[11]

The Combustible Material

The movement founded at Nanterre on March 22 by 142 students proclaimed as its purpose to destroy the bourgeois university and create "another Vietnam" in France. Consider the state of France a scant two months later: most factories occupied by workers and many converted into armed camps, topped by fluttering red flags; no mail, no public transport, no gasoline; no industrial production; all department stores shut; all universities occupied by students; thousands of people injured and considerable damage done to property in the riots that had swept Paris in the preceding three weeks; and even vacillation on the part of the police. The government seemed powerless, and opposition leaders were beginning to talk about the formation of a provisional government as if the regime had already disappeared. In the midst of this social and political chaos, on the afternoon of May 29, General de Gaulle secretly flew out of beleaguered Paris to consult with his generals commanding the French expeditionary force in Germany! Not a bad record of accomplishment for 142 students.

The detonator set off an explosion because the surrounding materials were combustible. The students had legitimate grievances in their schools and universities, as had the workers in their factories, and the middle classes in their offices. Elements of a revolutionary situation existed at each stage of the escalating violence. French social structures simply were not adapted to the needs of the time.

Nowhere has this been more evident than in the universities. Up until World War I and to a lesser extent until World War II, the French university was reasonably well attuned to social needs. Programs were designed for the children of the existing elite and of the hard working professional and middle classes. Most graduates found jobs as teachers at all levels of the state educational system; some entered the *Grandes Ecoles* and eventually were recruited into the policy-making positions of government and industry, or into the professions. Students from well-to-do families characteristically studied law or letters without too much expenditure of time or effort, passed their exams with ease, and embarked upon careers on the basis of family contacts rather than educational attainments. The demands upon the university were light and easily satisfied: to provide teachers for the state schools and a small number of highly intelligent graduates for the establishment.

But the old elitist structures of the French university were clearly inadequate in a rapidly modernizing society after the Liberation. The universities were not able to provide a sufficient number of trained technicians for the booming industrial sector. Only about one-half the positions available in industry were filled by university graduates. Instead, the universities were busily engaged in turning out huge numbers of students who had been exposed superficially to liberal arts subjects and were ill-adapted to the job market.

The virtues and defects of the French university system are illustrated by the contrast between the *Grandes Ecoles* and the other schools within the university system as of 1968. The *Grandes Ecoles,* accounting for about ten percent of the total university student body, include a half-dozen technical institutes, the famed Polytechnique, the Hautes Etudes Commerciales, Ecole Normale Supérieure, and the Ecole Nationale d'Administration along with its feeder institutions, the various Instituts d'Etudes Politiques. Candidates for each *Grande Ecole* must pass a stiff entrance exam; once accepted, they receive individual attention and the certainty of a good position after graduation.[12]

The "faculties" of the twenty-three French universities (subsequently tripled in number through decentralization) presented a sharp contrast. They were obliged to admit every student with a baccalaureate degree (the equivalent of a high school diploma). In theory, students attended lecture courses throughout the year and passed exams at the end of their course of study. In reality, only a small fraction of the registered students ever came to class. Many worked full-time, frequently in other cities. Others could not fight their way into overcrowded lecture halls; facilities were inadequate even for the small percentage of students that attended classes. Research papers were not required, and could not be prepared in any case; the library of the Sorbonne, serving 30,000 students, had only 300 seats. To beat the system, students bought and memorized mimeographed transcripts of the lectures (*polycopiés*). The attrition rate was harrowing. Fifty percent of all students dropped out at the end of the first year and seventy percent never received a degree. Those who finally earned degrees had trouble finding jobs that corresponded to their educational level. No direct links existed between industry, business, and the state administration on one side, and the universities on the other.

The Gaullist government did not remain indifferent to the problems of the university. An impressive program of construction was launched in 1960. Existing universities were greatly enlarged; new faculties were added to the University of Paris (Orsay, Nanterre, and Vincennes); seven wholly new campuses were built (Amiens, Limoges, Rouen, Nantes, Nice, Orléans, Tours); and a number of scientific institutes were created. In the period from 1960 to 1968, under the Gaullist Republic, more university facilities were created than had existed before then. The number of university teachers was greatly increased also—from less than 6,000 in 1958 to over 25,000 in 1968.

Tentative efforts were made to introduce new methods of instruction as a supplement to the mass lecture, and several experimental schools were founded. But for the most part the hordes of students that poured into the new campuses found themselves in the same crowded lecture halls, reading the same *polycopiés* and taking the same highly stylized exams. A feeble attempt to introduce selective admission procedures, though rational in itself, simply added to the fears of the high school students. This wasteful system generated massive irritation and frustration. Student associations became increasingly militant in demanding more buildings, more libraries, and more professors. It became customary for students to hold protest demonstrations each autumn, when school opened, leading inevitably to clashes with police.

Government and university officials alike agreed that university structures and instructional methods had to be adapted to education of masses rather than of a small elite, and that the university should provide trained people for the economy and the state as well as educate men and women to think for themselves. Decentralization of the cumbersome university structure was an urgent priority. Myriad decisions affecting some 600,000 students in the far-flung educational system could no longer be made at one central point. Some form of entrance exam or selective admission procedure was also called for in order to eliminate the intolerable waste of human resources in the first year of studies, and to bring the number of university graduates into line with job opportunities. The mass lecture had to be supplemented by other forms of instruction, since it inculcated a passive attitude on the part of students and perpetuated intellectual attitudes of dogmatism and abstraction wholly at variance with the decision-making process in modern enterprise and research activities in science. Introduction of discussion groups and seminars, in turn, required a great expansion of the teaching corps and of library facilities. Some observers believed that the heart of the problem was the relationship between the *Grandes Ecoles* and the rest of the university system. Either the *Grandes Ecoles* should be eliminated, they argued, and their functions absorbed by the whole university system, or they should be expanded and eventually replace the traditional faculties. In either case the point was to generalize the admission procedures, instructional methods, and sensitivity to employment opportunities then characteristic only of the *Grandes Ecoles.*

In addition to presiding over the greatest boom in the history of French higher education, General de Gaulle gave his ministers the assignment of reforming the University. The first far-ranging plan was drawn up by Christian Fouchet, who became minister of education in 1962. Shying away from rigorous admission procedures, he tried instead to offer students opportunities that it would be in their interest to take. His ministry created "University Institutes of Technology" to serve the needs of industry, and plans were drawn up for a system of student guidance. But little else was accomplished during his five-year term. Alain Peyrefitte succeeded Fouchet in 1967, and proceeded at a much faster pace. Among the innovations scheduled for introduction in the fall of 1968 were: guidance councils for high school students as a means of encouraging the choice of technical or scientific training; admission procedures based on a student's record, so that the high school diploma would no longer automatically ensure entrance to a university; and pedagogical techniques involving dialogue, original thinking by students, and group cooperation in research projects. Debate on these proposals was scheduled in the National Assembly for the month of May 1968. At that time the deputies instead debated the occupation of universities by self-styled revolutionaries seeking the overthrow of the whole political system.[13]

Student restiveness is widespread throughout Europe, but only in France has a student riot sparked a working class strike. Only in France has unrest among students crossed the great divide that separates universities from factories. Yet, by all the usual indices, workers in France seemed to be no worse off than elsewhere in Western Europe. The French economy has performed well since the Liberation. Beginning in 1950, when industrial production finally reached its prewar level, economic growth averaged close to 10 percent in most years. Reserves of gold and foreign currencies, practically zero in 1959, amounted to over 28 billion francs (5.5 billion dollars) in 1968. By that year there were 12 million cars on the road, almost one for each family. The general strike of 1968 took place at a time of relative prosperity, qualified, however, by a disappointing economic performance in 1967.

Alexis de Tocqueville observed that revolutions come not during periods of stagnation, but rather when a long period of economic growth and prosperity is followed by a sudden depression. Impoverished masses are less likely to revolt than are people who are used to rising prosperity and are then shocked when there is an economic downturn. De Tocqueville's dictum was particularly appropriate for France just before the

May Revolt. After twenty years of steady economic expansion, young people expected to find jobs, and adult workers counted on a steady increase in their standard of living. In 1967, however, the economy stagnated. To strengthen the franc (more accurately, to weaken the dollar), the Gaullist government took deflationary measures: tightening credit, encouraging exports, checking consumer spending, and reducing subsidies for the social security system. One result was an increase in the ranks of the unemployed by early 1968. Figures vary according to the criteria used but the total number of unemployed probably amounted to a half-million (out of twenty million employed). In early 1968, four times as many workers were receiving unemployment compensation as in 1964, but half of those unemployed were under twenty-five years of age. In 1967 the Gaullist government deliberately ran the risk of an increase in unemployment and a slowdown in economic growth in order to improve the international position of the franc; the gamble did not pay off.[14]

Nor was the relative prosperity in France spread evenly throughout the society. A disproportionate share of the wealth was in the hands of the upper-middle class. It was notorious that the progressive income tax in France was not steep enough to bring about the degree of equalization of income considered normal in other societies. To make matters worse, the Gaullist government introduced a special tax credit for stock dividends. Ostensibly to encourage private investment, the government decided in 1965 that taxes paid by corporations (about fifty percent of profits) should be considered as paid by individual shareholders. Not only were the dividends collected by shareholders free of tax—the virtuous citizen-capitalist received a tax credit for the amount previously paid by the corporation ("retained at the source," to use the picturesque phrase of the finance ministry). Thus, if a worker or other salaried person had an income of, say, $500 a month, he paid a full tax on that amount; but a person who received $500 a month from stock dividends paid no tax on that amount (on the assumption that the tax had already been paid by "his" corporation before distribution of profits). He even received a credit that could be applied to tax due on other types of income. The social injustice produced by this taxation system was deeply resented by workers.[15]

Added to fiscal discrimination were unusually great wage differentials, and depressed salaries for unskilled workers. For example, in 1965 the average wage of a plant manager or engineer was about $750 a month, a middle-level manager earned about half that sum, a skilled worker made about $200 a month, and an unskilled laborer about $130 a month. The minimum wage was a pitiful 40 cents an hour, and one-third of all French workers earned less than $110 a month. Although the standard of living of the French worker has improved steadily in the past twenty years, it remains low compared to other advanced industrial societies.

Even more important, French workers have a long tradition of class consciousness and political radicalism. Over one-fourth of the workers have voted consistently for the Communist Party in every election since the Liberation—a sure sign of alienation from the political system. Working class attitudes are dramatically illustrated by the situation at the Renault plant of Boulogne-Billancourt, which has the largest single concentration of factory workers in the nation and was also a focal point of activity in May 1968. A vivid portrait, based on intensive interviews with a sample of over 115 Renault workers, has been sketched by Jacques Frémontier in his book, *La Forteresse ouvrière: Renault*. The typical worker, says Frémontier, makes an initial self-identification on the basis of his family's class: "I am a worker." When he enters the factory he discovers the class struggle: "I am against the boss" (the fact that the "boss" at Renault is a democratically elected government is easily repressed). Finally, after participating in strikes he becomes conscious of the total situation: "The entire society is dominated by the class struggle." Almost three-fourths of the workers at Renault in 1968 voted for delegates sponsored by the CGT. That is, they voiced their confidence in a union controlled by the Communist Party and dedicated to the principles of class struggle and socialist transformation of society.

Frémontier also cites a startling statistic: approximately 12,000 of those working on the Renault assembly line, or 39 percent of the total, are immigrants; about one-half of these immigrants are North Africans, and almost one-fifth are black Africans. Among the native French who work on the assembly line, the overwhelming majority have not gone beyond elementary school. North Africans and black Africans, and to a lesser degree Spaniards and Portuguese, frequently live in abysmal circumstances, cooped up in shabby hotels or flophouses, and are constantly in fear of losing their work permits. They can hardly be considered firm supporters of parliamentary democracy in case of a showdown. Renault illustrates, in microcosm, the reasons why many French workers are receptive to anti-capitalist and revolutionary appeals.[16]

One of the surprises of the May Revolt was the participation of large numbers of people in clerical, professional, and managerial categories. A spirit of rebellion popped up in the most unlikely places—young executives staged a sit-down in the offices of the national business organization (CNPF), writers occupied the premises of the Society of Men of Letters, militant doctors attacked the national health insurance system, and many clerical workers and even managers joined enthusiastically in heated discussions within the occupied factories and enterprises. Only a minority of the professionals, technicians and managers took part in the May Revolt. But even this limited involvement was a significant indication of disaffection within social groups that had traditionally been mainstays of the liberal Republic.

In the case of many intellectuals—particularly writers, painters, cinema and theater personalities, lawyers, and teachers—it could hardly be said that the May Revolt crystallized a new political consciousness. Most of the intellectuals active in the events of May had long been fervent advocates of socialism or bitter critics of capitalism. A good many had been committed Communists, suffered the disillusionment with

Stalinism that was general after the Hungarian revolt and the revelations of Khrushchev, and saw in the May Revolt a providential affirmation that their youth had not been wasted, that a humanistic socialism free of Stalinist stains was still possible. They were delighted to have an opportunity to reaffirm their profound convictions.

Some in positions of authority collapsed under pressure, not out of weakness but because they had never really believed in what they were doing in the first place. Consider the story of the occupation of the Odéon theater, the result of an impulsive decision by a group of writers, artists, and actors, with the support of students from Nanterre and Censier. When they invaded the Odéon on the evening of May 15, Jean-Louis Barrault, the actor who was now director of the national theater, was called hastily to the scene. Obviously shaken, he at first tried to win the sympathy of the militants. "I am," he announced, "an old anarchist myself" (*"Je suis un vieil anar . . . ."*). He went on to praise his nonpaying audience as participants in a "movement of the young who wish to transform society. With all my heart I am with this movement." He then pleaded with these young idealists to allow his actors to continue to perform. The crowd hooted down his request, approving instead a resolution declaring the "Ex-Théâtre de France" a permanent, creative revolutionary forum.

The next night Cohn-Bendit spoke in the packed theater, declaring that henceforth the Odéon was a weapon in the struggle against the bourgeoisie. He heaped insults upon the hapless Barrault, seated in the audience. Taking the microphone, Barrault replied: "I am completely in agreement with this gentleman" (*"avec ce monsieur"*)—pointing to Cohn-Bendit. In view of the importance of the explosion, he declaimed, "Barrault is of no interest, the director of the Theater of France no longer exists . . . . Barrault is dead, there remains a living man." Exit Barrault, enter the revolutionaries without a fight and without even being challenged by the man responsible for the functioning of a national theater. Many intellectuals similarly found it more congenial to join in the fight against the despised bourgeoisie rather than resist demands of the militants.[17]

Some dissatisfaction within the middle class stemmed simply from low salaries, especially among clerical and sales personnel, and teachers. But the deepest protest was against French authority structures, which vest responsibility and decision-making power in a relatively few people at the top of the pyramid. The university was a microcosm of all collective enterprise. A given discipline in a university was allotted one "chair," occupied by a full professor; that exalted personage made all important policy decisions, including the appointment of assistants and associates, the organization of courses, the assignment of topics, and the drafting of examinations. There was always a possibility of abuse of power by the professor and humiliation of those under him. In hospitals and scientific laboratories as well, the "patron" ran everything in his little bailiwick. In the business world, too, authority was usually concentrated in the hands of the "patron," and his associates and subordinates suffered constant indignity. When government weakened in May, those in inferior positions within bureaucratic structures gave vent to their resentment at the way their lives were organized.

The pervasive unrest among professionals and intellectuals was especially evident in two groups of key importance in any modern society: journalists of radio and television, and research scientists. The Organization of French Radio and Television (ORTF) and the French Center for Nuclear Studies at Saclay both virtually ceased to function during the May Revolt. Journalists and scientists on strike incarnated the alienation of the middle class.

Radio correspondents of ORTF and the "peripheral" stations in Luxemburg and Belgium had a field day during the riots in the Latin Quarter. Many were sympathetic to the student cause. One young reporter, describing a battle in which students were being driven back by the police, exclaimed: "There is only one hope, that the workers will arrive by the first métro!" Direct coverage of the riots kept the students in a constant state of excitement. The state was engaged in a desperate struggle for survival, found itself slipping and gravely menaced, and its own radio and television was affording precious assistance to the revolutionaries. The government cracked down by prohibiting live coverage of street fighting and censoring some programs on television. On May 17 a general assembly of ORTF personnel voted for a strike; it dragged on long after the other strikes had been settled. The radio and television workers demanded complete autonomy of the ORTF from all governmental agencies, including especially the ministries of information and finance! Replacing the existing system would be an administrative council, half of whose members would be elected by the employees, and half chosen by the state; a director-general would be elected by and be responsible to the council. Their proposal expressed a profound desire on the part of broadcasters, writers, and producers for complete independence from the state and all other authority.[18]

The greatest concentration of research scientists in France, outside of the universities, is at the Centre d'études nucléaires de Saclay. Of the 10,000 employees in residence (half employed directly by the French Atomic Energy Commission, 3,500 by private enterprises, along with 1,500 students or apprentices) a solid majority are scientists, engineers, and technicians. Saclay is a vision of the society of the future—hardly any workers in the sense of a proletariat, almost everyone contributing his intelligence to the solution of a common problem. During the May Revolt these "workers of the future" rejected all external controls, ranging from security checks to the setting of research priorities by the state. A resolution adopted by a general assembly of Saclay employees demanded the replacement of the existing administration by a committee elected by and responsible to the "workers" alone; it also called for the creation of an elected council, or soviet, in each department. The scientists made it clear that they, and not the state, were to decide on research topics regardless of military need or commercial interests.[19]

The mood of dissidence spread to scientists everywhere. A

National Conference of Scientific Research Workers held at the Faculty of Science at Orsay in July 1968 was attended by 350 delegates elected by 11,000 researchers (out of 20,000 altogether employed in public laboratories and offices). The final report reflected the same longing of intellectuals to be free of political and administrative controls that had been manifested at Saclay. The assembled scientists proclaimed as their goal increased wealth and enhanced cultural values for the collectivity, not the furtherance of military or private interests, as demanded by the state. Scientists should therefore be free to engage in research that will, in their opinion, benefit the majority. The role of the state was simply to provide the necessary support.[20]

The specific mechanisms proposed by dissident journalists and scientists for the achievement of self-rule were not well thought out; their implications would be unacceptable in any functioning society. How could any state, and especially any socialist state, hand over money, credits, and facilities to be used as desired by the recipients, without any controls? Although the proposals for complete autonomy were altogether unreal, the dissatisfaction they expressed was all too real. The rigidity of French bureaucracy had produced an extreme reaction against all controls, setting people to dreaming of a world where they could do exactly as they pleased.

Rejection of political and social discipline spread even to the world of business. A preliminary survey of the attitudes of managers and administrators during the May Revolt in 120 firms throughout the nation revealed an orientation that had never before been expressed in previous strikes. Some managers and administrators actually took part in the work stoppage, making common cause with the workers. They demanded the right to *participate* in decisions affecting them, and in the elaboration of a national economic plan through elected professional delegates. Complaints were also voiced about the way in which orders were given and responsibility enforced within French enterprises.[21]

One major reason for the rapid spread of dissidence after

the explosion occurred was the political system that General de Gaulle saw fit to impose as a condition for his return to power in 1958. For De Gaulle the fatal weakness of the classic parliamentary system, as it had existed in France for almost a century, was the absence of a powerful executive. He had no taste for the kind of electioneering and horse-trading characteristic of all parliamentary democracies, but which had been pushed to an extreme, so he thought, in France. And so the presidency, occupied by General de Gaulle himself, was fashioned as the dynamo of the political process, the source of policy, the embodiment of the principle of energy within the political system.

But such a radical departure from the tradition of almost a century was bound to have repercussions. Diminishing the role of Parliament meant also reducing opportunities available to those in the opposition to influence policy. The Gaullists missed the point when they replied, almost in taunting fashion, that the people still had the right to vote and the opposition still had the right to try to win a popular majority. Of course France remained a parliamentary democracy; but it was an unusual kind of democracy in which the opposition parties, in fact supported by a majority of the voters, were not offered an honorable and creative role within the system. The result was increasing bitterness, frustration, anger, and irresponsibility on the part of opposition leaders. When the crisis came, they treated the regime with the same ill-will and disdain that had been directed at them as opposition. Gaullist policy successively alienated large groups within the electorate that, combined with the permanent defiance of the Communists, by 1968 amounted almost to a working negative majority.

The gravity of the institutional problem was especially evident in the aftermath of the legislative elections of 1967, which provided the setting for the riots of the following year. On the first ballot, on March 5, the candidates of the various Gaullist groups received about as many votes as they had in the previous election, or 38 percent of the total. To put it the other way round, the opposition parties, although hopelessly divided and unable to form a coherent alternative government, represented 62 percent of the electorate (22 percent for the Communists, 19 percent for the Federation of socialists and radicals, 13 percent for the Democratic Center, and the remainder divided among smaller opposition groups of both the left and the right). But on the second ballot, one week later, the parties of the left collaborated to a greater extent than ever before. The result was that the Gaullists squeaked through with the narrowest margin conceivable—exactly 244 deputies in a chamber of 488.

Under normal circumstances an opposition with as many deputies as the government would either have a good deal to say about policy formation (as in the United States Congress), or would be able effectively to challenge the government and either bring about a change in the party composition of the cabinet or overthrow the government. But the Fifth Republic is not a "normal" regime. In a brilliant move that eventually backfired, Pompidou asked the newly elected Parliament to delegate full power to the government to enact laws by decree for a range of troublesome issues (achievement of full employment, reorganization of the social security system, profit-sharing schemes, and modernization of enterprise). Debate would take place only once, at the beginning of the session, and then the government would have a free hand for one year.

The opposition, including Communists, Socialists, and Radicals, duly introduced a motion of censure. The three major trade unions called for a twenty-four hour strike in protest against the request for special decree powers, the first time under the Fifth Republic that there had been such a demonstration of working class unity on a strictly political question. After an unusually bitter debate, the motion of censure received 236 votes, or eight short of the required majority. The government was enabled to govern in effect without having a majority, but the opposition parties did not consider themselves fairly treated. By assuming decree powers the government deprived the Republic of the legitimacy that is its shield against adversity.[22]

It was not surprising that the Gaullist state floundered about in trying to manage the crisis produced by the student riots. Democracies are simply not capable of dealing with concerted attempts to destroy liberal values. Nothing works because a policy of tolerance leads to mob rule and repression destroys the very liberal values the state is supposed to be defending. But ultimately public opinion rallies behind the government, no matter what policy is adopted, and the riots peter out. In France the scenario took a different turn. Public opinion did not rally to the regime. When the Gaullist state seemed to be disintegrating, the militant trade unions and the Communist Party were tempted, if not to seize power, then at the very least to take advantage of the temporary weakness of their class opponent and extract as many concessions as possible. In the general revolutionary atmosphere of May, a whole society began to draw up its *Cahiers de doléances.*[23]

The Commune of Nantes

Almost wholly unobserved by the outside world at the time, a revolution of sorts actually took place in one large French city—Nantes (in the department of Loire-Atlantique), population 265,000. For one week (May 25-31) an ambiguous "dual power" came into being in Nantes, created by trade unions and farmer organizations as well as students. The events at Nantes are evidence that the utopianism of anarchists and Trotskyists was not altogether devoid of realism. Nantes presents in miniature a reenactment of the May Revolt, with almost the same cast of characters but an outcome favorable to the revolutionaries. On the side of the revolution in Nantes were: a weak student union controlled by leftists, plus local organizations of the FER, JCR, M.L.'s, a scattering of anarchists and situationists, local sections of all the major trade unions, and a strong section of the farmers' federation led by a radical. Confronting them was a representative of the Gaullist regime in command of security forces, Prefect Jean-Emile Vié; and the mayor, a nationally known centrist politician, André Morice. The various revolutionary groups in Nantes drew up audacious plans before May for the seizure of power, including all the tactics we have previously discussed: contestation by militants everywhere in order to arouse the people; inciting workers to strike and occupy factories; formation of strike committees coordinated by a central strike committee for the entire region; conversion of strike committees into a new form of social control and economic production; and suppression of the bourgeoisie by a dictatorship of the proletariat. The revolutionary program came closer to fulfillment in Nantes than anywhere else in the nation.[24]

The University of Nantes is one of the new campuses created under the Fifth Republic; unlike Nanterre, the campus was conveniently located and the facilities were adequate. By 1967, twelve thousand students were registered in its four faculties (Letters, Social Sciences, Law, Medicine), with an unusually large percentage from modest middle-class backgrounds. The local student union, the Association Générale des Etudiants Nantais (AGEN), like its parent organization, UNEF, was practically moribund as of 1967. The activist impulse came not from AGEN but from small groups of Trotskyists, Maoists, anarchists, and situationists, as elsewhere in France. In November 1967 AGEN was taken over by a coalition of revolutionaries who immediately emulated the militant actions of their comrades at Strasbourg and Nanterre.

The situationists were particularly active in Loire-Atlantique. Nantais students first encountered the situationists of Strasbourg at the time of the UNEF general assembly in January 1967; a year later they established links with the Enragés of Nanterre; and finally with the center of orthodox situationism in Paris. During the May Revolt the situationists considered the Commune of Nantes so important that they dispatched one of their troubleshooters and leading lights, Raoul Vaneigem, to help out. Situationist themes caught on immediately in this region of historic radicalism and nonconformism.[25]

The major trade unions and peasant organizations in Loire-Atlantique were led by unorthodox radicals, a reflection of the restive climate of opinion in west Brittany. The CGT was not as fully in control of the working class, or as fully supported by it, as in the nation as a whole. Force Ouvrière (referred to by the Nantais workers always as CGT-FO and never as FO) was a major influence, but with an unusual local accent. The departmental section of the CGT-FO rejected the moderate position of its national federation; the local leader, Alexandre Hébert, head of the teamsters at Sud-Aviation, was an anarcho-syndicalist and a powerful friend of student radicals of all stripes. There was also an active Trotskyist group within the local CGT-FO federation, led by Yvon Rocton, influential secretary of the union at Sud-Aviation. As Dansette has remarked: " . . . so long as the revolution has not triumphed, the anarcho-syndicalism of Alexandre Hébert and the Trotskyism of Yvon Rocton marry well."[26] To add another ingredient to this revolutionary cocktail, an extremist PSU group was active within the Christian Democratic trade union. The working class in Loire-Atlantique was constantly exposed to radical agitation by anarchists, Trotskyists, and Maoists, in addition to the standard revolutionary line of the Communist Party.

Of the twenty-thousand peasants in Loire-Atlantique, seventeen thousand are dues-paying members of the Fédération Nationale des Syndicats d'Exploitants Agricoles (FNSEA) which, on the national level, is a moderate organization representing the interests of relatively prosperous farmers. But—another peculiarity of the region of Loire-Atlantique—the local section of FNSEA was led by Bernard Lambert, a left-wing Catholic and fervent militant of the PSU. During the crisis Lambert spoke at a general assembly of students, denounced capitalism as the cause of the poverty and misery of farmers and workers alike, and called for revolutionary change. "What we demand finally," he concluded, to the cheers of the students, "is that capitalist society and the liberal Europe that it has engendered be put in the dock."[27] Rural radicalism falls upon favorable terrain in Brittany, where the average farm is too small for efficient cultivation. Protest demonstrations erupt periodically, and frequently go beyond the limits of peaceful confrontation. In June 1967 irate Breton peasants took a sub-prefecture by assault; in October a peasant protest rally at Quimper resulted in injury to 300 persons.

Militant students took the initiative at Nantes, as they had done previously at Strasbourg, Nanterre, and Paris, to create a confrontation and compel the university and the state to use force against them. Specific issues and tactics were a matter of improvisation. If one issue did not do the trick, the militants raised another, and another, until they could finally provoke a violent reaction. In December 1967 several hundred students staged a brief attack against the Prefecture. Tension continued to mount after the overnight occupation of dormitories. On February 14 about 800 student demonstrators occupied the Rectorate on the campus of the University of Nantes. After helping themselves to the rector's supply of cigars and liquor, tearing down curtains, and—the public was shocked to learn— urinating on the rector's rug, the militants obeyed a police order to leave. However, a clash between police and students occurred afterward, involving the usual assortment of injuries and arrests.

At the request of the prefect, the general council of Loire-Atlantique transferred a subsidy of 10,000 francs ($2,000) from AGEN to a student service organization, on the grounds that the state could hardly give public funds to the group that had led an "intolerable" attack against the rector. Escalation, and at last an issue. The Nantais students now agitated for restoration of the subsidy. On May 11 student militants conducted a surprise occupation of the railroad station, shouting slogans and disrupting traffic.

On May 13, the stage was set for a day of violence, at Nantes as at Paris. All trade unions and UNEF had called for a general strike to protest police brutality. Fifteen thousand workers and students marched in Nantes, listening to fiery speeches by anarchists of AGEN and by trade union leaders, including Hébert of the CGT-FO. A delegation was received by the prefect, who agreed readily to several demands, but not to the restoration of the subsidy for AGEN. Student militants, infuriated by his refusal, launched a full-scale assault on the prefecture—rocks, Molotov cocktails, barricades against tear gas bombs and billy club charges. It was the usual scenario. During heated talks at the prefecture, a professor at the University of Nantes finally extracted a promise from the rector that the 10,000 francs would be paid to AGEN, and announced triumphantly to the crowd, "You have won!"

Indeed they had; the money was subsequently used to support the revolution. A student militant later commented: " . . . many workers were astounded. What an enormous mass of peaceful and dignified demonstrators had not been able to obtain, a handful of rioters succeeded in gaining. Violence clearly revealed its efficacity . . . . "[28] There was a compelling reason for the prefect's suddenly flexible attitude. At this time the security forces under his command (about 1,200 policemen, gendarmes, and CRS) were outnumbered by the determined militants (including students, young workers, and some members of motorcycle gangs), ready to start a riot. The balance of coercive forces in Nantes had swung in favor of the revolutionaries.[29] On the following day, May 14, the workers at the Sud-Aviation plant at Bougenais (a suburb of Nantes) went on strike and occupied their plant, triggering a nationwide general strike. The events at Sud-Aviation offer a glimpse of what could have been a successful seizure of power.

The climate of labor-management relations in Brittany has been troubled for many years. Lack of employment opportunities in Brittany have caused an exodus of population to other areas. The government has undertaken a campaign to favor industrialization in the west of France, but an out of the way location and inadequate transportation facilities have been serious obstacles. Nearby St. Nazaire, a ship building center, was hard hit by a decline in demand for ocean going passenger liners. The textile and metal industries of west Brittany have not been modernized and are relatively inefficient; salaries are low and kept low by an abundant supply of labor. As part of a continuing program of protest against low living standards and structural unemployment, the leading trade unions, with the support of teacher and peasant organizations, decided in November 1967 to call for a twenty-four hour general strike and mass demonstrations throughout Brittany. Since months of preparation were necessary, the target date was set for May 1968. Events were conspiring to provide a shock.

In spite of the high percentage of engineers, managers and skilled workers employed there, the Sud-Aviation plant at Bougenais was a bastion of revolutionary syndicalism. In early 1968 the company (a nationalized enterprise under the control of the ministries of defense and finance) was in temporary difficulty, due to the phasing out of production of the Caravelle, Bréguet, and the Mirage IV. Management announced a reduction of the work week from forty-eight to forty-five hours and alluded to the possibility of retrenchment. The unions demanded that salaries not be reduced (or that salaries be increased seven cents an hour in order to maintain them at existing levels in spite of the reduced work week). The unions also wanted guarantees against unemployment. The director, however, refused to negotiate the issue, or even to receive a union delegation. Shortly thereafter several dozen workers spotted the director on his way to lunch at the nearby airport restaurant, pursued him, and laid siege to the air control tower where he had taken refuge. He was finally rescued by the police.

On May 2 about eighty percent of the workers at Sud-Aviation walked off the job. Fifteen-hundred workers then organized a "March on Nantes" to inform the public of the issues. On May 6 a mass meeting of workers at Sud-Aviation approved a motion of the CGT delegate to stop work four times a day for fifteen minutes. The CGT-FO delegate, Yvon Rocton (Trotskyist) proposed a general strike with occupation of the plant. Although his proposal was voted down at the time, it was a sign of things to come. On May 8 Sud-Aviation workers participated in the general strike throughout Brittany. Two days later the work stoppages were extended. A union delegation finally was received by the director, who rejected their demands. This was reported to two thousand workers of Sud-Aviation at a mass meeting on Tuesday, May 14. After an hour of discussion, the workers decided to occupy the plant until their demands were accepted by the central office of the company in Paris. They also determined to detain the director "for as long as necessary." In all these deliberations the anarchists and Trotskyists of CGT-FO played a leading role in crystallizing opinion.

A strike committee then took charge of the factory. The main gates were locked and twenty-five watch towers around the factory were converted into defensive bastions. According to an official report: "The first two nights the strikers forced the director to stay awake, prevented him from lying down, and broadcast the 'Internationale' continually over the loud-speaker. Outside, patrols were organized to capture anyone trying to escape from the plant. Some managed to do so. But the band in control of the plant did not leave them alone. Their homes, or their cars, were covered with paint and inscriptions."[30] The families of many strikers joined them inside the plant, and the strike committee organized food service and recreation. Students from the University of Nantes marched seven kilometers from town to the plant and joined the workers outside on the picket lines.

The strike movement spread quickly throughout Nantes. Within a week the economic life of the city was paralyzed. Everyone was on strike—factory workers and municipal employees, garbage collectors, and shopgirls—and the peasantry was in ferment. On May 25, at the call of the FNSEA, several thousand peasants converged on Nantes for a monster rally. Speakers protested against the condition of agriculture and also against the Gaullist regime and capitalism. As an indication of the political temperature, the crowd decided that the prestigious Place Royale would henceforth be known as the Place du Peuple. After the peasants dispersed, a thousand students tried to take the prefecture by storm; and set fire to its annex, but they were eventually repulsed. One hundred policemen and an equal number of demonstrators were injured in this unusually violent clash.

The originality of the Nantes experience was the unprecedented cooperation of student, worker, and peasant leaders through a Central Strike Committee—Comité Central de Grève (CCG)—created on May 24. It consisted of representatives of the three major trade unions (CGT, CGT-FO, and CFDT), two agricultural organizations, and later a student organization. The creation of a strike committee had been proposed by Alexandre Hébert, the firebrand of the CGT-FO, ostensibly to resolve problems created by the strike, such as supplying the population with food and essential services. But he hoped also that the strike committee would be the nucleus of an insurrectional power. The other union leaders accepted the idea of such a committee without sharing Hébert's revolutionary aim.[31] A communiqué to the people, published the following day in *L'Eclair*, signaled the emergence of another power in Nantes, alongside legally constituted authority.

> The Departmental Unions of the CGT, CFDT, FO and FEN of Loire-Atlantique inform the population of the creation of the Central Strike Committee sitting in permanence from 8 A.M. to 8 P.M. at the Nantes city hall. The goal of the Central Strike Committee is to deal with numerous concrete problems like that of food supply. It has organized, in accord with the strike committees directly involved: a municipal canteen in schools, where school children will be welcomed, under the responsibility of the strike committee of the establishment; a surveillance of prices charged by food shops that have been authorized to do business.
>
> In addition, the CCG has established contact with our peasant comrades of the FNSEA, sympathetic to our movement and wishing to supply the families of strikers through outlets in schools and neighborhoods.
>
> The CCG sitting in the Nantes city hall asks local strike committees to contact it in order to establish a better coordination of common efforts.

A mass rally on May 27, called by the trade unions, was attended by 20,000 people. In spite of their different union affiliations, the leaders of the CCG were remarkably unanimous in their views. On the next day the CCG assumed the power to ration gasoline since the prefecture could not effectively do so. Only those possessing CCG ration coupons were entitled to service at local gas stations. As the CCG stepped up its activities, the municipality placed more office space at its disposal. Striking municipal employees registered births and deaths, performed marriage ceremonies, and supervised garbage removal. Barricades were set up on all roads leading to and from the city, and traffic was controlled by representatives of the CCG. In short the CCG assumed major responsibility for running the city and maintaining public services. A deputy from Loire-Atlantique, Henri Rey (president of the Gaullist party in the National Assembly) returned to Paris with a tale of woe.

> It's incredible. At the city hall, the president of the strike committee conducts marriage ceremonies. Meetings of the mayor with his assistants are supervised. In the streets, civilians wearing armbands control traffic. And do you know how? Vehicles go on red and stop on green! Powerless, the police simply look on.[32]

Neighborhood strike committees were created throughout the city. All food stores were ordered to close, and only selected ones were permitted to reopen with the authorization of the CCG. Prices were carefully regulated. Workers and students helped the farmers bring in produce, which was distributed to the population directly and at lower than usual prices. The typesetters union established censorship of the press through a "vigilance committee," refusing to print any items critical of the strike or unsympathetic to the new order. On May 25, for example, both local newspapers were prevented from appearing because the vigilance committee did not want a speech by General de Gaulle to be accorded a bigger headline than a speech by CGT leader Georges Séguy! The anarchist press exulted:

> A reflection comes to mind when one sees and understands the reality of the Commune of Nantes. There is the solution, there is the revolutionary action to undertake everywhere! If there were 10, 20

Nantes in France and in Europe, the Gaullist administration and capitalism would collapse like a house of cards![33]

Did a "dual power" in Trotsky's sense actually exist in Nantes? It would be more accurate to call it the beginning of a dual power, which could easily have evolved into the real thing had there been sufficient time or more favorable conditions. The handicaps were too great: suspicion of the revolutionaries on the part of the CGT, CFDT, and moderate elements of the CGT-FO, who imposed a rule of unanimity within the strike committee; and lack of agreement on the role of that committee. Anarchists wanted to continue the strike movement until economic paralysis brought about the collapse of legal authority, while most others wished to prevent suffering on the part of the population by mitigating the effects of the strike. Nevertheless, by making daily decisions of an administrative nature the CCG was in the process of modifying the political attitudes of the people of Nantes and the balance of political power. Many members of the CGT, for example, began to change their minds about the possibility of revolution.

De Gaulle's speech on May 30 doomed the Central Strike Committee. Gasoline was made available throughout France, depriving the CCG of its principal stranglehold on the economy. Fearful of a clash, workers dismantled their road blocks on June 1, and the prefect was once again in control of his department. The ambiguous dual power collapsed without a fight. In the election that followed a few weeks later the Gaullists swept all three Assembly seats in Nantes by comfortable margins. The only party to manifest any sympathy toward the May Revolt—the PSU—received about 5 percent of the vote on the first ballot. One year later, during the presidential elections of June, there were two candidates who defended the revolutionary upsurge of May 1968: Michel Rocard of the PSU and Alain Krivine, leader of the Trotskyist JCR (converted after its dissolution into the Ligue Communiste). With 112,670 people going to the polls in the city of Nantes, Rocard received 6,249 votes and Krivine 1,240 (as compared to 6,000 for the Socialist Defferre; 17,000 for the Communist Duclos; 29,000 for the Centrist Poher; and 52,000 for the Gaullist Pompidou). No more than 7 to 8 per cent of the people of Nantes were willing to vote for the Revolution in June, yet the trend in May had been "all power to the soviet."

Nantes was an illustration in its purest form of the chain reaction that constituted the May Revolt. A climate of rebellion had been created by the students, who occupied the university, briefly took over a railroad station, assaulted the prefecture, and challenged all authority. The contagion spread to the workers at Sud-Aviation, who were particularly receptive because of their traditional radicalism and the difficulty of negotiating grievances with management. The local union leadership was militant; the idea of occupying the plant had been suggested in early May by the plant delegate of the CGT-FO, not merely by isolated anarchists and Maoists. When all of Nantes went on strike, the cooperating trade unions created a Central Strike Committee, in effect a local soviet, that largely displaced the legal administration in the daily running of the city. All this in an area where a majority of the people gave its support in elections to the Gaullist and moderate parties! Had the scenario unfolded in the capital city rather than a faraway province, the outcome of the May Revolt might well have been a revolution.

NOTES

1. "The Power [i.e., those in power] had the universities; the students seized them. The Power had the factories; the workers seized them. The Power had the ORTF [Office of French Radio and Television]; the journalists seized it. The Power has Power. Seize it." Cited by J. Besançon, ed., *Journal mural, mai 1968* (Tchou, 1968), p. 95.

2. For a lively account of contestation at Nanterre, see Jean Bertolino, *Les trublions* (Stock, 1969), pp. 262-94.

3. Declaration of M22M reprinted in Schnapp and Vidal-Naquet, *Journal de la commune étudiante* (Seuil, 1969), p. 149.

4. Anarchist view of the events of May 3 in M22M, *Ce n'est qu'un début,* (Maspero, 1968), p. 23. Trotskyist (JCR view in Daniel Bensaïd and Henri Weber, *Mai 1968, Une répétion générale* (Maspero, 1968), p. 113.

5. Jacques Sauvageot, Alain Geismar, and Daniel Cohn-Bendit, *La révolte étudiante,* (Seuil, 1968), pp. 29-30. M22M spokesman on "exemplary" action, M22M, *Ce n'est qu'un début,* pp. 59, 72.

6. On the theory of a "dual power" see in particular Bensaïd and Weber, *Mai 1968,* pp. 186-203. Also Thierry Pfister, *Le gauchisme* (Filipacchi, 1972), pp. 29-30; and on the tactics of street fighting, ibid., pp. 49-50.

7. The CIA is mentioned specifically by PCF spokesman Georges

Cogniot, *Les intellectuels et les étudiants devant la révolution socialiste* (Lecture at the Institut Maurice Thorez, 24 October 1968, mimeo.). On the East German intelligence service as a possibility, cf. François Duprat, *Les journées de mai 68, les dessous d'une révolution* (Nouvelles Editions Latines, 1968), pp. 49-61. On the role of Cuba and the Tricontinental: Raymond Marcellin, *L'ordre publique et les groupes révolutionnaires* (Plon, 1969), especially pp. 11-21, 42-52, 72-74.

8. On subsidies from China, cf. Michel Legris, "Qui sont les pro-chinois en France?", *Le Monde*, 31 March, 2 and 3 April, 1968. Pompidou's declaration in *Journal Officiel*, May 11, 1968, p. 1771. For the IFOP poll, *Sondages*, nos. 1 and 2, 1970, p. 41.

9. Adrien Dansette, *Mai 1968,* (Plon, 1971), pp. 354-56; Pierre Viansson-Ponté, *Histoire de la république gaullienne,* (Fayard, 1971), vol. II, pp. 405-06; Christian Fouchet, *Au service du Général de Gaulle,* (Plon, 1971), p. 234.

10. Trotsky's letter cited by Annie Kriegel, *Les communistes français* (Seuil, 1970, 2nd ed.), p. 128. Her estimate of Russian financial aid to the PCF, ibid., p. 130.

11. For tactics used in overthrowing the Fourth Republic, see R. C. Macridis and B. E. Brown, *The De Gaulle Republic* (Dorsey Press, 1960), chaps. 3, 4.

12. On the traditional French university see the excellent analysis by Raymond Boudon, "Quelques causes de la révolte estudiantine," *La Table Ronde* (Dec. 1968-Jan. 1969), pp. 169-83. On the contrast between the Grandes Ecoles and the regular "faculties": Michel Crozier, *La société bloquée,* (Seuil, 1970), p. 253; also Frédéric Bon and Michel-Antoine Burnier, *Les nouveaux intellectuels* (Seuil, 1971, 2nd ed.), pp. 107-20.

13. On university expansion and the Fouchet and Peyrefitte reforms, see Dansette, *Mai 1968*, pp. 31-41.

14. On the state of the French economy in 1968: P. Bénéton and J. Touchard, "Les interprétations de la crise de mai-juin 1968," *Revue Française de Science Politique,* 1970, xx:3:531-532.

15. The tax credit on dividend income was in the news again in 1972, when Prime Minister Chaban-Delmas's tax return was published by a right-wing journal. It revealed that through the tax credit mechanism the prime minister, who periodically exhorted the French to make greater sacrifices, had escaped paying taxes altogether one year.

16. Jacques Frémontier, *La Forteresse ouvrière: Renault* (Fayard, 1971), p. 60. Percentage of votes at Renault for the major trade unions, ibid., p. 307. On the immigrant workers at Renault, ibid., pp. 84-112. One-fourth of the workers vote consistently for the PCF, many vote for other parties (Gaullist and moderate as well as socialist), and about one-fifth do not vote at all.

17. On the occupation of the Odéon theater: Dansette, *Mai 1968,* pp. 153-54; Patrick Ravigant, *L'Odéon est ouvert* (Stock, 1969), p. 60; and letter of Barrault to *Le Figaro*, reprinted in Christian Bouyer, *Odéon est ouvert* (Debresse, 1968).

18. On the strike at the ORTF: Dansette, *Mai 1968,* pp. 214-16; also Claude Frédéric, *Libérer l'ORTF* (Seuil, 1968); Roger Louis, *L'ORTF, un combat* (Seuil, 1968); and J. P. Manuel and A. Planel, *La crise de l'ORTF* (Pauvert, 1968).

19. Soviets at Saclay: Dansette, *Mai 1968,* pp. 272-74; and Jacques Pesquet, *Des soviets à Saclay?* (Maspero, 1968).

20. On the Orsay conference: L. Gatineau et al., *Recherche et contestation* (Anthropos, 1969), pp. 27-29.

21. J. Blancherie et al., *Les événements de mai-juin 1968 vus à travers cent entreprises* (Centre national d'information pour la productivité des entreprises, n. d.).

22. On the request for decree powers in 1967, see the account by Viannson-Ponté, *Histoire*, vol. II, pp. 317-23.

23. *Cahiers de doléances* were the lists of grievances drawn up in each locality for submission to the Estates General in 1789.

24. On the Commune of Nantes, in general see: Dansette, *Mai 1968,* pp. 251-68; Yannick Guin, *La commune de Nantes* (Maspero, 1969); Seale and McConville, pp. 163-68; and the Nantes newspaper, *L'Eclair.*

25. On the influence of the situationists at Nantes, Guin, *La commune de Nantes*, (Maspero, 1969), pp. 12-14, 33-34, 85.

26. Dansette, *Mai 1968*, p. 171.

27. Quoted by Guin, *La commune de Nantes*, p. 68.

28. Ibid., p. 57.

29. Estimates of the balance of coercive forces in Nantes from Dansette, *Mai 1968*, p. 260.

30. Official report quoted by J.-R. Tournoux, *Le mois de mai du Général* (Plon, 1969), p. 186.

31. On the creation of the Central Strike Committee, Dansette, *Mai 1968*, p. 262; Guin, *La commune de Nantes*, pp. 67, 98-100, 125-29.

32. Quoted in J.-R. Tournoux, *Le mois de mai du Général, p. 186.*

33. Citation from anarchist press in Schnapp and Vidal-Naquet, *Journal de la commune étudiante*, p. 515. On revolutionary censorship in Nantes: Dansette, *Mai 1968*, pp. 265-66.

5

The
Revolt
Vanishes

"Un étudiant travaille pour apprendre. Il n'a pas de famille à faire vivre. Nous, les ouvriers, nous avons une famille. Et puis chez vous, il y a des anarchistes qui sèment la zizanie. Si nous voulons avoir quelque chose, il ne faut pas les suivre, ces gars-là . . . . "

"La Révolution ne se fera pas avec des bulletins de vote!" s'écrie l'étudiant.

"Qui parle de Révolution actuellement?" réplique brutalement un gréviste.

Jean-Claude Kerbourc'h, *Le piéton de mai*[1]

THAT A REVOLT took place in May 1968 in a highly industrialized society and a venerable parliamentary democracy is a fact of great importance; that the revolt failed is of equal importance, though generally downgraded by enthusiastic commentators. French revolutionaries by the afternoon of May 29 had succeeded beyond anyone's reasonable expectations. But they did not seize power. A month later the Gaullists triumphed at the polls and normalcy returned. Revolutionary hopes and dreams were blasted. The only visible reminders of the cataclysmic events of May were a few slogans scrawled on university walls. Bulldozers were laying down asphalt in the Latin Quarter so that paving stones never again would be used as weapons in an insurrection.

The following reasons may be suggested for the defeat of the revolution: [1] the contradiction between the revolutionary goals of the activists and the reformist inclinations of the mass of students, workers, and middle classes; [2] internal contradictions within the revolutionary coalition; [3] ambiguity of the concept of autogestion and widespread disillusion with its application in the universities; [4] the strength of the tradition of parliamentary democracy in France; [5] the hostility of the Communist Party toward the student revolutionaries; and perhaps the most important, [6] the unsuitability of guerrilla war tactics in an industrial society.

Revolution versus Reform

We have argued that at each stage of the chain reaction in May—as the revolt spread from students to workers to the middle classes—long-standing grievances suddenly came to the fore. But the grievances were not those imagined or desired by the revolutionaries who had set off the initial detonation. Only a small minority of the students, workers, and middle classes who participated in the May Revolt wanted a radical transformation of French society. As the masses became involved in the revolt, the gap widened between the apocalyptic vision of student militants and the moderate reformism most people found congenial. The differences of perception regarding the ills of French society and appropriate remedies worked to the disadvantage of the revolutionaries and were readily exploited later by both Communists and Gaullists.

The various revolutionary groups could no more agree on the role of the students in a modern society than on any other topic. Students are privileged, they are miserable; students are marginal, they are at the very center of the modern productive process—the controversy was never resolved. But the observation of Mustapha Khayati in the situationist tract, De la misère en milieu étudiant was compelling: "If there is a youth problem in modern society it is because the profound crisis of that society is felt with the greatest acuity by youth." Whatever their individual doctrines, the revolutionary groups viewed the students as completely alienated from French society, ready either to lead or support a movement to overthrow the bourgeois state and build socialism. The university was perceived as static and as exclusively serving the interests of a small ruling class, by keeping out or otherwise discriminating against children of workers and other low-income groups.[2]

But consider the nature of the changes that have taken place within the French university system since the turn of the century. In 1900 there were about 30,000 university students, double that number by the 1920s, and a total of 75,000 just before World War II. In 1950 the number had grown to 136,000 and in 1960 to about 195,000. Between 1960 and 1968—under the Gaullist Republic maligned by student rebels—the number of university students almost tripled (244,000 in 1962; 326,000 in 1964; 413,000 in 1966; 504,000 in 1968), and the trend continued thereafter (587,000 in 1969). There were more university students in 1968 than high school students before World War II; twice as many university students in France than in either Great Britain or West Germany. Indeed, this was part of the problem since the supply of university graduates greatly exceeded the demand. An enormous effort had to be made by the state to provide teachers and facilities for this massive student body.

The boom in higher education necessarily brought about a change in the social composition of the student body. In the prewar university most students were from high income families or the middle class, and very few were children of peasants and workers. By 1950 the student body had become more representative of the middle class, and, to a lesser extent, of low-income and working-class strata. In 1939 about 35 percent of the students came from families where the father was the head of an enterprise or a professional; 16 percent where the father was a shopkeeper, artisan or white collar worker; and only 2 percent where fathers were workers. In 1950 the corresponding figures were 33 percent, 17 percent, and 2 percent; and in 1960, 18 percent, 47 percent, and 3.4 percent. Since 1960 the percentage of students from working-class backgrounds has more than doubled, while the percentage of students from high income families has continued to decline. The student population of French universities is now much more representative of the population at large than was ever the case before, though middle-class students are still dominant. Students from working-class backgrounds in 1968 made up about ten percent of the student population.[3]

Some militants contend, nevertheless, that the social barriers are still up since students from middle-class and intellectual families have a natural advantage over those of working class origins. But this widely accepted belief is questionable. Recent studies of examination results have shown that the percentage of those who are successful is roughly the same for all social categories, and that, if anything, students of working class origin do a little better than average. The desire to climb the social ladder apparently more than makes up for lack of an intellectual atmosphere at home.[4]

The university in 1968 was neither static, nor the preserve of a small social elite. Most students, though dissatisfied with university structures and teaching methods, wanted reform that would enable the university to better serve the needs of a modern society. Only a small number—though they happened to constitute a highly active group—were revolting against the consumer economy and the society of spectacle. The notion that the student masses shared the revolutionary goals of those who had become their leaders was one of the many myths of May.

When the general strike broke out in mid-May, student militants were more convinced than ever that their strategy was correct. The workers had seized control of the means of production, revolution was at hand! Full of enthusiasm, ready to fraternize with the workers and march forward with them to the final victory of socialism, the students flocked to the gates of occupied factories. But the factory gates were shut in their faces, and workers on guard duty made it clear that no students would be allowed inside. How could such a thing have happened? Why weren't they welcomed with open arms? After all, students had started the revolt and now proclaimed that the workers should run the factories. For many militants the hostility of the working class was at first a rude shock, then an impenetrable mystery. Their surprise and confusion were reflections of a profound ignorance of working class life and politics in France. Ironically, the general strike turned out to be the beginning of the end of the May Revolt.

One of the illusions of student militants was that the strike movement had either started spontaneously or had been instigated by dedicated revolutionaries, and that therefore the "revisionist" CGT was no longer in control of events. It was true that Maoists, anarchists, and Trotskyists among the workers had some success as agitators. In the case of Sud-Aviation, where anarchists and Trotskyists have long held important positions of leadership in the unions, their influence was especially noticeable. But the established trade unions, particularly the CGT, also played an important role in launching the strikes. They were well aware of the plans of the revolutionaries to subvert their organizations and were determined at all costs to keep their troops in line. Once the strike had begun, no love was lost between leftists and CGT militants. Flying squads of *cégétistes* made the rounds of the occupied factories, interrupting debates started by leftists and their sympathizers, gently (and not so gently) forcing the leftists out of key positions in order to head off "adventurism."[5]

Reject the consumer society? The workers wanted more of it, all around! Through years of hard fighting at the plant level the workers were attuned to negotiations concerning safety procedures, reduction of work week, increased vacation time, higher salaries—in a favorite word, "beefsteak." Acts of sabotage and violence against individual foremen and union leaders repelled them. The revolutionary students simply did not understand the realities of the working class experience in France—at least as of 1968.

The contrast between revolution and reformism was apparent whenever students tried to engage workers in a dialogue, for example when students massed before the gates of the Renault plant at Boulogne on the evening of May 16, just after the strike had started. After one student criticized the Communist Party, a worker replied patiently that the party had nothing to do with it, the workers were simply looking out for their own interests. Another student tried vainly to persuade a worker to act now, since Lenin himself had not waited for all favorable conditions to materialize in 1917. The worker protested that the situation was not the same, that France was a complex industrial society, that a majority was against the revolution, would vote for De Gaulle in an election, and had the support of the army as well. A chasm opened between the perception of the student militant and the worker.

> Student: "If there had been ten million people in the street, who would have stopped them? Not even the army could have stopped them, or there would have been an enormous civil war, which would have been impossible."
>
> Worker: "If you were to take power, afterward you would have to hold elections. If you hold elections after that, well the guys who had taken power would be thrown out in the elections . . . ."[6]

The CGT secretary at Renault, Aimé Halbeher, relates why on May 16 the union decided to prevent the students from entering the occupied factory.

> We heard on the radio that a crowd of one to two thousand students was heading toward Billancourt. We were quite concerned, because we were afraid that they might come into the shop and thereby give the government and management a pretext for using force . . . . Some agitators wanted a discussion in the name of solidarity and student-worker power. There was a little trouble when some students tried to force their way in, but they didn't get very far.

Halbeher later complained that the students were ignorant about the condition of the working class, for example, "what a worker is, what a union is." Subsequently he tried to establish contact with the students, assuming that they had real organizations, like his own, with responsible leaders, secretaries who answered telephones, and complete dossiers on current problems. "He discovered a strange void," comments Frémontier, "an unbelievable mess, a total absence of doctrine. He was amazed, to put it mildly."[7]

Differences were even greater between the revolutionaries and the professionals, who were anxious to free themselves of all controls and not be subjected to iron discipline after the revolution. When the general assembly of employees of ORTF voted to strike on May 17, the revolutionaries were overjoyed. At last the mass media would be denied to the bourgeois state and placed in the service of the revolution. Student militants immediately proposed a march upon the Maison de la Radio to seal the new alliance. But the journalists, like the workers, balked. They asked the students not to hold a rally outside their building, since that would bring about a clash with the police and lead to forcible evacuation of the premises. "You are weaklings" (des mous), exclaimed Sauvageot, the art history student, in a telephone conversation with the leaders of the striking journalists. "Weaklings, perhaps," was the reply, "but we don't want the station blown up. If you come, we leave." In an effort to reach mutual understanding, several journalists went to the Sorbonne on the night of May 30 to set forth their position. A question from the audience: "What do you plan to do to help the revolutionary movements?" The journalists responded that they had to reflect the views of the entire nation, not of any one group. "We will fight against all governments," they cheerfully asserted, "and especially against revolutionary governments." The boos and catcalls greeting this declaration indicated what kind of "independence" journalists would enjoy under the new regime.[8]

That differences should exist between revolutionaries and reformists is hardly novel, and need not preclude the possibility of revolution. In 1917 Lenin did not bother to explain that collective or state farms were inherently superior to privately owned farms; he simply promised "land to the peasants." But this tactic, to work, requires an extraordinary docility or lack of political sophistication on the part of those being manipulated. French workers and intellectuals in 1968 were not comparable to the Russian peasants of 1917. Furthermore, the French revolutionaries did not promise reforms but offered the prospect of an authoritarian regime in which the masses and professionals would be mobilized and disciplined. The gap between a revolutionary elite and a reformist mass then became too great to be bridged.

Inner Contradictions

So long as the objective was to destroy the bourgeois university and state, doctrinal differences among the revolutionaries did not prevent limited collaboration. A pluralism of approaches to subversion and revolt may well be more effective than monolithic unity. Each group forwards the chain reaction of revolution by "doing its own thing." But the deep hatred among revolutionaries kept cropping up. Trotskyists detested orthodox Stalinists and their contemporary supporters, the Maoists, and considered anarchists and situationists to be totally unrealistic in their insistence upon spontaneity; anarchists and situationists denounced the bureaucratic proclivities of Trotskyists and Maoists; Maoists viewed Trotsky as a renegade, and his supporters as petty-bourgeois intellectuals completely cut off from the world of the workers, and so on. Each group of revolutionaries had its own ideology, each put forward a devastating and invariably convincing critique of all the others, and each had compelling reasons for maintaining complete autonomy.

The internal contradictions within the student movement came to the fore after the occupation of the universities. Trotskyists, Maoists, anarchists, and situationists could not agree on the appropriate organization of power within their new domain or on the future direction of their revolution—whether the factories would be run by workers alone or with the participation of managers; whether to drive forward to full industrialization based on atomic power and electronic calculators or to liberate man altogether from the tyranny of machines; whether to place a well-disciplined revolutionary party in power or govern through a network of local soviets; whether to permit all to express themselves or to wreak revolutionary vengeance upon the opposition.

There was also no agreement on the lessons to be learned from successful revolutions in the Third World. The model that generated most enthusiasm was Castro's Cuba. Every occupied university building boasted its Che Guevara Hall, bedecked with portraits of the fallen hero. Ho Chi Minh's Vietnam and Mao's China were also held in high esteem by most, and to a lesser extent Yugoslavia and the kibbutzim in Israel. But what was the relevance of "participatory democracy," workers councils, decentralization, and the immediate gratification of sexual desires to societies where power was highly centralized and sexuality closely supervised and regulated? The professed goals had no relation to any existing reality. The anarchists were critical of everyone. As Cohn-Bendit put it: "I do not think that Castroism is really a model and believe that Cuba is heading toward a redivision of society into classes . . . . Alas, . . . in the Third World . . . socialism does not really exist." What, then, is socialism? The answer was evasive, vague, unsatisfactory—and varied from group to group. Said Alain Geismar:

> I am not a theoretician. For me socialism is defined negatively, by relation to a certain number of existing structures, by a refusal of all bureaucratization, of all central management, by giving power to producers on the very site of production. Let us say that it is essentially *autogestion*, even though this, too, is a vague word . . . Autogestion and decentralization, the central power thus assuming a role of coordination and not of repression.[9]

Autogestion, called variously direct democracy and partici-patory democracy, derived from a combination of traditions: anarchism, orthodox Marxism, the Paris Commune, and workers councils during brief moments of glory in Russia, (1905), Germany (1918), Italy (1921), Spain (1937), and Hungary (1956). The common element in the Paris Commune and other workers' councils is election of delegates directly by the workers in a given enterprise or area; these delegates are responsible to the workers, subject to instant recall, and also are continually rotated in and out of office—a kind of Jacksonian democracy confined to the working class and appropriately certified intellectuals, with the bourgeoisie cast in the role of Seminole Indians.

The idea of autogestion was carried forward into the May Revolt primarily by anarchists and situationists, and, through them, by the *Enragés* of Nanterre and the March 22 Movement. The precondition for autogestion, spokesmen for M22M asserted, is the formation of revolutionary workers councils, within which all hierarchical divisions (among workers, managers, and intellectuals) would be dissolved, resulting in a new kind of creativity and the invention of "new forms of management" (unspecified, however). Autogestion must short circuit the trade unions, which have become a brake upon creativity, and reformist rather than revolutionary. The spark of revolution can come only from the "inside" (to reverse Lenin's phrase), from the unorganized masses, whose spontaneity should be interpreted, not directed, by revolutionary intellectuals. Interpretation is a kind of "collective psychoanalysis" that makes manifest the unconscious aspirations of the workers. As an example of "interpretation, not direction," it is the function of M22M to explain to the workers that their occupation of a factory expresses their profound desire to own the means of production.[10]

The distinction drawn by the revolutionaries between "interpretation" of the profound wishes of the proletariat and "direction" was not always clear to the beneficiaries or to the public at large. Suppose the workers who occupy factories assert that their goal is to improve conditions rather than expropriate capitalists—which is irrelevant anyway in the cases of Renault and Sud-Aviation, both nationalized enterprises. Suppose the workers shut the factory gates and refuse to allow students to enter the premises? Suppose workers continue to vote for delegates sponsored by the CGT, FO, and CFDT rather than the revolutionaries? Does autogestion mean that revolutionaries carry out the wishes of the workers? Of course not, since the masses would be expressing only superficial and not profound desires—as determined by the revolutionaries. Discussion is to take place in strike committees, actions committees, and general assemblies—on one condition only: that the correct revolutionary line is approved. A great deal of verbiage concerning autogestion concealed the revolutionaries' "profound desire" to manipulate the masses and shatter the unions which the workers, foolishly or not, preferred to support.

Even the revolutionaries were aware of the shortcomings of direct democracy as an alternative to organization and hierarchy. On June 1, the day after De Gaulle's speech, anarchists and Trotskyists debated the merits of direct democracy and organization. The problem was defined as follows: Spontaneity served a useful purpose in arousing the masses, in provoking revolt, in starting discussions and in crystallizing political consciousness. But now the forces of counterrevolution are rallying. In order to continue the forward march, is it not necessary to create a revolutionary organization?

Speaking on behalf of the action committees, J.-L. Vigier called upon the revolutionary movement to endow itself with a structure. "We need an organized instrument that will permit us to be not isolated individuals, atomized and dispersed forces, but really a coordinated force. An organization of one sole collective will that would be capable here and now, everywhere at once, to undertake a coordinated action." Cohn-Bendit replied for M22M that, yes, coordination is necessary—but not if it means sacrificing the ideals of the revolution. The only solution is to structure the movement in an organized manner, "elaborated at the base." He urged that debate be continued by all in small groups—hardly the effective structure required by the situation.[11] Nothing was done, and a few weeks later all revolutionary groups were dissolved by the government. The fruitless exchange between Vigier and Cohn-Bendit illustrates the unavoidable dilemma confronting the revolutionaries: to combat the organized forces of the opposition the movement must itself organize or perish; but organization means destruction of direct democracy, which is the very essence of the revolutionary cause.

Critics of autogestion asked how problems of production could possibly be resolved without some form of central direction. The revolutionaries replied that the people could be counted on to create new institutions combining efficient management and popular autonomy. It is unfair, they continued, to expect a detailed blueprint of direct democracy now; structures would be devised by the people in the future as they grappled with their real problems. The revolutionaries thus shrewdly placed themselves beyond criticism; they could airily dismiss opposition charges by saying, in effect, "first give us a chance, only then can you judge whether or not direct democracy works." It is impossible to deal with such an argument, except by expressing skepticism and thereby opening oneself to the charge of lacking confidence in the people.

Alas, the very success of the revolutionaries in occupying the universities and the Odéon theater gave them a chance to put their lofty notions into practice—and led to their undoing. It was not necessary to speculate on the possible implications of autogestion, or to await future developments; one only had to look closely at the Sorbonne and the Odéon. Autogestion, direct or participatory democracy, by any name was inglorious in practice. A *Le Monde* correspondent turned Rimbaud against the revolutionaries; "bateau ivre" (drunken ship) was the image he evoked of the liberated Sorbonne under "direct democracy."

On May 13 the sovereign students invaded the Sorbonne, swarmed all over the building, and jammed into the Grand Amphitheater (capacity, 3,500 persons). A fiery resolution was adopted: "The General Assembly of Monday, May 13, decides that the University of Paris is an autonomous, popular university and open permanently, night and day, to all the workers. The University of Paris henceforth will be run by committees of occupation and of administration, constituted by workers, students, and teachers." Here was an unprecedented opportunity to clarify the vague principles of autogestion and direct democracy, and to put them into practice. All power was vested in a general assembly of students, consisting of whoever could make their way into the Grand Amphitheater. To avoid the unspeakable evil of "bureaucratization," executive power was vested in a fifteen-member occupation committee, but only for one day and one night. The occupation committee was to report to and be reelected by the general assembly every twenty-four hours![12]

The first occupation committee elected on May 14 included representatives of the major groups. It created a network of subcommittees: secretariat, coordination, relations with the public, relations among faculties and with high schools, cultural services, press, food, hospital, and later on lodging, student-worker relations, nursery, and so on. In theory the subcommittees were responsible to the occupation committee; in practice they were colonized by the various revolutionary groups, became autonomous, and ignored the occupation committee.

On May 15 the occupation committee made its first report and was duly reelected. But the following meeting of the general assembly degenerated into sheer chaos. Led by Trotskyists, the members of the coordinating committee tried to displace the parent committee. The Trotskyist attempt to seize power was resisted by anarchists and situationists. Cooperation among the squabbling groups became impossible. When the time came for another report to the general assembly, thirteen members of the committee had disappeared and the remaining two had nothing to say. A new occupation committee, dominated by Trotskyists, was then elected, and that was the end of formal reports and responsibility to the general assembly. The *Enragés* and situationists withdrew in protest and formed their own Comité de maintien de l'occupation (Committee to Maintain the Occupation). Each revolutionary group took over as many subcommittees and as much office space at the Sorbonne as it could. The general assembly thereafter engaged in meandering and disorganized argument; it became a "society of spectacle."[13]

Direct democracy at the Sorbonne lasted perhaps 24 hours, if it ever existed at all. With the best of intentions, only 3,500 people could crowd into the amphitheater, so that participation by the 30,000 students of the Sorbonne, not to mention the 600,000 students of the nation, was a pure fiction. Once in the amphitheater the mob could neither govern nor even organize its own debates; it had to be "managed" by the leaders. But the leaders themselves were drawn from rival groups and were trying to gain control of executive committees for their own political purposes. Finally, there could be no continuous work in either the general assembly or the committees, since new faces appeared all the time. As one observer put it: "It could not have lasted indefinitely. Bit by bit, weariness overcame everyone."[14] The public got a taste of what "direct democracy," applied to the State, would have been like.

Within a month the student commune presented a spectacle that all but the most enthusiastic adult champions of liberated youth found utterly depressing. The public could not fail to notice that the students were unable to maintain elementary standards of sanitation and hygiene in the occupied Sorbonne. Garbage piled up in corridors attracted a small army of rats. Liberated schools were overrun by neighborhood bums, young hoodlums, juvenile delinquents, and drug addicts. By late June, for example, when the police evacuated the Ecole des Beaux Arts they found that only forty-six of the one hundred and three persons on the premises were students. Many were just drifters and twenty-eight had criminal records. Physical damage to the facilities of the University in Paris was later estimated at about two million dollars.

The "direct democracy" was also unable to cope with the problem of maintaining order in the liberated university. Criminal elements ("*la pègre*") flocked to the barricades and joyously helped the students battle with their common enemy, the police. At first the students welcomed them as poor victims of capitalist society, and some hailed the thugs as rebels against bourgeois law, order and inhibitions. One tough new ally, who went by the name of "Lulu," offered his services as a specialist in keeping order, presumably on the basis of his experience (which proved to be imaginary) as a white mercenary in Katanga. He recruited about thirty similarly minded young nonintellectuals, calling themselves the "Katangais," and formed a flying squad of troubleshooters. The Katangais took over a section of the Sorbonne by force, and began to make policy decisions. The generous ideals of the youth revolution were now in the hands of storm troopers. The occupation committee ordered the Katangais to leave; but it took a pitched battle, in which about eighty appropriately armed students participated, before the "poor victims of capitalist society" were expelled from the Sorbonne. Many of the Katangais subsequently went on a spree of automobile theft, robbery, and even murder, winding up once again in the prisons they knew so well.[15]

Autogestion was even less successful at the Odéon than at the Sorbonne. At first, several strong leaders emerged and created a semblance of order. They reported to a so-called general assembly (whoever drifted into the theater) each night. Several militants were then dispatched to the Odéon by anarchists with the mission to "contest" these leaders because they had created a rudimentary organization—and hierarchy is the enemy of liberty. The anarchists demanded that leaders be changed every day, or at least be given different functions, in order to head off dictatorship. The general assembly dissolved into a formless mass, and within two weeks the original leaders of the occupation resigned in disgust. The Odéon was taken over by the all too familiar cast of hippies, bums, thugs, and especially drug addicts, who helped themselves to costumes, stage accessories, and anything else portable. As at the Sorbonne, toilets were clogged and garbage accumulated. The chief medical advisor caused a panic when he declared that there was a danger of cholera; by that time, both theater and part of the audience were crawling with vermin. When the Odéon was evacuated by the police on June 14, among the hundred or so occupants there was only one student.[16]

But the fervent activity within the occupied universities had some positive results. By far the most impressive work was accomplished by art students, who turned out superb posters. Some serious proposals for reform were put forward by students in medicine, science, and political science. But by and large, the "liberation" courses conducted by student leaders were disappointing. The students went from one extreme to another. Before the May Revolt they had listened docilely to the all-knowing professor, committing his lectures to paper and then to memory. Now they discussed current political topics—without information or critical apparatus. One teacher who participated in the strike at a lycée in Paris proudly reported that in three weeks, "unpoliticized youngsters were discussing questions of revolution and reformism, apathy, trade unionism, the relations between leaders and the masses, the quelling of spontaneous revolutionary movement by the forces of reaction, movements designed especially for 'social warfare,' the conflict between generations, the definition of culture, etc." But he also mentioned casually that many students asked their leaders to set up "political information committees," since they did not know what a party or a trade union was and had never read the *Communist Manifesto*, for example.[17]

Typical of the contrast between promise and reality was the work of the revolutionary film students. *Le cinéma s'insurge* (the cinema revolts) was the enticing title of a new documentary projected in June 1968 at the Faculty of Science. The camera picked up a middle-aged man as he wandered about the courtyard of the liberated Sorbonne, happily leafing through revolutionary literature at the various stands of this "ideological drugstore." A voice from nowhere: "Pardon me, sir, but is this your first visit?" "Yes, indeed, and it's wonderful, you see I'm a railroad worker—" and for a painful half hour he droned on about the evils of labor-saving devices recently introduced in the French railroad system. The message was that technology had to serve man, and not vice-versa. How this noble end could be achieved by retaining archaic work procedures in an industrial society (or by inflicting boring films upon the public, for that matter) was not explained.[18]

Repudiation of Democracy

The obvious contradiction between libertarian pronouncements and authoritarian practices also lost the revolutionaries popular support. *"Il est interdit d'interdire"*—it is forbidden to forbid—was one of the most appealing slogans of the May Revolt, capturing the selfless idealism of students revolting against repression and inhibitions. A companion slogan inevitably made its appearance on the walls of the universities: *"Pas de liberté aux ennemis de la liberté"*—no freedom for the enemies of freedom. Maoists and Trotskyists were contemptuous of bourgeois liberalism and made no bones about the kind of "freedom" enemies of the people would be allowed to enjoy. Even those self-styled libertarians, the anarchists and situationists, inspired little confidence.

One incident of many involving the anarchists of M22M: On April 25 Cohn-Bendit burst into a seminar and invited the "comrade-students" to participate in the committees set up by the M22M, listen to political debates, and then join the "active resistance." One of the students present happened to be a leader of the moderate FNEF; he opined that the university was destined for work, not political activism, and that if Cohn-Bendit wanted to make propaganda he should do so elsewhere. A deadly look from Cohn-Bendit, and an ominous reply: *"Toi, fasciste, on aura ta peau"* ("you little fascist, we'll have your hide"). No sooner out the classroom door than the "little fascist" was set upon by about forty determined revolutionaries. University guards rushed to help and managed to drag the victim away from his ardent critics. A journalist, in sympathy with the anarchists, describes the scene: "The martyr, saved in the nick of time, no longer looked human. Blood gushed from his forehead all over his swollen cheeks. It took him ten days of rest and seven stitches to recover."[19] The victim lodged a complaint against Cohn-Bendit, who was picked up by the police and questioned. He denied that he had had anything to do with the attack, claiming instead that he often acted as a moderating influence during fights. He was released almost immediately, to be acclaimed as a hero by the revolutionaries, while the student who had been beaten up was forgotten. A broadside distributed immediately thereafter made the playful comment: "Every self-respecting student is ready to reply to fascist provocations by means of the most striking arguments."

The situationists, in the spirit of their Dada forebears, have been equally menacing in their attitude toward opponents. Letters addressed by situationists to nonbelievers usually begin with appellations like *"petite-tête"* (pinhead) or *"ordure"* (shit). Situationist sympathizers chased Jean-Jacques Servan-Schreiber off the stage when he dared to address students at a Spanish university. Freedom of discussion is not to be enjoyed by enemies of the people, such as liberals and reformers, was the comment in the I.S. journal. Another revealing incident took place in the wake of the May Revolt, when a special issue of the journal, *Le Mouvement Social*, was devoted to the occupation of the Sorbonne. A situationist document was presented in abridgement rather than its entirety, and it was also implied that an obscure anonymous tract expressed the situationist line. The I.S. demanded a written apology for both these affronts from the issue editor, the historian Jean Maître. As recounted later in the I.S. journal, Riesel and Viénet went to Maître's residence, rang the bell, "insulted him as he merited," and also broke some of the objects he had accumulated through participation in the consumer economy and society of spectacle.[20]

The justification offered for their behavior was the absolute necessity of defending "truth and nonfalsification," the indispensable condition for everything else. "Everything that falsifies must be discredited, boycotted, treated as contemptible . . . . We say all revolutionaries must now recognize as their immediate task to denounce and *deter*, by any means and at any price, those who wish to continue to falsify." Yet it must be remembered that the situationists proudly use the technique of *détournement*, that is, the deliberate falsification of reality in order to expose it to ridicule and to prepare the way for revolutionary transformation. *Détournement* by the situationists, then, is legitimate; but those who dare to present a situationist document in abridged form will be dealt with by violence, if need be. Similarly, *"l'esprit ludique"* or the spirit of playfulness, is acceptable only when directed at the stodgy bourgeois. Under no circumstances can it be used against situationists who, of course, are in deadly earnest.

Repudiation of bourgeois notions of freedom led naturally to repudiation of parliamentary democracy. In the best Marxist tradition, student militants argued that revolutions are made not by counting votes but rather by direct action in factories and in the streets. Alain Geismar's comments on parliamentary democracy were typical:

> A parliamentary regime endowed with a majority and an opposition, let us even say a majority of the left and a bourgeois opposition, cannot in my view impose . . . the necessary social transformation . . . because from the moment the struggle envisages the liquidation of the bourgeois opposition, it cannot possibly take place within the framework of a parliamentary debate . . . . That, at a later time, diverse modes of expression can coexist does not in any way detract from the fact that during the months, the years of social transformation, when the class struggle is practically a fight for the survival of the bourgeois class, the dear parliamentary colleague is an element that has no place and no meaning.[21]

Relating how little interest the revolutionary students have in parliament, Jacques Sauvageot even referred to that venerable institution as the "Chamber of Deputies"—a title it has not had since the Third Republic, though it remains the name of the nearby métro station. The student revolutionaries gave the appearance of being opposed to the right of the electorate to determine its own fate, and their distrust of elections was fully justified on pragmatic grounds. They had no electoral organization, no taste for electioneering, and would be easily out-maneuvered by the old hands in an electoral campaign. In the balloting on June 23 candidates of the only party in any way sympathetic to the revolution, the PSU, received 3.9 percent of the vote—ludicrous in view of the actual power of the revolutionaries on the barricades. This almost total lack of electoral support was confirmed when Alain Krivine, leader of the JCR, ran for the presidency in June 1969. He received a bare 1 percent of the vote, and PSU candidate Rocard, 3.6 percent.[22]

Whatever may be said about the shortcomings of parliamentary democracy, ever since 1875, and except during the Vichy period, the French have been in the habit of holding periodic elections in which all organized political forces could participate freely. The tradition that opposition parties, as well as individuals, have the right to criticize those in power, and if possible vote them out of office, is strongly engrained. By draping themselves in the mantle of the republic, even renaming their party *Union pour la Défense de la République* (UDR), the Gaullists appeared the incarnation of parliamentarism. French voters, in refusing to support the candidates of revolution in June, were expressing deep skepticism about cataclysmic revolution as a means of improving society. They clearly preferred the parties with which they were familiar, the parliamentary system, and piecemeal reforms to a desperate gamble for an ambiguous utopia. Parliamentarism, despite or perhaps even because of the traditional scorn for politicians in France, permits the French to view their state as a servant of the people. It was widely sensed that aspiring revolutionaries might reverse that cherished relationship.

Left versus Left

The Communist refusal to join forces with the student militants in May 1968 puzzled many observers. Was not the PCF a Marxist party dedicated to the overthrow of capitalism and the installation of a socialist regime based on workers soviets? Why did the PCF not rally to the standard of revolution, cooperate with the students, and at least help liquidate capitalism? Even if there were large policy differences between student groups and the Communists, in the struggle for power that would surely follow De Gaulle's retirement, the PCF, as the most important organized political force on the left, would stand an excellent chance of elbowing the others out of the way.

From the outset, the PCF was opposed to "adventurism" on the left. After all, the anarchists and Trotskyists were engaged in vilification of the PCF. They claimed that the party bureaucracy within the Communist movement in France was playing the same exploitive role as the bureaucracy in the Soviet Union. The left extremists were deliberately trying to undermine the PCF apparatus. They demanded discussions at the "base" while condemning the leaders at the top, seeking constantly to drive a wedge between the leaders and the masses. There is no mystery, then, about the Communist reaction to the activists at Nanterre and the Sorbonne. These were the very elements that had been expelled from the UEC in the previous two years. After the mass protest parade of May 13, Cohn-Bendit exulted: "The Communist Party? Nothing gave me greater pleasure than to be at the head of a demonstration with all that Stalinist filth (*ces crapules Staliniennes*) bringing up the rear." The PCF took pains to prevent the "adventurers" from contaminating their own student followers and, above all, the workers.

The PCF leadership correctly viewed the threat from student revolutionaries as a matter of life and death for the party, which thrived on attacks from the right but could not survive if effectively outflanked on the left. The tone was set by Georges Marchais in *L'Humanité* of May 3, 1968, one of the first occasions that the leftists were dignified by mention in the communist press. In an intensely hostile article, Marchais referred sarcastically to Cohn-Bendit as "the German anarchist" and to Herbert Marcuse as "the German philosopher who lives in the United States." Agitation by the "groupuscules" (splinter groups) goes against the interests of the mass of students and favors fascist provocation, said Marchais; it serves the interests of Gaullism and monopolistic big business. The "false revolutionaries" are a joke, he continued, especially since they are the sons of comfortable bourgeois who cannot conceal their contempt for the workers. "That is why we must fight against and completely isolate the leftist groupuscules that seek to do harm to the democratic movement by covering themselves with revolutionary phraseology."

The vitriolic attack was not an expression of momentary rage. In the months that followed the May Revolt, the Communist leadership took up and expanded each of the points in the Marchais indictment. Georges Cogniot hinted that the force behind the "anarcho-Trotskyist sects" was none other than—the American C.I.A.! Jacques Duclos pointedly remarked that Herbert Marcuse had served with the American O.S.S., a precursor of the C.I.A., during the war, and was later attached to a suspicious sounding "Institute of Research on the Soviet Union" at Harvard. Another possibility, according to party spokesmen, was that the French police were manipulating extreme leftist groups to split the democratic forces and arouse popular hatred of the entire left. For René Andrieu, editor of *L'Humanité,* there is little doubt that the barricades of May 10 were created at the instigation of secret police agents, so that the resulting disorders would drive the middle classes into the waiting arms of the Gaullists. Georges Séguy comments that the anarchists, Trotskyists, and Maoists "constitute, for the class enemy, an ideal milieu for the recruitment of *agents provocateurs.*" After a Maoist commando group kidnapped an administrative employee at Renault to avenge the murder of one of their comrades by a guard at the factory in February 1972, the Communists were more convinced than ever of the existence of a "plot" by the Gaullist police to stimulate terrorism and put the entire left in a bad light.[23]

The new leftists were also denounced by Communist leaders as "children of the bourgeoisie" practicing a form of "social racism," by daring to suggest that they, not the workers, would lead the revolution. The PCF rejected the pretensions of the students, most of whom they argued would eventually sell out to the system. Party leaders recalled Lenin's warning that the revolutionary petty bourgeois, though outraged by the horrors of capitalism, is unstable, unreliable, incapable of sustained action. Left-wing communism, that celebrated infantile disease, reflects a lack of confidence in the revolutionary capacity of the working class, leading to purely verbal and meaningless violence. For the Party, the anarchists and Trotskyists of the past were the forerunners of Maoists and Guevarists today. They were all unfortunate examples of "how not to make the revolution."[24]

May 1968 was no aberration, but firmly in the tradition of relations between the Communist Party and the extremist groups that have always existed and occasionally flourished on its left. The squabble between Georges Marchais and Cohn-Bendit is in a long line of similar duels between Marx and Bakunin or Proudhon, Trotsky and the left opposition, Lenin and the anarchists. The Communist Party is the incarnation of organization and hierarchy, and is, therefore, the antithesis of libertarianism. What could be more natural than bitter antagonism between advocates and opponents of this hierarchy to end all hierarchies. Anarchists and Communists have always tried to use each other. Some anarchists hope that the unpleasant features of communism are merely a painful transition to the withering away of the state, while Communists occasionally encourage the anarchists—on condition that they attack the bourgeoisie and prepare the way for a communist takeover. The lack of coordination among Trotskyists, anarchists, and Communists thus was built into the structure of the situation in 1968.[25]

Although the Communists remained bitterly opposed to the "adventurism" of the leftists, their policy in other respects underwent an evolution in the course of the May Revolt. At first the Communist obsession with the leftists resulted in a virtual paralysis of policy. The leftists had seized the initiative and the Communist Party was reacting to events. But a policy change took place after workers began to occupy factories on May 14. A similar situation had existed in 1947, when Trotskyists at the Renault plant provoked a strike against the wishes of the union leadership. The Communists took over the strike, which led ultimately to their expulsion from the tripartite governing coalition. In 1968, again, not to be outflanked on the left, the CGT and the Communists took charge of the strike movement.

While continuing to denounce the "adventurers" the Communists were tempted to press for immediate political advantage. In a meeting at CGT headquarters on May 16, several Communist leaders (including Séguy and Krasucki) offered an alliance to a delegation of leaders from the Federation. They proposed in effect the creation of an insurrectional situation through a general strike, followed by a motion of censure in Parliament. The left would then doubtless win an election under the pressure caused by paralysis of the economy. But this proposal was not pressed by the Communist leadership, and soon was forgotten. Communist strategy in mid-May was to respect legality, defend the material interests of the workers, and enter willingly into negotiations with the government in order to win concessions for the party's working-class clientele.[26]

When the Grenelle Accord was turned down by the striking workers at Renault, PCF policy changed again. Gingerly, but methodically, the Communists now sought to make it impossible for the Gaullist regime to remain in power—not through an insurrection, but simply through the force of circumstances. The PCF troops began to make purely political demands—for De Gaulle's resignation, and for a *gouvernement populaire*. Careful to avoid any move that might alarm the non-Communist public or the army, the Party tried to draw a recalcitrant Federation into its orbit. If the Gaullist regime collapsed the Communists would be in an excellent position to return to power as part of a coalition, and if De Gaulle called for elections they would be beyond reproach.

Francois Mitterrand and the other leaders of the Federation were not about to cooperate. In his press conference on May 28 Mitterrand spoke at length about the political crisis; he offered himself as a successor to De Gaulle, virtually designated Mendès-France as his prime minister—but neglected to mention the Communist Party. PCF secretary-general Waldeck Rochet immediately went to see Mitterrand, and demanded to know where the Communists stood in his calculations. Mitterrand offered the Communists "a seat" in the government, which Waldeck Rochet referred to derisively as a *"strapontin"* (folding chair). The alliance between Socialists and Communists made sense only so long as the Gaullists were a threat; on the assumption that the Gaullists were collapsing, the Socialists were preparing to turn toward the center. The Communists were not going to depend upon Mitterrand's benevolent intentions. To remind all concerned that they still had the biggest battalions and could control the street, the CGT announced a mass parade through Paris, from the Bastille to the Gare Saint-Lazare—skirting the Hôtel de Ville (where tradition favors the proclamation of new republics) and the Elysée (a tempting target for assault). "The people of France," ran a declaration of the Communist Party on May 29, "require that, in the new regime, the working class and its Communist Party have their rightful place."[27]

In a brief meeting at the Elysée, Prime Minister Pompidou told General de Gaulle that he believed, for the first time, the Communists might try to take power. He ordered that the Hôtel de Ville and the Elysée be defended by massive police forces. De Gaulle may have shared his prime minister's fears. When he asked his son-in-law, General de Boissieu, to arrange for a meeting with General Massu, he gave the following reason for his sudden departure: "The Communists are going to parade in the afternoon from the Bastille to the Gare Saint-Lazare; I do not want to give them an opportunity to attack the Elysée; it would be a pity if blood were to flow for my personal defense. I have decided to leave; one does not attack an empty palace."[28] After he learned of De Gaulle's disappearance, Pompidou confided to the close friends who flocked to the Matignon his fears of a Communist insurrection. "The situation is really revolutionary," he declared; "the Communist Party has done a turnabout."[29]

It did not turn out that way. Several hundred thousand Communist marchers shouted hostile slogans concerning De Gaulle and capitalism, but they dispersed peacefully. The next day, after De Gaulle's comeback speech, the party agreed to the elections and abandoned any plans that may have been harbored to convert unrest into insurrection. Communist tactics were apt and shrewd—but did not work. In spite of the care the party had taken to avoid the appearance of illegality, De Gaulle centered his attacks during the election campaign on the PCF, virtually disregarding the student revolutionaries, and successfully revived the specter of "totalitarian communism." Nevertheless, the party survived the election, retained its organization and its bastions, and made a remarkable electoral comeback in the presidential contest of June 1969.

A Revolutionary Party?

It is true that the PCF did not join forces with the Trotskyists and anarchists in May. Had it done so, and had the revolution succeeded, one can only speculate about the grim fate that would have awaited the leaders of the March 22 Movement at the hands of a Communist minister of the interior. Student militants and anti-Communists alike hastily concluded— for diametrically opposed reasons—that the Communists had ceased to be "revolutionary." Militants denounced the party for "selling out" in return for the dubious privilege of being able to contest meaningless elections, and accused the party of failure of nerve. To Jean-Paul Sartre, Communist policy in May indicated not merely that the Communists were no longer revolutionary, but that they "were afraid of revolution." The Communists, he contends, accepted the elections offered by De Gaulle knowing they would lose, because under no circumstances did they want to take power. Only the formation of an authentic revolutionary party to the left of the PCF, Sartre continues, can "de-block" Communist policy.[30] In contrast, some liberals welcomed Communist caution as evidence of the party's readiness to accept the parliamentary system while continuing to pay lip service to a vague notion of revolution. Wishful thinking was combined with oversimplification on both sides of the barricades. It was not the first time that the Communist Party had been accused of revisionism by an extreme left, or wished out of existence by liberals.

Georges Lavau, in a stimulating interpretation of the function of the Communist Party within the French political system, suggests that one of the party's major roles now is that of a "tribune" organizing and defending the plebian social categories and giving them a feeling of strength and confidence. The party thus caters to the desires of workers, peasants and low income groups, favoring those groups when it comes to power either as part of a coalition or in a municipality that falls under its control. Gradually, the party has adapted itself to the routine of elections and municipal administration. After thirty years of this kind of reformism, comments Lavau, it is difficult for any party, Marxist or not, to remain or to reconvert into a truly revolutionary party. In his judgment the PCF, at least since 1936 and perhaps in spite of itself, has made a "positive" contribution to the functioning of the French political system even while remaining outside the system in certain respects.[31]

If the PCF is now a "tribune" of the people, the future evolution of the French political system will be profoundly affected. On the assumption that the PCF seeks to further the interests of the Soviet Union and to create a one-party proletarian dictatorship, the other parties are condemned to perform the double task of governing and opposing by themselves. The natural divisions among conservatives, liberals, and socialists make for complex cross-cutting cleavages under the best of circumstances. When twenty-five per cent of the electorate throws its support to a Communist Party, the task of forming governments becomes exceedingly difficult. If the PCF indeed ceases to be an "opposition of principle," and begins to cooperate with the other parties as a loyal partner respecting the rules of democracy, then the parliamentary system will be strengthened immeasurably.

Yet Lavau's argument is hedged at every key point, so that we are never sure whether the party is really reformist or only waiting for a favorable opportunity to hoist its true colors. Says

Lavau: "Our hypothesis is not that the PCF today has arrived at the same point as the social democratic parties, but that since 1936 it has started out on the same road. This does not necessarily signify that it will end up the same way, nor that it will lose its zest; it is one thing to no longer be a 'revolutionary party,' another thing to betray the cause and the groups for which one struggles."[32] Lavau does not explain, however, what difference there is between being on the same road and not ending up the same way, between defending and betraying the interests of the workers, between a "true" revolutionary party and any other kind. From this highly ambiguous "hypothesis" it would be premature to draw the conclusion that the PCF has become a "party like the others."

More nuanced is Annie Kriegel's analysis of changes in the French Communist Party since its creation at the Congress of Tours in 1920—expanding and contracting, altering tactics, rethinking goals, taking on the responsibilities of government and withdrawing into opposition. But, she points out, constant change does not mean that the party is repeating the experience of the mass social democratic parties of the late nineteenth century—evolving from revolution to reformism. One reason why it is difficult to discern any clear evolution is that policy has been in flux, especially since 1962, and major options are still open. As is evidenced by the revelations of those who have fallen into disgrace—such as André Marty, Charles Tillon, Auguste Lecoeur, Piêrre Hervé, and most recently Roger Garaudy— there have been serious policy disputes within the party in the past between advocates of "hard" and "soft" lines, revolution and reformism, independence from and fealty to the Soviet Union.

As Kriegel shows, Waldeck Rochet made a conscious effort to "de-Stalinize" the French Communist Party during his tenure as secretary-general. Very cautiously, he moved the party closer to the position of the Italian Communists, denying that there was any "center" in the international movement of comradely parties. He also called into question the dogma that a "dictatorship of the proletariat" must necessarily follow a

Communist accession to power, holding out the hope that a pluralism of parties and opinions would continue to exist after the passage to socialism. In 1966 he pointedly remarked that: "The recognition of the plurality of democratic parties and of the necessity of a lasting collaboration between the Communist Party and the Socialist Party supposes a political regime entailing broad democratic liberties."[33]

Even though the French Communists took the position that there is no longer *a* center or *several* centers of international communism, the Russians were not deterred from invading and occupying Czechoslovakia in August 1968, and proclaiming their right to safeguard the precious accomplishments of the socialist revolution wherever their armies could march with impunity. After initially disapproving the Russian invasion, the French Communists obediently fell into line, refusing to join the Socialists in studying, much less condemning, the situation in occupied Czechoslovakia.

The critical question has remained the sincerity of the Communist commitment to a "pluralism of parties" under socialism. In a country like France, explained René Andrieu (editor of *L'Humanité*) in 1968, there is bound to be a multiparty system. Criticism is a good thing. The constitution of a socialist France should guarantee the plurality of political formations "whether on the Left or the Right." But he saw fit to add: "On condition that the latter respect the law of the majority and that they resort neither to violence nor to sabotage."[34] The Socialists—future partners of the Communists in the coalition that would presumably usher in the new era—had great difficulty in pinning down the PCF on the exact meaning of a "pluralism of parties." In December 1967, during discussions with Federation leaders on a common program, the Communists insisted that there would be no freedom for the "enemies of socialism" after the coalition of the left was installed in power. In numerous public declarations Waldeck Rochet stated as a matter of course that the bourgeoisie would be forcibly prevented from returning to power in a socialist state. During discussions in 1971 the Socialists were still pressing the same point. Would their partners accept a decision by the voters in a free election turning the Socialist coalition out of power? The Communists hedged: they could not imagine why free-thinking and sensible people would ever want to inflict such an error upon themselves; the real problem was to deprive the bourgeoisie of its monopoly over the mass media.

When asked directly whether there is "pluralism of parties" in Eastern Europe, the Communists answer with an enthusiastic "Yes"! Does freedom of expression exist in the Soviet Union? But of course it does! In other words, the "real democracy" advocated by the French Communists, according to their own clarification of the phrase, is the kind that now exists in the Soviet Union and Eastern Europe, or would be a preliminary stage "opening the way" to this real democracy. Since the French Socialists were perfectly aware of the fate of their colleagues in other countries during both the preliminary and final stages of this real democracy, their reluctance to enter into an agreement with the Communists was understandable.

Negotiations between the Socialists and Communists on a "common program" finally came to fruition in June 1972, when both parties agreed on a policy combining muscular socialism and respect for democratic liberties. Immediately afterwards, Georges Marchais asserted that this agreement was valid only for the first five years of the newly elected Assembly (assuming that the left gained a majority), and would usher in an "advanced democracy"—not to be confused with socialism itself. He explained that only after the "passage to socialism" could all of the problems confronting French society be resolved, presumably in the same manner as in the Soviet Union. François Mitterand defended the common program in altogether different terms. In his view, most of those who vote Communist do so out of "desperation." By becoming more militant, through the common program, it is his hope that the French Socialists will compete more effectively with, and eventually replace, the Communist Party! Although the Socialists and Communists need each other in forging electoral alliances, their conceptions of socialism and democracy remain completely at variance.

It is part of Kriegel's thesis that, through all their twists and turns, one point remains fixed for the French Communists: the party seeks power, all else is a means to that end. When the party defends the interests of the workers or any other social category it makes sure, above all, to gain control of whatever structures exist (unions, factory committees, university councils, social security committees, and so on). Progressively, the Communist Party weakens, then surrounds, finally takes over as many structures as it can within French society. To try to comprehend the phenomenon that is the French Communist Party in terms of classic social democracy is futile. As Kriegel puts it, the party is, and always has been "a power other than the established power"—a power that is a rival to and seeks to replace the bourgeois state.[35] The party hopes to create a dual power by utilizing all the possibilities offered it in the existing system, and then to transcend dual power in the same way that Lenin did. This is neither social democracy, nor revisionism, nor reformism.

But one consequence of this patient, gradual conquest, sector by sector of French society, is that the revolution is always postponed. In Marxist terms, the revolutionary situation is *never* sufficiently "ripe" since some sectors always are yet to be conquered, and some conquered sectors slip away or turn to dust. Defense of the interests of workers and others meanwhile requires constant negotiations with the bourgeois state; habits of consultation begin to develop. The result is a domestic version of Soviet foreign policy; instead of "no peace, no war" we have "no reform, no revolution." Liberals hope that negotiations will gradually become institutionalized and result in the integration of the party and the working class into the system; Communists hope that by extending their control, they will undermine the bourgeois state. So far the result has been a stalemate.

One of the most interesting explanations of Communist policy during the May Revolt was offered spontaneously by

Aimé Halbeher, the secretary of the CGT section at Renault Billancourt. Jacques Frémontier relates that one day, in a bistro near the factory, he asked Halbeher how he envisioned the making of a revolution in France. The frank reply, which is not contradicted by anything ever said by Waldeck Rochet, Georges Marchais, or Georges Séguy: "As in Prague in February 1948. Everything is legal, everything takes place without violence. We participate legally in a coalition. One day the adversary makes a mistake. It is enough that the masses exert their pressure at the right moment and that the bourgeoisie no longer disposes of a sufficient force of repression."[36] In this view, the exact way in which power will be seized cannot be foreseen. Perhaps as a result of an opening to the left, coalition with the Socialists, and use of the state power to expropriate the bourgeoisie—which accounts for the keen interest of the French Communists and Socialists in the Chilean experiment under Allende. Another possibility materializes during the unsettled conditions created by a general strike; the bourgeoisie suddenly vacillates, and for a brief moment there may be an opportunity for a "democratic alternative."

The lesson of revolutionary uprisings in the modern era is that power is seized not against the state, but through the state. A necessary condition for gaining control of social and state structures is to preserve intact the party apparatus as the instrument of the future revolution. Writing shortly after the May Revolt, René Andrieu confirmed the party's appraisal at the time—that to attempt to seize power would have been "adventurism" endangering the very existence of the party.

> The truth is that there was no "revolutionary situation" because the Gaullist power, even though weakened, had kept intact its repressive striking force (the professional army), because it still influenced large sections of the population, frightened by the specter of civil war (as shown by the elections), because the millions of workers on strike were far from all being won over to the idea of a revolution and finally because there was not a sufficiently solid agreement among the political formations of the left and the trade unions around a common program.[37]

Perhaps the anarchists had forgotten about the French army, but the PCF leadership had not. When conditions are not favorable for an armed revolt, Waldeck Rochet pointed out, an attempt at insurrection may lead to disaster "by affording a pretext for repression by reactionary forces." He cited the example of Indonesia in 1965, when an attempt was made by some leaders of the Indonesian Communist Party, inspired by the ideas of Mao Tse-tung, to overthrow "reactionary generals" through a putsch. But they did not have the support of the masses.

> Thus, the attempt failed, and we know the result: the reactionary forces, which went berserk, were able to massacre more than 300,000 Communists and decapitate a party which counted 2.5 million members without the popular masses of Indonesia being in any position to react effectively. This example—and there are others—demonstrates that the adventurism of the "left" which consists in advocating armed struggle "everywhere" and "any time" can cause the greatest harm to the revolutionary movement.

All Communist leaders, in reviewing the events of May, are persuaded that the May Revolt was a trap prepared by the Gaullists to strike a mortal blow at the PCF and the working class. According to Waldeck Rochet the plan was to bring about a violent, bloody confrontation between the workers and the police and army, enabling the bourgeoisie to install a military dictatorship. "Well before the 30th of May," he later commented, "a military force including numerous tanks was positioned near the capital, ready to intervene. It is under these conditions that some dubious and irresponsible people would have wanted our Communist Party to launch itself, alone, into a test of strength."[38]

It is impossible to know how the officers and men of the armed forces would have reacted had they received the order to attack and clear occupied factories, or to fire upon workers and students. But that such an order would be given by Georges Pompidou and General de Gaulle in the event of civil strife was a reasonable supposition. The security dispositions of the government could hardly have gone unnoticed by the Communist leaders. Indeed, Pompidou and De Gaulle wanted the Communists to know of their determination to use force if need be. As related by Dansette, on May 17 Pompidou decided to mobilize a part of his reserve forces. On the 20th he began to study the conditions under which the army would be called into action; on the 25th he ordered the transfer of several units stationed in the provinces to the Paris region. Plans were drawn up to place these troops under the command of General Le Doyen, and a regular order of battle was prepared. By the 30th troops and armored columns were in movement all over the outskirts of Paris. After De Gaulle's departure from Baden Baden, General Massu met with subordinates, briefed them on the legal authority vested in the President of the Republic to use the army to maintain order, and instructed key units to be ready to move at short notice.[39] Was this simply De Gaulle's favorite tactic of "the ruse," as outlined in a celebrated passage of his prewar book, *L'armée de métier*? If the intention was to convince the Communist Party that the army remained loyal and would crush any armed revolt, the ruse worked.

The prospect that the PCF might come to power in the foreseeable future is not bright. Consider either of the two major alternatives: a policy of violent confrontation with the bourgeois state, prepared and directed by a small core of professional revolutionaries; *or* a policy of legality, pursued by a mass party seeking to gain a majority, or at the very least entering into a coalition with other forces of the left preparatory to the achievement of "real democracy." Either alternative can work under favorable conditions, but such conditions have not existed in France in the more than fifty years since the PCF was created, nor does it appear likely that they will exist soon. Suppose the PCF were to convert itself into a paramilitary organization, and attempt to seize power forcibly. Some elements within the party were tempted by this prospect during the Liberation, and also in the period following the expulsion of the PCF from the tripartite governing coalition in 1947. In

1944 the presence of allied armies made a Communist seizure of power too risky; and in 1947-48 the Republic was able to defeat the attempt of the Communists to transform widespread strikes into an insurrection—though it was touch and go for a while. The disconcerting fact is that the masses who are appreciative of the way in which the PCF defends their interests are not receptive to a call for violence and revolution. Marching into battle without the masses, the party must face the police and armed forces by itself, and such a confrontation could result in the physical extermination of the Communist leadership.

On the other hand, legality means a commitment to defense of the interests of the masses, so that inevitably the party becomes involved in elections and parliamentary negotiations. Revolution becomes an increasingly remote prospect, and gradually drops entirely out of the calculations of the party leaders. Since other parties are making similar appeals to the masses, there is no guarantee that the PCF will ever increase the percentage of its vote—which seems to have leveled off at between 20 and 25 percent of the total. The one best hope remaining for the PCF is to form a genuine coalition of the left, win a majority, and then dominate that coalition. But the other partners are wary, and insist on guarantees that will hamstring the Communist Party in the event of victory at the polls.

The drawbacks of Communist strategy were evident again in the legislative elections of March 1973. Nine months earlier the Communist leadership achieved its goal of forging an alliance with the Socialist Party, sealed by a "common program" and an ironclad agreement to support whichever member of the left coalition won the greatest number of votes on the first ballot. The hopes of the Communists were almost—but not quite—fulfilled. On the first ballot Communist candidates received 21.3 percent of the votes, and Socialist and allied Radical candidates 19.2 percent—for a total of 40.5 percent. When the PSU vote of 3.3 percent, and some scattered "diverse left" votes, were added, the total vote of the left approached 45 percent, as compared to about 38 percent for

Gaullist candidates and 13 percent for the Reformist movement. But this kind of combined left vote was simply not enough, for one crucial reason. Whenever a Communist candidate represented the left on the second ballot a certain number of Socialists and Radicals abandoned their ally. The Gaullists were thus able to win a comfortable majority in the Assembly.

In preparation for the presidential election that is due no later than 1976, Socialists and Communists again eyed each other warily, calculating their chances of duplicating Allende's success in Chile. Assuming that a strong Socialist candidate (like François Mitterrand) allied with the Communists could count on at least 45 percent of the vote, the margin of victory might be provided by accumulated popular dissatisfaction with the Gaullists, an unforeseen scandal or crisis, or a defection of the center. But, unlike the electoral system in Chile, a run-off is required in France in case no candidate for the presidency receives an absolute majority, which permits the anti-Communist reflex full sway. Had there been a run-off in Chile, Allende would have been soundly beaten. If the tactic of an alliance with the Communists fails to produce results, the Socialists inevitably will be tempted to explore the possibility of an alliance with the center instead. In short, the conditions of politics in contemporary France are highly unfavorable to professional revolutionaries, even when they are supported by one fifth of the electorate.

The dilemma of revolution versus reformism has bedevilled the PCF ever since the day it was founded. There is one way in which the dilemma can be resolved, probably the only way in a country like France: as a result of a shift in the balance of international power. It is impossible to understand the PCF—either its policy on the seizure of power or its decision-making procedures—without considering the global context. Not that the party is simply a tool or agency of the Soviet Union—an absurd notion at the present time, although not far from the truth in the first few years of the party's existence. The PCF leadership views itself, and must be viewed, as part of a universal phenomenon and in a "special relationship" with the fraternal Communist Party of the Soviet Union. French Communists believe they are making significant contributions to a common cause in a variety of ways—if only by creating difficulties in the heart of an aggressive Western alliance. Habits of internationalism are deeply engrained in French Communists. The PCF has well served the international Communist movement in the past fifty years; there is no reason why it cannot continue to do so, even though it is blocked from power regardless of the tactics it employs.[40]

Urban Guerrillas

Probably the most important reason for the failure of the May Revolt was the misinterpretation by student revolutionaries of the nature of guerrilla war and particularly of the Cuban model. Why the attraction of the Cuban Revolution for French students? Castro and Guevara were intellectuals of European origin, expressing themselves in a European language, and therefore closer to aspiring French guerrillas than distant, exotic Asians. In no other major revolution of the modern era is it so clearly evident that intellectuals lead and workers follow. The workers hardly existed as an important social class in Cuba, yet the revolution took place. That the French working class is now reformist would thus not be an obstacle to revolution, provided that students and intellectuals were prepared to change the course of history by an act of will, and thereby gain the confidence of the masses.

Even the militarization of the Cuban economy and society, which began in earnest in 1968, did not detract from the appeal of Castroism among French students. To consider the problems of production in military terms, with the army in charge of all key sectors of the economy and intellectuals in charge of the army, recalls the heroic period of the Russian Revolution—Leon Trotsky at the head of the Red Army dealing hammer blows to the enemies of the Revolution and at the same time mobilizing workers on the army model for the great task of socialist reconstruction. Hierarchy, authority, command, and strict labor discipline—how else can the masses be mobilized? Castro's total disregard, bordering on contempt, for the details of managing an economy or holding elections added to his romantic luster and corresponded to the inclinations of the French student revolutionaries.[41]

Inspired by the Cuban example, the student militants in France raised high the banner of socialism, proclaimed their intention to destroy the existing social order, and plunged into battle with the mercenaries of capitalism. Anarchists of the March 22 Movement proudly referred to themselves as "fidélistes d'Europe." Many of the French student militants made the pilgrimage to Cuba, and some attended the Tricontinental Congress in Havana in January 1966. J.-P. Vigier, a former Communist expelled from the party because of his pro-Cuban position, and who later became editor of *Action* (widely read during the early days of the May Revolt), explained in July 1968 in what respects the Cuban model is applicable to an industrial society:

> In many ways the action committees resemble the Castro model. As the Moncada assault was a prelude to the successful guerrilla war in Cuba so the May events are the pattern of future political activity in France . . . . Just as the group of the twelve *Granma* survivors were able to raise a revolutionary army through a correct strategic appreciation, so we hope that our centers of action will expand to encompass the revolutionary potential in contemporary French society. Like the Cuban *focos* the action committees try to create an explosive situation by setting off simultaneous sparks in industrial centers throughout the country. We will attempt to build *focos* of extra-parliamentary political activity and mass violence against the system. Our aim is to polarize the social forces to such an extent that the finely-balanced social fabric will be destroyed and those who destroy will, in a parallel movement, construct a new society.[42]

In taking literally the slogans of Castro and Guevara *after* the seizure of power, the French students mistook the end result of revolution for the revolutionary process itself. Mass support for an effective guerrilla war is secured through a reformist, moderate, and nationalist program. Only after the revolutionaries are in control of the state apparatus can the people be mobilized to "build socialism." During the period of armed struggle the program of the Cuban rebels stressed the bourgeois notions of land ownership and liberalism. Ché Guevara held that the motor force of the revolution is not the working class, but the guerrilla. The guerrilla fighter, he continued, "interprets the desires of the great peasant mass to be owners of land . . . . Whatever the ideological aims that inspire the fight, the economic aim is determined by the aspiration toward ownership of land." Castro's program at the time was moderate, well within the established left-reformist tradition. He called for restoration of the Constitution of 1940, guarantees of political freedom, and early elections. In his New York press conference of April 17, 1959, Castro summed up his position: "I have said in a clear and *definitive* fashion that *we are not communists* . . . . The doors are open to *private* investments that contribute to the development of industry in Cuba . . . . It is absolutely impossible for us to make progress if we do not get along with the U.S."[43] No one knows whether Castro really was, as he later declared, a "Marxist-Leninist" from the very outset. But in any case, his moderate line before 1960 won the support of the middle and professional classes, as well as of the peasantry and workers.

Once in power Castro quickly dismantled the old armed forces and replaced them with a popular militia. The state, its army and police were then used to bring about the real revolution. In the beginning the Cuban revolution was not socialist in any sense—neither Marxist nor social democratic. But within eighteen months of his New York press conference, Cuba officially entered the "socialist camp." This was a "sliding" revolution that gradually was extended from the state to the people. Similarly, in Asia the revolutionaries were careful to put themselves forward as reformers and nationalists. They appealed not only to workers and peasants, but also to the "urban petty bourgeoisie" and even to the "national" capitalists (as opposed to those subservient to foreign powers).

Had the student leaders in France really adapted the tactics of Guevara, Mao, and Ho to their own situation, they would have tried to gain mass support for short-term and reformist objectives, toning down the revolutionary content of their program. In the *Communist Manifesto*, Marx reserved his choicest epithets for those Socialists who sought to raise the banner of revolution prematurely. These "German" or "true" Socialists, these "fantastic" Utopians are all fundamentally reactionary, Marx observed, because they succeed only in frightening the bourgeoisie and bringing about a political alliance of the middle class and feudal elements in society against the proletariat. The leaders of the May Revolt did everything that Marx warned against and brought about the very triumph of conservatism that Marx had predicted.

NOTES

1. "A student works to learn. He doesn't have a family to support. We, the workers, we have families. And then among you, there are anarchists who stir up trouble. If we want to have something, we can't follow those guys . . . . " "The Revolution will not come through ballots! " cried out a student. "Who's talking about Revolution now?" brutally replied a worker. J.-C. Kerbourc'h, *Le piéton de mai* (Julliard, 1968), pp. 33-34.

2. *De la misère en milieu étudiant*, p. 13. The thesis that the university serves the interests of a ruling class is developed at length in P. Bourdieu and J.-C. Passeron, *Les héritiers* (Editions de Minuit, 1966). Their book was influential in student circles.

3. Estimates of student registration are approximate, since many students were not full-time or serious. Figures presented here are from Raymond Boudon, "Quelques causes de la révolte etudiantine," *La Table Ronde* (Dec. 1968-Jan. 1969), pp. 171-72. Analysis of social composition of student body: ibid., pp. 172-73.

4. Studies of exam results cited by P. Bénéton and J. Touchard, "Les interprétations de la crise de mai-juin 1968", *Revue Française de Science Politique,* 1970, xx:3, pp. 513-15.

5. On CGT hostility toward the leftists in occupied factories, cf. Jacques Frémontier, *La forteresse ouvrière: Renault,* (Fayard, 1971),

pp. 342-67. Contradictory objectives of students and workers are also evident in the study by Pierre Dubois et al., *Grèves revendicatives ou grèves politiques?* (Anthropos, 1971).

6. The dialogue between student and worker was recorded on tape by a filmmaker during the strike at Renault, and is reprinted by Frémontier, *La forteresse ouvrière,* p. 363.

7. Ibid., pp. 361-62, for declaration by Aimé Halbeher, and Frémontier's comment about the unbelievable mess.

8. The dealings between journalists and Sauvageot, and the appearance of journalists at the Sorbonne, related in Claude Frédéric, *Libérer l'ORTF,* (Seuil, 1968), pp. 47-48, 88.

9. Cohn-Bendit quote on socialism in the Third World, in J. Sauvageot, A. Geismar, and D. Cohn-Bendit, *La révolte étudiante,* (Seuil, 1968) p. 68. Geismar quote on socialism, ibid., p. 55.

10. M22M views on autogestion are set forth in *Ce n'est qu'un début* (Maspero, 1968), especially pp. 89-99.

11. The June 1 debate is reprinted in J.-L. Brau, *Cours, camarade, le vieux monde est derrière toi!* (Albin Michel, 1968), pp. 310-18.

12. On the occupation of the Sorbonne, and resolution of May 13: A. Dansette, *Mai 1968,* (Plon, 1971), p. 146. In general, ibid., pp. 145-53, 190-204, 336-38; and P. Seale and M. McConville, *French Revolution, 1968* (Penguin, 1968), pp. 101-07.

13. For a good account of the power struggles within the occupation committee by a situationist: René Viénet, *Enragés et situationnistes dans le mouvement des occupations,* (Gallimard, 1968), pp. 71-106. Also *I.S.,* no. 12 (Sept. 1969), pp. 17-18, 22-23.

14. Jacques Perret, *Inquiète Sorbonne* (Classiques Hachette, 1968), p. 47.

15. On the Katangais: Dansette, *Mai 1968,* p. 337; Viansson-Ponté, *Histoire de la république gaullienne,* vol. II, pp. 490-91. Benjamin Barber makes some trenchant observations on the affinity between anarchism and the *lumpen,* in *Superman and Common Men* (Penguin, 1972), pp. 23-27.

16. On the contestation by anarchists at the Odéon, cf. Patrick Ravigant, *L'Odéon est ouvert,* (Stock, 1969), p. 154; and the collapse of

direct democracy at Odéon, ibid., pp. 179-96. Also Dansette, *Mai 1968*, pp. 336-37. For sensible comments on the illusion of mass participation: André Philip, *Mai 68 et la foi démocratique* (Aubier, 1968), p. 123.

17. In Charles Posner, ed., *Reflections on the Revolution in France: 1968* (Penguin, 1970), pp. 129, 138.

18. Among those in the audience was the author.

19. Jean Bertolini, *Les trublions*, (Stock, 1969), p. 369, who relates the entire incident in detail.

20. Comment on Servan-Schreiber in *I.S.*, no. 12 (Sept. 1969), p. 86. Incident involving Maîtron, ibid., pp. 88-90.

21. In J. Sauvageot et al., *La révolte étudiante*, pp. 50-51.

22. Alain Krivine presents a Leninist justification of his candidacy in *La farce électorale* (Seuil, 1969).

23. Statements by Communist leaders: Georges Cogniot, *Les intellectuels et les étudiants devant la révolution* (Institut Maurice Thorez, 1968); Jacques Duclos, *Anarchistes d'hier et d'aujourd'hui* (Editions Sociales, 1968); René Andrieu, *Les communistes et la révolution* (Julliard, 1968), pp. 91-100; Georges Séguy in his preface to Henri Krasucki, *Syndicats et lutte de classes* (Editions Sociales, 1969), p. 9.

24. The phrase, "social racism," is from René Andrieu, *Les Communistes et la révolution* (Julliard, 1968), p. 83. For a more serene justification of the Communist attitude toward the gauchistes: Pierre Juquin, *Le sens du réel* (Bernard Grasset, 1971), especially chap. 2; and Claude Prévost, *Les étudiants et le gauchisme* (Editions Sociales, 1969).

25. On the past relations between anarchists and Communists, see Annie Kriegel, *Les Communistes français* (Seuil, 1970), pp. 107-08.

26. The intriguing incident of May 16 is related by Dansette, *Mai 1968*, pp. 174-75. That PCF policy evolved in May is also stressed by Kriegel, *Les Communistes français*, pp. 211-14.

27. Mitterrand press conference and subsequent meeting with Waldeck Rochet: Dansette, *Mai 1968*, pp. 286-89. See also François Mitterrand, *Ma part de vérité* (Fayard, 1969).

28. Dansette, *Mai 1968*, p. 314.

29. Viansson-Ponté, *Histoire de la république gaullienne*, vol. II, p. 536.

30. See Jean-Paul Sartre, *Les Communistes ont peur de la révolution* (Didier, 1968), pp. 10-12, 29.

31. Georges Lavau, "Le parti communiste dans le système politique français," in *Le Communisme en France* (Armand Colin, 1969), pp. 7-82.

32. Ibid., p. 22.

33. Citation in Annie Kriegel, *Les Communistes français*, p. 228; in general, ibid., pp. 6, 227-37.

34. René Andrieu, *Les Communistes et la révolution*, p. 243.

35. Annie Kriegel, *Les Communistes français*, p. 252. In general, ibid., pp. 245-60; and François Borella, *Les Partis politiques dans la France d'aujourd'hui* (Seuil, 1973), pp. 174-89.

36. Citation in Jacques Frémontier, *La forteresse ouvrière*, p. 235.

37. René Andrieu, p. 179.

38. Citation on Indonesian repression: Waldeck Rochet, *L'avenir du parti communiste français* (Grasset, 1969), p. 105; on the readiness of armed forces to intervene in May, ibid., pp. 21-23.

39. Military movements recounted in Dansette, *Mai 1968*, pp. 299-300.

40. The international dimension is emphasized by Annie Kriegel, *Les Communistes français*, pp. 177-208; George Lichtheim, *Marxism in Modern France* (Columbia University Press, 1966), pp. 129, 198; and Jacques Fauvet in his *Histoire du parti communiste français* (Fayard, 1965), especially vol. I, p. 154, vol. II, pp. 227-28.

41. On the attractiveness of the Cuban Revolution for French students, see the insightful comments of Gilles Martinet, *Les cinq communismes* (Seuil, 1971), pp. 214-32.

42. In Charles Posner, ed., *Reflections*, p. 210.

43. Citation from Che Guevara, *Guerrilla Warfare* (Vintage, 1968), p. 5. Castro's New York press conference statement cited by René Dumont, *Cuba, est-il socialiste?* (Seuil, 1970), p. 19.

6

Modernization and Revolt

Parce que la prospérité s'est accrue, les désirs sont exaltés. La proie plus riche qui leur est offerte les stimule, les rend plus exigeants, plus impatients de toute règle, alors justement que les règles traditionnelles ont perdu de leur autorité. L'état de dérèglement ou d'anomie est donc encore renforcé par ce fait que les passions sont moins disciplinées au moment même où elles auraient besoin d'une plus forte discipline.

Emile Durkheim, Le suicide, étude de sociologie.[1]

STUDENT DEMONSTRATIONS, revival of working-class demands, alienation of the middle classes—each phase of the May Revolt can be understood separately. But when the elements are put together there remains a residue of mystery. What led to the explosion of student discontent in the first place? What can account for the depth and intensity of the revolt of so many intellectuals and apprentice intellectuals against the liberal state? Why has there been such a pervasive uneasiness throughout the society ever since? A fundamental change took place in France in May 1968, sensed by all observers, whether sympathetic or hostile.

That the May Revolt was no run-of-the-mill political crisis is evident from the public statements made in the heat of battle by a tenacious prime minister and an anguished president of the republic. During the debate in the National Assembly on May 14, Georges Pompidou reflected upon the profound meaning of the crisis. "Nothing would be more illusory than to believe that the events we have just lived through constitute a temporary flare-up." It is not simply a question of reforming the university, he continued, it is the whole problem of the place of youth in modern civilization, its obligations, and its morals. The social discipline of the past has disappeared; social relations among parents and children, teachers and pupils, have been weakened, and the advance of technology has eliminated the incentive to work. "Why is it surprising then if the need of man to believe in something, to have solidly anchored in himself some fundamental principles, is contradicted by the constant questioning of everything on which humanity has depended for centuries: the family is often dissolved or abandoned, the nation questioned, often denied. God is dead for some. The Church itself is debating the path to follow and is overturning its traditions." Under these circumstances the students are at loose ends. Some are searching for solutions; others turn to negation, total refusal, and the desire to destroy. "Destroy what? What they have close at hand, and for the students that is the university. And then the society ... society itself, modern society, materialistic and soulless." There followed a solemn conclusion:

> I see no other precedent in our history but that desperate period that was the fifteenth century, when the structures of the Middle Ages were collapsing and when, even then, the students were revolting at the Sorbonne. At this stage, it is no longer, believe me, the government which is at stake, nor the institutions, nor even France. It is our civilization itself.[2]

General de Gaulle a few weeks later, during the election campaign, also viewed the May Revolt as a chilling development that might presage the death of liberal democracy. Yet one could sense in his remarks a strange affinity, a grudging admiration for the revolt against modern society and its inhuman emphasis on consumption and machinery. De Gaulle himself had always been a critic of the modern world, even as he called on his countrymen to increase industrial production and build atomic bombs.

In French society, he commented in his televised interview with Michel Droit on June 7, the machine is "absolute master" and pushes man onward at an ever faster pace, toward incredible transformations. After describing the sweeping changes in French society in the past fifty years, he added: "How could anyone possibly imagine that such a society is placid and, at bottom, satisfied? It certainly is not." Of course, mechanical civilization brings with it many benefits, including a growing prosperity. But—and here De Gaulle resembles the situationists—it remains mechanical, making man in his work and his daily life a mere cog in an overwhelming machine. "So, everything is organized and functions in an automatic, standardized, and technocratic manner in such a way that the individual, for example, the worker, no longer has an influence on his own destiny . . . . " In the spirit of the situationists, he condemned both communism and capitalism for enslaving man to the machine. "How to work out a human balance for civilization, for mechanical society? There is the great question of our century!"[3]

De Gaulle's purpose in this declaration was to prepare the public for the crowning reform of his regime: to implant the principle of *participation* and thus change the condition of man in the context of "modern, mechanical society." The analysis also had the happy effect of relieving him and his government of the responsibility for the outbreak of the May Revolt, since modern civilization was the culprit, not the Fifth Republic. Who would want to vote against modern civilization in the upcoming elections? But there can be no doubt that General de Gaulle was truly shaken by this "terrible crisis," as he called it. A year later, Georges Pompidou, now De Gaulle's successor as president of the republic, continued to express deep pessimism about the viability of modern society. He spoke gloomily even of a possible "collective suicide."[4] The disorientation of Pompidou and De Gaulle was understandable. The very fabric of the society was rent, and all social structures and discipline seemed to be collapsing. It may be suggested, however, that the May Revolt can best be understood not as a crisis of civilization but as a crisis of modernization involving more than a reaction to its "mechanical" nature.

Modernization and Ideology

The May Revolt took place in a country that for two centuries has been in the forefront of political and social change in the world, and today is undergoing further transformation at an exceptionally rapid pace. Not "future shock," but permanent shock would be an appropriate characterization of this process. The May Revolt is the most recent dramatic tremor produced in the course of the French experience of modernization.

By modernization we mean the transformation of human relationships that has accompanied the enormous development of science and technology in the past two centuries. Modernization is the economic, social, political, and cultural equivalent of the scientific revolution. When a society undergoes the process of modernization, it is shaken to its roots, changed in every one of its aspects. No sector of the society is spared. For analytic purposes it is useful to tie together the characteristics of each sector of the society into a package, as models or ideal-types of traditional and modern societies. A contrast may then be drawn between traditional and modern societies as regards the economy, social structure, political institutions, and the values that permeate the whole and justify coercion. All attempts to construct ideal-types are bound to be distortions of complex realities. But distortion through analytic abstraction is unavoidable if we seek to understand the evolution of a society. History has meaning, even though we can never fully grasp that meaning, even though we are condemned to oversimplify in our attempts at understanding.[5]

The drive toward modernity has been viewed by social scientists from many different angles. It may be considered a movement toward greater rationality, a result of the seeping of science into the fabric of the society; or a movement toward greater division of labor and specialization of function, a necessary condition of industrialization that characterizes all social life as well as the economy; or a movement toward greater centralization of decision-making through bureaucratic organization, a reflection of the increased importance of knowledge and expertise in the productive process. Observers like Max Weber and Emile Durkheim have concentrated on one or the other of these aspects of modernization; any approach may be fruitful so long as it focuses our attention on the reality of the evolution of European society.

The typologies of traditional and modern societies can be illustrated by comparing, for example, the France of 1968 and of 1768. Prerevolutionary France was governed by a monarch whose rule was justified, literally, in terms of divine right; the economy was primarily agricultural, with significant beginnings of industry; the family was the predominant social unit and the basis not only of monarchical and aristocratic lineage but also of economic enterprise; and religious themes permeated the society, though increasingly challenged by men of science. The France of 1968 was a parliamentary democracy whose leaders attained their position through elections; political decisions were implemented, and in many cases inspired, by a vast bureaucracy; the economy was predominantly industrial and dominated by giant enterprises run by large bureaucracies, both private and public; and science—not religion or witchcraft— provided the underpinning of a complex economy. The point need not be belabored: like all other European nations France experienced an evolution from feudalism to modernity in the course of the past three centuries. The process was complex, systematic, and inexorable. In some European nations modernization was compatible with the slow evolution of constitutional monarchy, and the introduction of parliamentary democracy; in other cases modernization took place under the auspices of authoritarian monarchies, later succeeded by Fascist or Communist regimes. In western Europe, and especially in nations aspiring to the role of great powers—Britain, France, and Germany—modernization proceeded at roughly the same pace (when compared to the rest of the world). Since national defense was dependent increasingly on the development of heavy industry, production of sophisticated armaments, and rapid application of scientific advance to military uses, each European nation had good reason to press forward along the path of complete modernization. Those who hesitated ran the risk of defeat and domination by their enemies—or allies.

In the face of the total transformation of society brought about by the general movement away from traditional and toward modern forms, each individual must make a choice. Is he for or against modernization, and under what conditions? Similarly, the spokesmen for such social categories as capitalists, managers, workers, and peasants, must opt either for or against the emergence of an industrial and scientific civilization. In this context, anarcho-surrealism may be viewed as the ideology of total, unyielding *resistance* to modernization in all of its aspects. Every feature of modern society is repudiated, or called into question, by anarchists and surrealists: the centralized state, hierarchy, bureaucracy, division of labor, science, technology, assembly lines, urban living, rationality, and organization. Instead an alternative vision is put forward: emotion, passion, and chance replace cold rationality; men live close to nature, are awed by the mysteries of the universe, and participate spontaneously and joyously in their social rites. Since workers are too easily caught up in the rational materialism of modern society, anarcho-surrealists instinctively turn to the peasantry, small artisans, and even the *lumpen* and criminal elements, all of whom are far removed from or hostile toward modern society, and therefore are more likely to strike out against it in rage. Who says modernization also says resistance to modernization, and in the front line of the resistance are the anarchists and surrealists.[6]

On the other hand, orthodox Marxists—including Trotskyists and Maoists—although equally determined to overthrow capitalism and the liberal state, fundamentally accept modernization and its implications. They value science, proudly proclaim themselves scientific socialists, see organization as the key to revolutionary change, and promise rapid industrialization and increased production through central planning. One of their major claims is precisely that capitalism has now become a fetter upon the full development of the productive capacity of modern technology. Trotskyist and Maoist interpretations especially manifest a profound desire to hasten the transformation of society by eradicating the last vestiges of primitive and traditional mentalities, eliminating all hereditary privileges that might be left over from feudal or capitalist times.

The great issue that divides the revolutionary coalition—rejection or acceptance of modernization itself—erupted in the middle of the nineteenth century, when Proudhon, Bakunin and Marx sought to interpret and direct the social evolution of their time. In his early, unpublished manuscripts, Marx castigated the German society of which he was a part—a conglomeration of feudalism and nascent capitalism—and seemed to long for the reconstitution of the unity of preindustrial and even prefeudal society. But he moved quickly into the phase of scientific socialism, coming to terms with the modern world (though retaining dislike for many of its features), and elaborating an ideology that purported to express the interests of one of the social groups being generated in the process of industrialization. Proudhon and Bakunin, however, feared that the Marxist solution might be just as bad as the capitalist society they all wanted to destroy, that humanity would continue to be exploited but by an authoritarian bureaucracy rather than by capitalists. Merged with their pleas for libertarian socialism was an aversion to modern civilization. Proudhon's scheme for mutualist associations of producers linked in communes and federations is appropriate for a society of yeoman farmers and sturdy artisans (reminiscent of his beloved province of Jura before the coming of the railroad), hardly for a complex industrial economy. Bakunin saw in science the potential threat of dictatorship by an elite and a means of brutalizing mankind. His ideal society was the American frontier, where the individual farmer was virtually self-sufficient. Throughout the works of Proudhon and Bakunin—and in young Marx's *German Ideology*—runs a profound distaste for the specialization of labor at the heart of the process of industrialization.

Anarchism and Marxism in the nineteenth century reflected the tensions of European society in the period of early industrialization. Similarly, the revival of interest today in Proudhon, Bakunin and the young Marx, as well as the sudden popularity of Trotskyism and Maoism, must reflect the new tensions produced by the transition from an industrial to a scientific civilization. Ever greater rationalization of economic and social behavior inevitably provokes a contrary impulse, a romantic desire to save as much as possible of the traditional society—leading back naturally to the founders of anarchism. At the same time many socialist intellectuals have been appalled by the end result of socialism in the Soviet Union and Eastern Europe. In their search for an ideology that will enable them to continue to fight for their ideals, they are reappraising the course of socialism, looking for the point at which the express train of history went off the track. Some go back to the break between Khrushchev and Mao, others to the conflict between Stalin and Trotsky. In either case they retain a commitment to a civilization of science and technology. But many believe that the seeds of authoritarianism were planted by Lenin, or even by Marx. They trace the trouble to the formative period of socialism, when the European working class moved away from the libertarianism of Proudhon and Bakunin, and fell under the baleful influence of Marx (or at any rate, of the older Marx).[7]

The contradictions within the socialist movement came to the fore in the May Revolt. Most students, workers, and professionals accepted modernization as a goal and wished to eliminate archaic barriers to facilitate mass participation in the modern society. Some wished to quicken the march toward ever elusive modernization by imposing totalitarian control and ruthlessly eliminating all leftovers of traditionalism. Still others were revolting against modern society and all its works in order to return to an idyllic or imagined past. The May Revolt thus reflected the ambiguity of all political reactions to the process of modernization, involving a mix of reformism, revolution, and reversion to the past.

The Crises of Modernization

One fruitful way of studying the complex process of modernization is to view it as a series of crises or challenges, to which a number of different responses are possible. A distinction can be made among the crises of legitimacy, participation, and tension-management (occurring roughly in that chronological order). As European societies went through the experience of modernization they necessarily had to cope with each of these crises. Feudal societies could not survive the Enlightenment, and the concept of divine right gave way to more rational theories of political legitimacy. With industrialization new groups emerged (an energetic entrepreneurial class, a managerial and clerical class, and a massive working class), and the existing political elites somehow had to deal with the demands of these new groups and integrate them into the political system. As the European economy became more complex each national society had to devise a system of controls, enabling it to coordinate the activities of increasingly specialized associations.

Nothing is fated to work out in favor of modernization in any of these crises. Revolt against the monarchy may be crushed; reactionary forces may overthrow a republic and reestablish monarchy; new or greatly expanded social groups, in particular the working class, may not be effectively integrated into the political system; and a society may be unable to cope with the problems of coordination. But punishment for failure is severe. A country that falls behind is likely to come under the influence or even the rule of those who have been more successful in meeting these challenges.

Each of the crises of modernization has posed serious problems for the French. Take, for example, the crisis of legitimacy.[8] One of the basic assumptions of modernization theory is that as a society becomes more complex, the values serving to legitimize political authority become more rational. Or, rather than imply any causal relationship, rationalization of authority proceeds along with industrialization and increasing complexity of social structure. This assumption is borne out in a striking manner by the French experience, because of the great divide of the Revolution of 1789. The Tennis Court Oath, the August decrees abolishing feudalism, and the Declaration of the Rights of Man and Citizen marked an irrevocable break with absolutism and feudalism, and signaled the emergence of more rational principles of political legitimacy. Although France was converted almost overnight into a modern state as regards its official pattern of legitimacy, it did not thereby achieve a large popular consensus on its basic institutions. The revolution was repudiated by conservatives, and the revolutionaries were themselves divided. The result was a long period of constitutional instability. The transformation of French society continued. But the way in which the French tackled the successive crises of modernization was drastically affected by inability to agree on political structures. In the first great crisis of modernization in France, bursting forth in the Revolution of 1789 but continuing to this day, intransigeance rather than compromise became characteristic of the political process.

Dissensus carried over from one historical phase to another. When the French turned to the problem of integrating the working class into the political system a pattern of rejection, opposition, and violence had already taken hold and made it more difficult (though not impossible) to formulate policy. The French working and business classes, from the outset, have been reluctant to bargain with each other—although compelled to do so by circumstances. The heritage of class distrust and conflict continues to interfere with the smooth functioning of the political system. That twenty to twenty-five percent of the electorate votes fairly consistently for the Communist Party, and that the Communist-led CGT is the most powerful of the French trade unions, are indications of profound dissatisfaction within the French working class. In turn, exclusion of the Communist Party from governing coalitions drives the political balance to the right, placing the working class at a disadvantage in the political process and further intensifying feelings of class consciousness and alienation from the political system. Without having completely resolved the crises of legitimacy and participation, the French have plunged into the later phase of modernization, for the alternative is national decline. But the carryover of dissensus creates friction and grievances throughout the society. Much of the May Revolt—in particular the readiness of masses of students, workers, and even professionals to defect—can be explained by the relative failure of the French, compared with other industrial nations, to cope with the successive crises of modernization.

However, revolutionary dissent combined with an intensive destructive urge is a general trend among students and middle class intellectuals in all liberal-industrial societies today. The May Revolt never could have begun in a stagnant or traditional society. It came about in the first place only because, despite all the difficulties in their way, the French managed to create an advanced industrial nation by 1968. We are led to the paradoxical conclusion that not only the failures, but also the very *success* of a society in meeting the challenges of modernization may lead to its own downfall.

Anomie

Accompanying modernization in France, and everywhere else, is the phenomenon of *anomie*—a term popularized almost a century ago by Emile Durkheim. We have already encountered explanations of the May Revolt along the lines of Durkheim's theory, for example in Raymond Aron's *La révolution introuvable,* and the remarks of Georges Pompidou (before the National Assembly on May 14, 1968) and of General de Gaulle (during the television interview with Michel Droit on June 7, 1968). Durkheim asserted that the appetites and desires of men are infinite and that every society must impose a discipline or "regulator" in order to survive. In traditional society the family and religion constitute the regulator. Every person knows his role in family and religious activities; his desires are limited by his own perception of social status. But when a traditional society breaks up, the family structure and the church are brought into question. New values and new social structures arise (science, the republic, the corporation, the university, and so on); but frequently the individual in transition cannot accept them. Caught between the traditional and modern forms, his reactions may be those of resignation (ranging from apathy to suicide) or of rage against established authority. It is Durkheim's great insight that every modern society carries within itself the seeds of its own destruction. The more the individual is encouraged by society to realize his individuality, the greater is the risk that he will reject discipline and become perpetually discontent.[9]

The "anomic" reaction to social change in France has taken the form of violent opposition to the modern state and to urban industrial life. Hostility to industrial life has been especially vigorous in France among artists and writers, who have drawn a sharp contrast between bucolic nature and the polluted inhumanity of cities. As we have seen, under the influence of Proudhon and Bakunin, French anarchists have traditionally celebrated the glories of village and farm society. Such literary movements as Dada and surrealism have questioned science, rationality, and modern society, exulting instead in the gesture of the child, the unpredictable happening, and the immediate gratification of desires. The anarchist, dadaist, and surrealist traditions resurfaced in the May Revolt with astonishing force.

The anomic opposition to modernization is only one form of protest against poverty and exploitation. The dominant wing of the global revolutionary movement fully accepts modernization, though not through capitalism. The goal is to eliminate the capitalist, not science and technology—to base socialism on a modern, not a primitive economy. The question of whether to fight against exploitation by recapturing the spirit of traditional societies, or by transcending that spirit altogether has been a running controversy among revolutionaries ever since the industrial revolution started, and was especially pressing in May 1968.

Anomie is an unexpected consequence of the ability of modern societies to triumph over obstacles that seemed insurmountable a century ago. The development of science and technology has resulted in extraordinary increases in economic production and national wealth, in France and elsewhere; and though income differentials persist, it would require an excessive devotion to nineteenth-century Marxist texts to believe that workers in France, Britain, the United States, or any other industrial society have become increasingly miserable and impoverished in the past hundred years. There are always enough grave instances of social injustice, no matter how productive an economy, to inspire any number of protest movements—but this cannot account for the astonishing spurt of revolutionary activity in all modern societies today.

It is not only poverty that causes protest and revolt in a modern society, but also prosperity—a fatal defect in societies whose very rationale is to create more wealth. Poverty, however lamentable may be its consequences for individuals, is a school for discipline. A man fearful of losing his job because he will cease to eat is remarkably receptive to commands from his superiors. He may rebel from time to time but even in revolt he continues to carry out orders. In contrast, prosperity gives people the illusion that they are totally independent of others, that any obstacles can be overcome by an effort of individual will. When life is easy there is no reason to obey commands and no penalty for insubordination or indiscipline. When an individual successfully defies one authority he is tempted to defy another, and another, until finally the very notion of authority becomes unbearable. Prosperity unaccompanied by a strong sense of social responsibility undermines collective effort and may undo a society.[10]

The possibility of the dissolution of social discipline is especially great when wealth increases suddenly or when opportunities open up for a previously depressed class of people. It was precisely this kind of change in the condition of life that fascinated Durkheim from the time he first noticed that suicide rates increase sharply along with the progress of civilization. It is the dream of the poor that sudden wealth (winning first prize in the national lottery, an unexpected inheritance, a fabulous marriage) will open wide the gates of paradise—and in some cases it may. But the struggle to be successful may be more satisfying than success itself, in all walks of life. It is classic that the writer or artist who finally gains recognition after many years of effort goes through a crisis of confidence, fearing that he cannot repeat his success or, worse, so disappointed with the fruits of success that going on seems pointless. Similarly, the active businessman thrives on his work, telling himself that his goal is to retire young and enjoy life, only to discover later that he is incapable of savoring an existence without the challenge of work.

When the moorings of a society give way, everything goes—social discipline, political authority, the incentive to produce, and sometimes the incentive to live. As Durkheim perceptively remarked, "one cannot remain in contemplation before a vacuum without being progressively drawn into it."[11] He had in mind primarily suicide; lesser variations on the same theme are to "drop out" of normal society or to escape the real world through the use of drugs. This form of anomic behavior is especially noticeable among the children of parents who themselves had to work hard to succeed. The corroding effect of prosperity is most evident at one remove.

Once in a condition of anomie, the individual may react in altogether unforeseeable ways. One tendency, we have noted, is toward renunciation, withdrawal, loss of zest for life, or suicide. But, as is stressed by Durkheim in a less well-known part of his analysis, anomie gives birth to a state of exasperation and irritated lassitude, "which can, depending upon circumstances, turn the individual against himself or against others . . . . "[12] He was referring not only to the extreme cases of suicide and homicide, but also to alternating political attitudes of apathy and violent attacks upon authority, the attempt either to escape from reality or to destroy it. Apathy and terrorism are related aspects of the same continuing reaction to modernization.

The May Revolt displayed many of the characteristics of

the instability characterized by Durkheim as anomie. It took place in a society that had just experienced twenty years of unprecedented economic growth and was more prosperous than at any other time of its history. Poverty and injustice had hardly been eliminated, but the workers scraping along on the minimum wage, and other unfavored groups, took no initiatives and even throughout the general strike remained primarily concerned with improvement of material conditions rather than with revolution. Those who were in the forefront of the revolutionary movement were precisely those labeled by Durkheim as prime candidates for anomie—the children of the newly prosperous middle classes. It is significant that the most raucous and undisciplined campus in the entire French university system was Nanterre, whose students are drawn from the comfortable sections of the west of Paris. It was striking that students from modest backgrounds were more interested in their own social mobility than in abstract revolution in May.[13] Also noteworthy was the interaction and in many cases interchangeability between the two related anomic tendencies of apathy and rage. Once they had lost their ties to French society, many students and others glided back and forth between a diffuse counterculture of dropouts and organized revolutionary groups. Extreme individualism blossomed into extreme collectivism only to disintegrate again upon meeting the slightest resistance. Those who wanted to escape all authority and those who wanted to impose iron discipline upon everyone else were the two marching wings of the revolutionary coalition; the ease with which many people switched from one to the other called attention to anomie as the common element of the diverse revolutionary groups.[14]

The May Revolt highlights in dramatic fashion the existence of a new dimension in the continuing crisis of participation or "entry into politics" of important social groups. Anomie was Durkheim's formulation of the problem of integrating the middle and working classes into political systems that had previously been dominated by a landed aristocracy. He saw that the working class was becoming increasingly isolated from the owning class. The life style of the capitalists was more and more remote from the reality of workday experience. A point is reached where it is beyond the capacity of workers and capitalists even to understand each other. He later broadened the meaning of anomie to include the lack of purpose in life under capitalism where individuals are engaged in the single-minded pursuit of wealth.[15]

In later stages of industrialization the social force undergoing the greatest rate of expansion is the intellectual class—the scientists, engineers, technicians, administrators, and so on—who receive their training in scientific institutes and universities. This newly massive intellectual class follows in the tradition of its predecessors by making demands upon the political system. Just as hereditary monarchy was repudiated by the bourgeoisie, and parliamentary democracy questioned by the revolutionary wing of the working class, so many intellectuals find the dominant liberal synthesis inadequate. Liberalism seems to many to be a cover for the supremacy of money or numbers. Intellectuals are uncomfortable with political values that give an advantage to the wealthy and to demagogues. The life style of the intellectuals is also distinctive. In Durkheim's sense, many intellectuals are in a condition of anomie because they are increasingly isolated from the rest of society.[16]

In addition, a certain amount of alienation is generated simply because there is a confrontation between an existing elite and a rising social group. At every stage of the modernizing process there is an anomic reaction due to the weakening of traditional values and the failure of the new values to replace them. The conflict between old and new norms must affect the intellectuals in the scientific civilization, as it affected workers in the industrial civilization. Just as the assembly line provoked irritation and revolt among workers, so the organization of social activity on the basis of scientific and rational criteria creates a feeling of "dehumanization" in many intellectuals. It is to be expected that a certain number of individuals will be left, at least during a transitional period, in a state of normlessness, or "deregulation." Those who repudiate the old and fear or disdain to accept the new display the symptoms of anomie.

That there should be an anomic reaction to modernization among intellectuals is not unusual; but the depth and intensity of this reaction—expressing itself in withdrawal and rage, political apathy and political terrorism—is startling. Why should the mass of anomie increase so sharply? At least three reasons may be suggested.

First, a large number of people break under the greater strain. In a scientific civilization there necessarily are rigorous standards of education and performance. There is no short cut to acquisition of scientific knowledge. Those who are not capable of acquiring this knowledge, or are not sufficiently motivated, fall by the wayside. Furthermore, the amount of knowledge to be mastered is increasing at an enormous rate, and with it the pressure on students. While examinations and student anxiety have always existed, in the past there have also been many ways of getting ahead on the basis of a modest education. When the major avenue to success is the university, those who cannot meet its demands are at a greater disadvantage than ever before.

Secondly, the productivity of the scientific civilization makes it possible to carry a marginal element within the society. Technically, it is feasible for any advanced industrial society to support a large class of dropouts and drones—provided that this class remains within manageable bounds and does not deprive the productive classes of their motivation to work. Many young people are able to enjoy—or endure—a life of anomie with the bemused support of their parents. Poverty is a highly effective social technique for imposing limits on anomie; prosperity, however, creates the conditions for the existence of a large alienated group.

Freedom itself may be a major cause of anomie in the intellectual class. Modernization makes possible a great expansion of individual freedom. As Durkheim points out, primitive man is merely an extension of the group, hemmed in by custom and taboo. He has no mind of his own. Modern man enjoys greater autonomy and is free to think as he pleases.[17] But the heavy responsibility of making a free choice can be utterly demoralizing, leading either to a desire to escape or to revolt. In authoritarian regimes the masses and the intellectuals can be conditioned, mobilized, and commanded. Problems may not actually be solved, but the over-pressured individual is relieved of the burden of choice. The disorder inherent in liberalism and the scientific civilization is eliminated. Anomic groups serve as pile drivers, splitting the foundations of the liberal state. Authoritarian elites pick up the pieces and impose the discipline that so many desperately crave.

In the scientific civilization what Durkheim called the "regulator" is more essential than ever. The intellectual must be imaginative, creative, and even enthusiastic if the collective scientific enterprise is to flourish. Doubts, hesitation, and withdrawal will block the system. The political integration of the intellectual class may well prove to be inherently more difficult than was the case for the capitalist and working classes. The landed aristocrats and capitalists were numerically weak in relation to the rest of the society and could be outmaneuvered in politics. But while the working class had the advantage of numbers, its function within the economy was to carry out orders rather than to give them, to obey rather than to innovate. As a class the workers were unable to direct themselves, let alone the rest of society. The intellectual class is not subject to the same handicaps. Unlike the old aristocrats or the capitalists, intellectuals are a large social force. Unlike the workers, they have ability, inculcated by their social function, to direct and command.[18]

The question may be raised whether parliamentary democracies like France can cope with the entry of the intellectuals as a massive social force into the political system. Wherever freedom of criticism is permitted, opportunities for exploiting tensions are almost unlimited. In a climate of freedom the intellectuals are even more likely to rebel than the old working class, and more likely to withdraw their cooperation from the establishment. The parliamentary democracies that experienced great difficulty in securing the integration of the working class probably will continue to be unstable as they move into the scientific civilization and deal with the intellectual class. Even relatively consensual parliamentary democracies may have difficulty in adjusting to these new circumstances. It may well be that integration of the intellectuals into the political system can be accomplished only by an authoritarian elite (whether of the left or right) in order to eliminate that anarchy which is incompatible with the continued functioning and further development of a scientific civilization.

We are living through an era of reversal of values and of social relationships perhaps best comprehended through Hegel's parable of the master and the servant in which the servant, compelled to live by his work, becomes self-reliant, while the master comes to depend completely on the servant. Thus, capitalists may be overturned by proletarians, any dominant group may be subverted by any dominated group, the most contradictory and unforeseen developments may occur in the unfolding of history.

Most social scientists postulate that science is sweeping all before it, thrusting aside magic, superstition, and religion, bringing about the rationalization of social behavior, laying the basis for modern industry, unprecedented prosperity, and the full flowering of human freedom. In the model modern society it is assumed that the ideological conflict of early industrialization will be transcended and replaced by pragmatic negotiation among claimant groups for larger shares of ever increasing national revenues. The long-term trend would thus be toward stability, prosperity, and freedom. But, through an irony of history, mastery can be converted into dependence, political trends can be reversed. A complex economy can be paralyzed by the determined opposition of relatively few people in key positions. An abundance of material wealth can lead to dissipation of individual motivation and disintegration of social ties. The privilege of exercising a free choice can turn into an agony. From stability may come instability, from prosperity may come misery, and out of freedom may come a new and fearful discipline.

NOTES

1. "Because prosperity has increased, desires are exalted. The richer prey offered stimulates them, makes them more demanding, more intolerant of any regulation, just when traditional regulations have lost their authority. The state of deregulation or of *anomie* is then deepened by the fact that the passions are less disciplined at the very moment when they are in need of a stronger discipline." E. Durkheim, *Le suicide, étude de sociologie* (Presses universitaires de France, 1969), p. 287.

2. *Journal Officiel, Assemblée Nationale,* May 14, 1968, p. 1772.

3. De Gaulle's televised interview of June 7 is reprinted in *Année Politique, 1968,* pp. 382-86.

4. An interview reported in *Le Monde,* August 27, 1969.

5. For a fuller treatment of the theory of modernization and its utility in interpreting French historical development, see my article, "The French Experience of Modernization," *World Politics* (April 1969), pp. 366-91, and the bibliographic citations therein.

6. On the incompatibility between anarchism and the development of modern society, see the perceptive comments by one of its leading historians: George Woodcock, *Anarchism* (Penguin,1963), pp. 23, 28, 444.

7. For an eloquent defense of Proudhon and critique of orthodox Marxism: Robert Aron, *Le socialisme français face au marxisme* (Grasset, 1971).

8. The following passages on the crisis of legitimacy are drawn from my article, "The French Experience of Modernization."

9. For Durkheim's views on anomie: *De la division du travail social* (P.U.F., 1967, 8th ed.), pp. 343-65; and *Le suicide* (P.U.F., 1960), pp. 264-311. An excellent contemporary interpretation is in Robert M. MacIver, *The Ramparts We Guard* (Macmillan, 1950). For a literary version of Durkheim's concept of anomie as applied to the May Revolt, see the interesting essay by Jean Dutourd, *L'école des Jocrisses* (Flammarion, 1970).

10. On the connection between poverty-wealth and discipline-anomie, see the suggestive comments of Durkheim in *Le suicide,* p. 282. Note also Raoul Vaneigem's call for a revolt against prosperity, in *Traité de savoir-vivre à l'usage des jeunes générations* (Gallimard, 1967), pp. 73, 88-91.

11. E. Durkheim, *Le suicide,* p. 316.

12. Durkheim quote on the link between suicide and homicide, ibid., p. 322. See also, ibid., p. 408, and on the correspondence between suicide-homicide and apathy-terrorism, ibid., p. 424.

13. That revolutionary students came in large proportion from "comfortable" situations is remarked by R. Boudon, "Quelques causes de la révolte estudiantine," *La Table Ronde* (Dec. 1968-Jan. 1969), p. 180. Also generously represented are Jews—corresponding to Durkheim's category of previously depressed groups suddenly enjoying new opportunities for advancement. Alain Krivine has publicly charged that the French police are now using Vichy records because so many Jews are in the New Left.

14. We have previously commented on the way in which surrealists suddenly became Communists or Trotskyists, and just as suddenly returned to anarchism. Note the recent overnight conversion of a leading American activist to an Eastern religion. In a press conference reported by the *New York Times* (May 6, 1973) one of the "Chicago 7" defendants, Rennie Davis, relates that during a flight to Paris on his way to meet Vietcong negotiators in January 1973 he heard about a fifteen-year-old guru in India called Maharaj Ji. His immediate reaction was skepticism and even hostility. But he went to India and after eight days "received knowledge" from a disciple of the guru, whom he now calls "the one perfect master" on earth at this time. Although at first uncomfortable

with the boy (who was about 10 years old at the time of the Chicago riots), Mr. Davis told the press conference that he now loved him. "I would cross the planet on my hands and knees," he said, "to touch his toe." The guru has been under investigation by the government of India on the charge of smuggling money, jewels and watches (all gifts from devoted followers) into the country.

15. For general treatments of the "entry into politics" problem, see T. H. Marshall, *Citizenship and Social Class* (Cambridge University Press, 1950), S. M. Lipset, *Political Man* (Doubleday, 1960), Reinhard Bendix, *Nation-Building and Citizenship* (John Wiley, 1964), Barrington Moore, Jr., *Social Origins of Dictatorship and Democracy* (Beacon, 1967), and J. G. LaPalombara and M. Weiner, editors, *Political Parties and Political Development* (Princeton University Press, 1966).

16. On the emergence of the intellectuals as a massive social force in France, see F. Bon and M.-A. Burnier, *Les nouveaux intellectuels* (2nd ed., Seuil, 1971).

17. For Durkheim's views on freedom in primitive and modern societies, cf. *De la division du travail social,* pp. 35-102. See also Alvin Toffler, *Future Shock* (Bantam Books, 1971), pp. 98, 319-22.

18. See the stimulating comments on the workers as a revolutionary force in F. Bon and M.-A. Burnier, *Classe ouvrière et révolution* (Seuil, 1971).

BIBLIOGRAPHY

Note: All footnote references are to works and specific editions listed below. Some of the items are not referred to in the text but are of general interest. Unless otherwise noted, place of publication of French books is Paris.

Gérard Adam et al., *L'ouvrier français en 1970*. Armand Colin, 1970.

Philippe Alexandre, *Le duel De Gaulle-Pompidou*. Grasset, 1970.

Philippe Alexandre, *L'Elysée en péril*. Fayard, 1969.

René Andrieu, *Les communistes et la révolution*. Julliard, 1968.

Année Politique. Presses Universitaires de France, annual.

John Ardagh, *The New French Revolution*. Harper, 1969.

Raymond Aron, *La révolution introuvable*. Fayard, 1968.

Raymond Aron, *Marxismes imaginaires*. Gallimard, 1970.

Robert Aron, *Le socialisme français face au marxisme*. Grasset, 1971.

Henri Arvon, *L'anarchisme*. Presses Universitaires, 1971.

Benjamin R. Barber, *Superman and Common Men*. Penguin, 1972.

André Barjonet, *La CGT*. Seuil, 1968.

André Barjonet, *La révolution trahie de 1968*. Didier, 1968.

Jean-Louis Bédouin, *Vingt ans de surréalisme*. Denoel, 1961.

Reinhard Bendix, *Nation-Building and Citizenship*. John Wiley, 1964.

Philippe Bénéton and Jean Touchard, "Les interprétations de la crise de mai-juin 1968." *Revue Française de Science Politique,* vol. XX, no. 3 (June 1970), pp. 503-44.

Daniel Bensaïd and Henri Weber, *Mai 1968: Une répétition générale*. Maspero, 1968.

Jean Bertolino, *Les trublions*. Stock, 1969.

Julien Besançon, editor, *Journal mural, mai 1968*. Tchou, 1968.

J. Blancherie et al., *Les événements de mai-juin 1968 vus à travers cent entreprises*. Centre national d'information pour la productivité des entreprises, n. d.

François Bloch-Lainé, *Pour une réforme de l'entreprise*. Seuil, 1963.

Frédéric Bon and Michel-Antoine Burnier, *Classe ouvrière et révolution*. Seuil, 1971.

Frédéric Bon and Michel-Antoine Burnier, *Les nouveaux intellectuels*. Seuil, 1971. 2nd edition.

François Borella, *Les partis politiques dans la France d'aujourd'hui*. Seuil, 1973.

Raymond Boudon, "Quelques causes de la révolte etudiantine." *La Table Ronde* (Dec. 1968-Jan. 1969), pp. 169-83.

P. Bourdieu and J.-C. Passeron, *Les héritiers*. Editions de Minuit, 1966. 2nd edition.

Christian Bouyer, *Odéon est ouvert*. Debresse, 1968.

Eliana Brau, *Le situationnisme ou la nouvelle internationale*. Nouvelles Editions Debresse, 1968.

Jean-Louis Brau, *Cours, camarade, le vieux monde est derrière toi!* Albin Michel, 1968.

Robert Bréchon, *Le surréalisme*. Armand Colin, 1971.

André Breton, *Manifestes du surréalisme*. Gallimard, 1971.

Bernard E. Brown, "The French Experience of Modernization." *World Politics,* vol. XXI, no. 3 (April 1969), pp. 366-91.

Zbigniew Brzezinski, *Between Two Ages, America's Role in the Technetronic Era.* Viking, 1971.

M.-A. Burnier and B. Kouchner, *La France sauvage.* Editions Publications Premières, 1970.

Antoine Casanova et al., *Les intellectuels et les luttes de classes.* Editions Sociales, 1970.

Ce que veut la Ligue Communiste. Maspero, 1972.

Georges Chaffard, *Les orages de mai.* Calmann-Lévy, 1968.

Georges Cogniot, *Les intellectuels et les étudiants devant la révolution.* Institut Maurice Thorez, 1968.

Daniel and Gabriel Cohn-Bendit, *Le gauchisme, remède à la maladie sénile du communisme.* Seuil, 1968.

Jean Coin, *J'en appelle à cent mille hommes.* Plon, 1969.

Michel Crozier, *La société bloquée.* Seuil, 1970.

Michel Crozier, *The Bureaucratic Phenomenon.* University of Chicago Press, 1964.

Adrien Dansette, *Mai 1968.* Plon, 1971.

Guy Debord, *La société du spectacle.* Buchet-Chastel, 1971.

Guy Debord and Gianfranco Sanguinetti, *La véritable scission dans l'internationale.* Editions Champ Libre, 1972.

Jean Defrasne, *La gauche en France.* Presses Universitaires, 1972.

De la misère en milieu étudiant. Strasbourg, 1967. Attributed to Mustapha Khayati.

Isaac Deutscher, *The Prophet Outcast.* Oxford University Press, 1963.

Maurice Druon, *L'avenir en désarroi.* Plon, 1968.

Pierre Dubois et al., *Grèves revendicatives ou grèves politiques?* Anthropos, 1971.

Isidore Ducasse (Comte de Lautréamont), *Oeuvres complètes.* José Corti, 1969.

Jacques Duclos, *Anarchistes d'hier et d'aujourd'hui.* Editions Sociales, 1968.

René Dumont, *Cuba, est-il socialiste?* Seuil, 1970.

Georges Dupeux, *La société française, 1789-1960.* Armand Colin, 1964.

Yvonne Duplessis, *Le surréalisme.* Presses Universitaires, 1971.

François Duprat, *Les journées de mai 68, les dessous d'une révolution.* Nouvelles Editions Latines, 1968.

Gérard Durazoi and Bernard Lecherbonnier, *Le surréalisme.* Larousse, 1972.

Emile Durkheim, *De la division du travail social,* 1893. 8th edition, Presses Universitaires, 1967.

Emile Durkheim, *Le suicide,* 1897. New edition, Presses Universitaires, 1960.

Jean Dutourd, *L'école des Jocrisses.* Flammarion, 1970.

Maurice Duverger, *Janus, les deux faces de l'occident.* Fayard, 1972.

Epistémon, *Ces idées qui ont ébranlé la France.* Fayard, 1968.

Claude Estier, *Journal d'un fédéré.* Fayard, 1970.

Alfred Fabre-Luce, *Le général en Sorbonne.* La Table Ronde de Combat, 1968.

Edgar Faure, *Ce que je crois.* Grasset, 1971.

Edgar Faure, *L'âme du combat.* Fayard, 1970.

Jacques Fauvet, *Histoire du parti communiste français.* 2 vols. Fayard, 1965.

Jean Ferniot, *Mort d'une révolution.* Denoel, 1968.

Pierre Feuerstein, *Printemps de révolte á Strasbourg.* Strasbourg, Saisons d'Alsace, 1968.

Claude Fohlen, *Mai 1968, révolution ou psychodrame?* Presses Universitaires, 1973.

Christian Fouchet, *Mémoires d'hier et de demain,* vol. 1, *Au service du Général de Gaulle.* Plon, 1971.

Claude Frédéric, *Libérer l'ORTF*. Seuil, 1968.

Jacques Frémontier, *La forteresse ouvrière: Renault*. Fayard, 1971.

Roger Garaudy, *Le grand tournant du socialisme*. Gallimard, 1969.

Roger Garaudy, *L'itinéraire d'Aragon*. Gallimard, 1961.

Roger Garaudy, *Toute la vérité*. Grasset, 1970.

L. Gatineau et al., *Recherche et contestation*. Anthropos, 1969.

Alain Geismar, *Minutes du procès d'Alain Geismar*. Halliers, 1971.

Alain Geismar, Serge July, Erly Morane, *Vers la guerre civile*. Editions et Publications Premières, 1969.

Pierre Genève, *Histoire secrète de l'insurrection de mai 1968*. Paris, 1968.

André Glucksmann, *Stratégie et révolution en France 1968*. Christian Bourgeois, 1968.

Richard Gombin, *Le projet révolutionnaire*. Mouton, 1969.

Richard Gombin, *Les origines du gauchisme*. Seuil, 1971.

Hugh Davis Graham and Ted Robert Gurr, *The History of Violence in America*. Bantam, 1969.

John Gretton, *Students and Workers: An Analytical Account of Dissent in France, May-June 1968*. London, Macdonald, 1969.

Alain Griotteray, *Des barricades ou des réformes?* Préface de Valéry Giscard d'Estaing. Fayard, 1968.

Yves Guéna, *Maintenir l'état*. Fayard, 1970.

Daniel Guérin, *L'anarchisme*. Gallimard, 1965.

Che Guevara, *Guerrilla Warfare*. Vintage, 1968.

Yannick Guin, *La commune de Nantes*. Maspero, 1969.

Stanley Hoffmann, "Paradoxes of the French Political Community," in S. Hoffmann, ed., *In Search of France*. Harvard University Press, 1963.

Stanley Hoffman, "The French Psychodrama," *The New Republic*, August 31, 1968, pp. 15-21.

Jules Humbert-Droz, *"L'oeil de Moscou" à Paris.* Julliard, 1964.

James Joll, *The Anarchists.* London, Eyre & Spottswoode, 1964.

Maurice Joyeux, *L'anarchie et la société moderne.* Debresse, 1969.

Pierre Juquin, *Le sens du réel.* Grasset, 1971.

Jacques Jurquet, *Le printemps révolutionnaire de 1968.* Gît-le-Coeur, 1968.

Jean-Claude Kerbourc'h, *Le piéton de mai.* Julliard, 1968.

Patrick Kessel, *Le mouvement "maoiste" en France.* vol. 1. Union Générale d'Editions, 1972.

Charles P. Kindelberger, *Economic Growth in France and Britain.* Harvard University Press, 1964.

Henri Krasucki, *Syndicats et lutte de classes.* Editions Sociales, 1969.

Marc Kravetz, editor, *L'insurrection étudiante.* Union Générale d'Editions, 1968.

Annie Kriegel, *Aux origines du communisme français.* Flammarion, 1969.

Annie Kriegel, *Les communistes français.* Seuil, 1970. 2nd edition.

Alain Krivine, *La farce électorale.* Seuil, 1970.

Philippe Labro et al., *Ce n'est qu'un début.* Publications Premières, 1968.

Joseph G. LaPalombara and Myron Weiner, eds., *Political Parties and Political Development.* Princeton University Press, 1966.

André Laude, "Les anarchistes." *La Nef* (June-Sept. 1972), pp. 117-28.

Georges Lavau, "Le parti communiste dans le système politique français." In *Le communisme en France.* Armand Colin, 1969.

Henri Lefebvre, *La proclamation de la Commune.* Gallimard, 1965.

Henri Lefebvre, *L'irruption de Nanterre au sommet.* Anthropos, 1968.

Michel Legris, "Qui sont les pro-chinois en France?" *Le Monde,* 31 March, 2 and 3 April, 1968.

George Lichtheim, *Marxism in Modern France.* Columbia University Press, 1966.

Seymour Martin Lipset, *Political Man.* Doubleday, 1960.

Roger Louis, *L'ORTF, un combat.* Seuil, 1968.

Robert M. MacIver, *The Ramparts We Guard.* Macmillan, 1950.

Roy C. Macridis and Bernard E. Brown, *The De Gaulle Republic.* Dorsey Press, 1960.

Serge Mallet, *La nouvelle classe ouvrière.* Seuil, 1969.

Serge Mallet, *Le pouvoir ouvrier.* Anthropos, 1971.

Michèle Manceaux, *Les maos en France.* Gallimard, 1972.

J. P. Manuel and A. Planel, *La crise de L'ORTF.* Pauvert, 1968.

Raymond Marcellin, *L'ordre publique et les groupes révolution-naires.* Plon, 1969.

T. H. Marshall, *Citizenship and Social Class.* Cambridge University Press, 1950.

Gilles Martinet, *Les cinq communismes.* Seuil, 1971.

J. H. Matthews, *An Introduction to Surrealism.* Pennsylvania State University Press, 1965.

François Mitterrand, *Ma part de vérité.* Fayard, 1969.

Jules Monnerot, *Sociologie de la révolution.* Fayard, 1969.

Barrington Moore, Jr., *Social Origins of Dictatorship and Democracy.* Beacon, 1967.

Jean Moreau, "Les 'Maos' de la Gauche Prolétarienne." *La Nef* (June-Sept. 1972), pp. 77-103.

Edgar Morin, Claude Lefort, and J. M. Coudray, *Mai 1968: la brèche.* Fayard, 1968.

Jean-Claude Mouret, "La famille Trotskiste." *La Nef* (June-Sept. 1972), pp. 57-75.

Mouvement du 22 Mars, *Ce n'est qu'un début, continuons le combat.* Maspero, 1968.

Maurice Nadeau, *Histoire du surréalisme*. Seuil, 1964.

Claude Paillat, *Archives secrètes, 1968-69: Les coulisses d'une année terrible*. Denoel, 1969.

Jacques-Arnaud Penent, *Un printemps rouge et noir*. Laffont, 1968.

Jacques Perret, *Inquiète Sorbonne*. Hachette, 1968.

Jacques Pesquet, *Des soviets à Saclay?* Maspero, 1968.

Pierre Peuchmaurd, *Plus vivants que jamais*. Laffont, 1968.

Thierry Pfister, *Le gauchisme*. Editions Filipacchi, 1972.

André Philip, *Mai 68 et la foi démocratique*. Aubier, 1968.

Charles Posner, ed., *Reflections on the Revolution in France: 1968.* Penguin, 1970.

Claude Prévost, *Les étudiants et le gauchisme*. Editions Sociales, 1969.

J.-J. Raspaud and J.-P. Voyer, *L'internationale situationniste*. Champ Libre, 1971.

Patrick Ravigant, *L'Odéon est ouvert*. Stock, 1969.

Piotr Rawicz, *Bloc-notes d'un contre-révolutionnaire ou la gueule de bois*. Gallimard, 1969.

Charles A. Reich, *The Greening of America*. Bantam, 1971.

Lucien Rioux and René Blackman, *L'explosion de mai*. Laffont, 1968.

Michel Rocard, *Le PSU*. Seuil, 1969.

Waldeck Rochet, *L'avenir du parti communiste français*. Grasset, 1969.

Waldeck Rochet, *Les enseignements de mai-juin 1968*. Editions Sociales, 1968.

Michel Sanouillet, *Dada à Paris*. Pauvert, 1965.

Jean-Paul Sartre, *Les communistes ont peur de la révolution*. Didier, 1968.

Jacques Sauvageot, Alain Geismar, and Daniel Cohn-Bendit, *La révolte étudiante*. Seuil, 1968.

Alain Schnapp and Pierre Vidal-Naquet, *Journal de la commune étudiante*. Seuil, 1969.

Patrick Seale and Maureen McConville, *French Revolution, 1968.* Penguin, 1968.

Jean-Jacques Servan-Schreiber, *Le réveil de la France.* Denoel, 1968.

Daniel Singer, *Prelude to Revolution, France in May 1968.* Jonathan Cape, 1970.

André Thirion, *Révolutionnaires sans révolution.* Laffont, 1972.

Alvin Toffler, *Future Shock.* New York, Bantam Books, 1971.

Jean Touchard, "Introduction à l'idéologie du parti communiste français." In *Le communisme en France.* Armand Colin, 1969.

Alain Touraine, *The May Movement, Revolt and Reform.* Translated by L. F. X. Mayhew. New York, Random House, 1971.

J.-R. Tournoux, *Le mois de mai du Général.* Plon, 1969.

Raoul Vaneigem, *Traité de savoir-vivre à l'usage des jeunes générations.* Gallimard, 1967.

René Viénet, *Enragés et situationnistes dans le mouvement des occupations.* Gallimard, 1968.

Pierre Viansson-Ponté, *Histoire de la république gaullienne.* 2 vols. Fayard, 1971.

Gérard Walter, *Histoire du parti communiste français.* Somogy, 1948.

Claude Willard, *Socialisme et communisme français.* Armand Colin, 1967.

Alfred Willener, *L'image-action de la société ou la politisation culturelle.* Seuil, 1970.

George Woodcock, *Anarchism.* Penguin, 1963.

Gordon Wright, *France in Modern Times.* Chicago, Rand McNally, 1960.

INDEX

Note: n refers to footnotes.

A

Alexandre, Philippe, 31 n.2, 32 n.7
Algeria, as model for revolutionaries, 126-127
Althusser, Louis, 78
Anarchists
  and autogestion, 86-87, 167-168
  and contestation, 119-120
  and May Revolt, 67, 80-88
  and modernization, 36, 215
  in Nantes, 144
  and other revolutionary groups, 165
  and the PCF, 178-180
  and spontaneity, 121
  and surrealism, 106
  See also Michael Bakunin, Daniel Cohn-Bendit, Pierre-Joseph Proudhon
Andrieu, René, 179, 186, 189, 200 n.23, 201 n.37
Anomie, 44-45, 214-222
Aragon, Louis, 103, 106-109, 114 n.44, 47
Army, French, 190-191. *See also* General Massu
Aron, Raymond, 37-45, 50, 61 n.4-7, 62 n.10-14, 214

Aron, Robert, 223 n.7
Association Générale des Etudiants Nantais (AGEN), 143, 145-146
Autogestion, 13, 47, 77, 86, 102, 158, 166-172

B

Baden Baden, meeting of De Gaulle and Massu, 25, 191
Bakunin, Michael, 83, 84-85, 87-88, 180, 210-211, 215
Barjonet, André, 22
Barrault, Jean-Louis, 17, 136
Bénéton, Philippe, 62 n.20, 63 n.30, 154 n.14, 198 n.4
Bensaïd, Daniel, 153 n.6
Bertolino, Jean, 31 n.4, 110 n.4, 5, 153 n.2, 200 n.19
Blancherie, J., 155 n.21
Boissieu, General Alain de, 25, 182
Bon, Frédéric, 154 n.12, 225 n.16, 18
Boudon, Raymond, 154 n.12, 198 n.3, 224 n.13
Bourdieu, Pierre, 198 n.2
Bouyer, Christian, 155 n.17
Brau, Jean-Louis, 111 n.10, 12, 199 n.11

Breton, André, 103-108, 114 n.40, 43
Brown, Bernard E., 154 n.11, 223 n.5,
    224 n.8
Bureaucracy, revolutionary critique of,
    70, 72, 97
Burnier, Michel-Antoine, 154 n.12,
    225 n.16, 18

Conseil National du Patronat Français
    (CNPF), 20, 135
Coudray, Jean-Marc, 57, 63 n.29
Couve de Murville, Maurice, 13
Crozier, Michel, 50-57, 63 n.22-24,
    26-28, 154 n.12
Cuba, 124-125, 165-166, 194-197

C

Castro, Fidel, 7, 195-196
Central Intelligence Agency (CIA), 123,
    153 n.7
Centre d'Etudes Nucléaires de Saclay,
    137, 138
Chaban-Delmas, Jacques, 26
Charléty Stadium, rally at, 22
China, and French revolutionaries,
    124, 125
Cogniot, Georges, 153 n.7, 179, 200 n.23
Cohn-Bendit, Daniel
    and anarchists, 81-84
    and autogestion, 166, 168
    cited, 111 n.10, 12, 112 n.15, 199 n.9
    in occupied Odéon, 136
    and the PCF, 178
    and the student uprising, 6, 9, 11, 18,
        45, 49, 87, 88, 174
    See also Mouvement du 22 Mars
Cohn-Bendit, Gabriel, 82
Comité de Liaison des Etudiants
    Révolutionnaires (CLER), 69
Comités Vietnam de Base, 78
Communist Party, French. See Parti
    Communiste Français
Confédération Française Démocratique
    du Travail (CFDT), 14, 22, 35, 167
Confédération Générale du Travail (CGT)
    and the general strike in May, 13, 14
    in Grenelle Conference, 18, 20
    in Nantes, 144, 149
    and PCF, 134, 213
    and revolutionary students, 162,
        167-168
Confédération Générale du Travail-Force
    Ouvrière (CGT-FO), 73, 144, 145,
        148, 151, 167

D

Dada, 99, 104-105, 108, 112 n.17,
    114 n.41, 215
Dansette, Adrien, 31 n.2, 4, 32 n.5, 6, 8,
    11, 110 n.2, 111 n.6, 124, 144,
    154 n.9, 155 n.29, 156 n.31, 191,
    199 n.12, 15, 200 n.26-28,
    201 n.39
Davis, Rennie, 224 n.14
Debord, Guy, 90, 91, 93-97, 100, 109,
    112 n.22, 23, 113 n.24-28, 30-32,
    35-36, 115 n.48
    See also Internationale Situation-
        niste
Dérive, situationist technique, 98, 105,
    113 n.29
Détournement, situationist technique,
    99-100, 105, 113 n.32, 175
Deutscher, Isaac, 110 n.6
Direct Democracy. See Autogestion
Dual power, 76, 119, 122-123, 143,
    151, 188
Ducasse, Isidore. See Comte de
    Lautréamont
Duclos, Jacques, 179, 200 n.23
Duhamel, Alain, 37
Dumont, René, 201 n.43
Duprat, François, 154 n.7
Durkheim, Emile, 37, 41, 44, 61 n.3,
    62 n.8, 95, 204, 208, 214-222,
    223 n.1, 224 n.9, 11, 12, 225 n.17
Dutschke, Rudi, 81, 87, 123

E

Economy, French, 133, 134
Elections, legislative

March 1967, 140-141
June 1968, 28-30, 176
March 1973, 192-193
Eluard, Paul, 103, 107
Enragés, les (of Nanterre), 7, 48, 51, 52, 93-94, 167, 170
Epistémon, 32 n.5, 57, 63 n.29

F

Fauvet, Jacques, 201 n.40
Fédération Anarchiste, 83
Fédération Communiste Libertaire, 83
Fédération des Etudiants Révolution- naires (FER), 67, 73-74, 81, 121
Fédération Nationale des Etudiants de France (FNEF), 68
Fédération Nationale des Syndicats d'Exploitants Agricoles (FNSEA), 144, 148
Feuerstein, Pierre, 31 n.3
Fifth Republic, defects as cause of May Revolt, 42, 140
Flins, incident at, 27-28
Force Ouvrière (FO). *See* Confédération Générale du Travail, Force Ouvrière
Fouchet, Christian, 5, 8, 10, 13, 32 n.8, 124-125, 131, 154 n.9
Fourth International (Trotskyist), 72-77
Frachon, Benoît, 21
Frank, Pierre, 74-76
Frédéric, Claude, 199 n.8
Frémontier, Jacques, 32 n.10, 134, 135, 155 n.16, 163, 189, 198 n.5, 199 n.6, 7, 201 n.36
Front de Libération Nationale (FLN), 126-127

G

Garaudy, Roger, 114-115 n.47, 185
Gatineau, L., 155 n.20
Gaulle, General Charles de
    disappearance on May 29, 23-27, 182
    explanation of May Revolt, 205-206

hostility toward opponents, 140
    role in student uprising, 10, 11, 13, 17, 19
Geismar, Alain, 4, 22, 80, 87, 111 n.7, 112 n.15, 126, 166, 176, 199 n.9
Gombin, Richard, 110 n.6, 111 n.7, 112 n.14, 17
Grandes Ecoles, 128, 129, 131
Grappin, Pierre, 6, 8
Grenelle Conference, 18, 20, 22, 24, 181
Guérin, Daniel, 111 n.13, 112 n.14
Guevara, Che, 7, 75, 194, 195, 196, 197, 201 n.43
Guin, Yannick, 155 n.24, 25, 27, 28, 156 n.31

H

Halbeher, Aimé, 163, 189
Hébert, Alexandre, 144, 145, 149
Hegel, G. W. F., 222
Hervé, Pierre, 185
Hoffmann, Stanley, 51, 53, 54, 63 n.25
Huvelin, Paul, 20

I

Intellectuals, entry into the political system, 219-222
Internationale Lettriste, 90
Internationale Situationniste (I.S.), 5, 89-109, 120, 143, 167, 170, 175
Isou, Isidore, 90

J

Jeanson, André, 21
Jeunesses Communistes Révolutionnaires (JCR), 67, 69, 75, 76, 77, 81, 121
Joxe, Louis, 8
Juquin, Pierre, 200 n.24

K

Katangais, les, 171-172

Kerbourc'h, J.-C., 198 n.1
Khayati, Mustapha, 92, 94, 110 n.1, 159
Khrushchev, Nikita, 71, 75
Krasucki, Henri, 181, 200 n.23
Kriegel, Annie, 125, 154 n.10, 185, 188, 200 n.25, 26, 201 n.33, 35, 40
Krivine, Alain, 75, 151, 176-177, 200 n.22, 224 n.13
Kronstadt rebellion, 73, 84, 86, 88

L

Lagaillarde, Pierre, 127
Lambert, Bernard, 144
Lambert, Pierre, 73-74
Lautréamont, Comte de (Isidore Ducasse), 105, 106, 109, 115 n.48
Lavau, Georges, 184-185, 201 n.31
Le Bon, Gustave, 39
Lecoeur, Auguste, 185
Le Doyen, General, 191
Lefebvre, Henri, 57, 63 n.29, 87
Lefort, Claude, 57, 63 n.29
Legris, Michel, 154 n.8
Lenin, V. O., 85, 125, 162, 164
Lettrists, 90
Lichtheim, George, 201 n.40
Lorenz, Konrad, 39
Luxemburg, Rosa, 71, 76, 87

M

McConville, Maureen, 31 n.2, 155 n.24, 199 n.12
MacIver, Robert M., 224 n.9
Macridis, Roy C., 154 n.11
Maîtron, Jean, 175
Makhno, Nestor, 86
Malraux, André, 2, 43
Manceaux, Michèle, 111 n.7
Mandel, Ernest, 74
Maoists, 11, 28, 67, 69, 78-80, 121, 144, 165, 174
Marcellin, Raymond, 123, 154 n.7
Marchais, Georges, 178-179, 180, 187, 189

Marcuse, Herbert, 87, 178
Martinet, Gilles, 201 n.41
Marty, André, 185
Marx, Karl, 36, 85, 96, 210, 211
Massu, General Jacques, 25, 32 n.12, 182, 191
Mendès-France, Pierre, 22, 23, 181
Missoffe, François, 6
Mitterrand, François, 22, 23, 24, 69, 75, 181, 193, 200 n.27
M.L's. See Union des Jeunesses Communistes, Marxistes-Léninistes
Modernization, and the May Revolt, 207-214
Monnet, Jean, 55
Morice, André, 143
Morin, Edgar, 57, 63 n.29
Mouvement du 22 Mars (M22M), 7, 8, 31 n.5, 67, 76, 81, 83, 120, 121, 167, 168, 174, 195
Mouvement pour un Bauhaus Imaginiste, 90

N

Nadeau, Maurice, 114 n.44, 47
Nanterre, University of, 5-8, 50, 56, 120, 218
Nantes, Commune of, 13, 142-152
Nantes, University of, 143, 145, 148
Noir et Rouge, 83

O

Occident, 8, 9
Odéon, occupation of, 17, 28, 136, 169, 172
Office de la Radio, Télévision Française (ORTF), 15-16, 137-138, 163
Organisation Communiste Internationaliste, 73

P

Pablo, Michel, 77

Pannekoek, Anton, 87
Pareto, Vilfredo, 39
Paris Commune, 85, 166
Participatory democracy. *See*
    Autogestion
Parti Communiste Français (PCF)
    during May Revolt, 12, 18-19, 22-23,
        29, 142, 181-182
    and other revolutionary groups, 79,
        119, 124, 159, 177-183
    as a revolutionary party, 39, 40, 59,
        134, 183-194, 213
    and the Soviet Union, 125-126
Parti Communiste Internationaliste,
    74-76
Parti Communiste Marxiste-Léniniste de
    France (PCMF), 79-80
Parti Socialiste Unifié (PSU), 5, 22, 68
Passeron, J.-C., 198 n.2
Péret, Benjamin, 103
Perret, Jacques, 199 n.14
Pesquet, Jacques, 155 n.19
Peyrefitte, Alain, 8, 9, 10, 132
Pfister, Thierry, 153 n.6
Philip, André, 200 n.16
Police, in May Revolt, 11, 20
Pompidou, Georges
    and the Communists, 24, 40, 182,
        191
    and De Gaulle, 24, 25, 26, 190-191
    and the Grenelle Conference, 18,
        20-21
    and the May Revolt, 8, 11-12, 141
    explanation of the May Revolt, 124,
        204-206
Prévost, Claude, 200 n.24
Proudhon, Pierre-Joseph, 36, 84-85, 86,
    180, 210, 211, 215
Provos, in Holland, 91
Psychogeographical Committee of
    London, 90

R

Ravigant, Patrick, 155 n.17, 199-200 n.16
Reich, Wilhelm, 105
Rémond, René, 120

Renault (Billancourt), strike and inci-
    dents at, 21, 134-135, 162, 167,
        179, 180
Rey, Henri, 150
Riesel, René, 93, 95, 175
Rimbaud, Arthur, 36, 104
Rocard, Michel, 151, 177
Roche, Rector Jean, 8, 9
Rochet, Waldeck, 22, 181-182, 185-186,
        189, 190, 201 n.38
Rocton, Yvon, 144, 147

S

Sade, Marquis de, 105
Salan, General Raoul, 28
Sanguinetti, Gianfranco, 112 n.22
Sanouillet, Michel, 114 n.41
Sartre, Jean-Paul, 71, 87, 111 n.7,
        201 n.30
Sauvageot, Jacques, 4, 22, 69, 121-122,
        164, 176
Schnapp, Alain, 110 n.3, 111 n.6,
        153 n.3, 156 n.33
SDS (German Socialist Students), 81,
        120, 124
Seale, Patrick, 31 n.2, 155 n.24, 199 n.12
Séguy, Georges, 20, 21, 150, 179, 181,
        189, 200 n.23
Servan-Schreiber, Jean-Jacques, 175
Servir le Peuple, 78
Situationists. *See* Internationale
        Situationniste
Socialist Party, 36, 186-187. *See also*
        François Mitterrand
Sorbonne, student occupation of, 8-10,
        16-17, 28, 121, 169-172
"Stalemate Society" thesis, 51-57
Stalin, Joseph, 70-72, 78, 107, 136
Strasbourg, University of, 5, 91-92
Sud-Aviation plant, strike at, 13, 121,
        144, 147-148, 152, 162, 167
Surrealists
    and the May Revolt, 80, 81, 215
    political views of, 88-109
    See also Internationale
        Situationniste

Syndicat National de l'Enseignement
    Supérieur (SNESup), 4, 9

T

Tendance Marxiste Révolutionnaire, 77
Thirion, André, 114 n.39, 46, 47
Tillon, Charles, 185
Tocqueville, Alexis de, 41, 42, 51,
    62 n.9, 132
Toffler, Alvin, 225 n.17
Touchard, Jean, 62 n.20, 63 n.27, 30,
    154 n.14, 198 n.4
Touraine, Alain, 45-50, 62 n.15-19,
    63 n.21
Tournoux, J.-R., 31 n.2, 156 n.30, 32
Tricontinental Organization of People's
    Solidarity, Havana, 123-124, 195
Triolet, Elsa, 108
Trotsky, Leon, 36, 70-77, 84, 86, 99,
    110-111 n.6, 122, 125
Trotskyists, 10, 11, 121, 144, 170, 174,
    178. *See also* Jeunesses Com-
    munistes Révolutionnaires; Fédé-
    ration des Etudiants Révolution-
    naires
Tzara, Tristan, 103, 109

U

Union des Etudiants Communistes
    (UEC), 69, 75, 78
Union des Jeunesses Communistes,
    Marxistes-Léninistes (M.L.'s), 67,
    69, 78-80
Union Nationale des Etudiants de France
    (UNEF), 4, 8, 9, 12, 16, 22, 27,
    29, 68-69, 143
Union of Soviet Socialist Republics,
    Trotskyist criticism of, 71-73

Union pour la Défense de la République
    (UDR), 29-30, 177
Universities, French
    as combustible material, 128-132
    composition of student body,
        160-161
Urban guerrilla, 102, 123, 159, 194-197

V

Vaillant-Couturier, Marie-Claude, 29
Vaneigem, Raoul, 93, 96, 98, 99, 101,
    102, 109, 112 n.17, 113 n.24, 25,
    28, 31, 32, 35, 37, 115 n.48, 143,
    224 n.10
Viansson-Ponté, Pierre, 3-4, 31 n.2, 4,
    32 n.5, 8, 11-13, 61 n.2, 124,
    154 n.9, 155 n.22, 199 n.15,
    201 n.29
Vidal-Naquet, Pierre, 110 n.3, 111 n.6,
    153 n.3, 156 n.33
Vié, Jean-Emile, 142
Viénet, René, 95, 112 n.17, 21, 175,
    199 n.13
Vietnam war, 7, 75
Vigier, J.-L., 168, 195
Voix Ouvrière, 77

W

Weber, Henri, 153 n.6
Weber, Max, 37, 208
Willener, Alfred, 112 n.17
Woodcock, George, 111 n.13, 112 n.14,
    223 n.6
Workers
    attitudes toward students, 161-163
    councils, 83, 101-102, 166, 167.
        See also Autogestion
Workers Opposition (Soviet Union), 76